American Thinking
About Peace
and War

American Thinking About Peace and War

New Essays on American Thought and Attitudes

KEN BOOTH
Department of International Politics,
University College of Wales, Aberystwyth

AND

MOORHEAD WRIGHT
Senior Lecturer in International Politics,
University College of Wales, Aberystwyth

THE HARVESTER PRESS · SUSSEX
BARNES & NOBLE · NEW YORK

First published in 1978 by
THE HARVESTER PRESS LIMITED
Publisher: John Spiers
2 Stanford Terrace, Hassocks, Sussex

and in the USA by
HARPER AND ROW PUBLISHERS INC.
BARNES & NOBLE IMPORT DIVISION
10 East 53rd Street, New York 10022

British Library Cataloguing in Publication Data

American thinking about peace and war.
  1. War   2. Peace
  I. Booth, Ken   II. Wright, Moorhead
  327'.1   U21.2

  ISBN 0–85527–859–5

Barnes & Noble
ISBN 0–06–490581–0

Photosetting by Thomson Press (India) Ltd., New Delhi
Printed in England by
Redwood Burn Ltd., Trowbridge and Esher

Contents

Preface

In July 1976 the Department of International Politics at the
University College of Wales, Aberystwyth celebrated the bicentenary of the United States of America by holding a conference
entitled 'American Thinking About Peace and War: Reflections
Two Hundred Years On'. Papers were commissioned from British
and American scholars, and the conference was held at Gregynog
Hall in Powys, between 5–9 July 1976; it was attended by a number
of British and American academics and by representatives of the
Foreign Office and the US Embassy in London. Preliminary drafts
of all but one of the essays (Chapter 8) were read and discussed.
Each author was asked to write a new essay reflecting upon
American attitudes towards various facets of peace and war from
the perspective of the two hundred year experience of the Republic.
A bicentenary might be thought a somewhat trite occasion for
an academic enterprise, but there can be no doubt about the
seriousness of this venture: no issues are more important to
students of international politics than those pertaining to peace
and war, and no set of attitudes are more pervasive, yet elusive,
or more in need of illuminating, than those of the United States.

*   *   *

The editors and several contributors wish to thank the following
for reading and commenting on specific essays: Christopher
Carr, John Gaddis, James E. King, Patricia McArdle, Eric
Quackenbush, Lucinda Quackenbush, and Phil Williams. A
debt is owed by all the contributors to all the other participants
at the original conference for the valuable contributions which they
made towards making the occasion both friendly and constructive.
For their help in a variety of administrative roles, the editors

wish to express their genuine appreciation of Jane Davis, the Research Officer in the Department, and of Doreen Hamer and Marian Weston, the Departmental secretaries. Special thanks are due to Jane Davis for preparing the index to this book. The funds for the conference were met by the University College of Wales, the Wilson Chair Advisory Board, and the U.S. Embassy. Without their generous help the conference could not have been held. Particular mention should be made of Robert E. McDowell, the Cultural Affairs Officer of the U.S. Embassy, for his valuable support and assistance in the initial stages of the organisation of the conference. The conference was supported and various assistance was provided by the Principal of the University College, Sir Goronwy H. Daniel, and the Registrar, T. Arfon Owen. For providing the delightful setting for a memorable meeting, we thank Glyn Tegai Hughes, the Warden of Gregynog Hall, and all his staff. In helping them so quickly and smoothly to transform the conference papers into a book, the editors wish to thank Frances Kelly of Curtis Brown Academic Ltd. and John Spiers of The Harvester Press. The proceeds of this book, together with those of Brian Porter's *The Aberystwyth Papers: International Politics* 1919–1969 and Ieuan G. John's *EEC Policy Towards Eastern Europe*, are being used to establish an annual student essay prize, to encourage thinking and writing about the problems of international relations. Finally, but most important of all, we wish to acknowledge our debt to our friend and colleague, Ieuan G. John, the Woodrow Wilson Professor of International Politics at the University College of Wales. Throughout the venture he shouldered some of the more troublesome administrative chores, and was a constant source of encouragement and advice.

Aberystwyth
March 1977

KEN BOOTH
MOORHEAD WRIGHT

Introduction

With American thinking about peace and war, as with social and political matters everywhere, there is no clear dividing line between image and reality. Not surprisingly, therefore, American attitudes towards peace and war have often been prone to the influence of myths and stereotypes, distortions and misconceptions; and there has often been a parallel awareness and exploitation of these over-simplifications. The essays in this volume attempt to explore various aspects of this complex dialogue between image and reality.

The focal point of this book is American thinking about peace and war. The subject is explored by proceeding from an examination of war as an instrument of policy through to an examination of American thinking about institutionalising peace. On the way, examination is made of such important features as strategy, alliances, the causes of war, popular reactions to war, peace movements, the legal and ethical dimensions of thinking, and institutional matters relating to the war-peace nexus. In addition to its main focal point the book is given additional coherence by the complementary perspectives from which the essays have been written. The diversity which characterises the United States is to some extent matched by the different academic backgrounds of the various writers.

In the opening chapter Ken Booth re-examines traditional images of the 'American way of war' from a strategist's viewpoint. In exploring some of the myths which have grown up around the subject, he argues that many of the well-established views about American strategic history are misconceived, and further-more that the American approach to strategy has had many more positive features than are usually recognised. The paper concludes that the conventional image of 'American Strategic Man' is not only more complex than the literature suggests, but also that what it represents does not deserve the reputation of universal 'bad guy'.

In the following chapter Harvey Starr focuses upon one aspect of strategy, namely tradition and change in the American view of foreign military entanglements. He takes international relations theory as the starting point of his analysis, and in particular he attempts to use 'collective goods' concepts to improve our understanding of alliance policies. On the basis of his survey of the evolution of U.S. alliance policy, he argues that isolationist and moralising rhetoric has obscured the essential realism and stability of American attitudes towards alliances. This essential continuity of approach he embodies in the concept of 'unilateralism', by which American policy-makers have sought to further American interests with the most appropriate instruments at hand. Both joining and casting off alliances have been consistent with this essentially independent posture.

Turning to American attitudes towards the causes of war, Anatol Rapoport shows that until World War I the phenomenon of war was such a 'natural' occurrence in people's lives that Americans scarcely thought it necessary to examine its 'causes'. Like the seasons or natural disasters, wars just happened, or were something which befell mankind. As a result of the widespread disillusionment which followed World War I, however, inquiries into the 'causes of war' began in earnest in the United States. This commitment became ever-more systematic in the aftermath of World War II, and during the terrors of the Cold War. Adopting a peace research perspective, the paper goes on to argue that the chief threat to peace is now the growth, strength, character, and pervasiveness of the very military establishment to which Americans have traditionally looked for their security.

The broad currents of social and political history provide Edmund Ions with the raw material for his study of the complex national attitudes to the series of foreign wars in which the United States has been involved. After examining the character of U.S. involvement in these wars, and the various factors which shaped national and sectional attitudes, he concludes that the pendulum between 'isolationism' and 'interventionism' is not a satisfactory explanation of U.S. behaviour: instead, he prefers to characterise the mainspring of the American reaction as one of 'vigilant ambivalence'. This is an outlook shaped by the unique historical experience of the United States, the peculiarities of its political system, and the multifaceted character of American society.

From this large historical canvas, Moorhead Wright's essay turns to three fictional portraits of Americans at war in order to discern the continuity and change in the relationship between the individual and war. Here he finds a tension between the pressures of participation and detachment; parallel with the evolution of warfare, he notes a steady trend towards individual detachment, for modern war has become increasingly technological and therefore impersonal. In this process, individuals become progressively more peripheral, and feel a growing sense of futility: they are, to quote Vonnegut, 'the listless playthings of enormous forces'.

After this literary perspective, Charles Chatfield brings the historian's resources to an understanding of the developments and ideals of American peace movements. He reveals that these movements have had a long and respectable history, dating back almost to the beginning of the Republic, and that they have varied greatly in scope, aims, and ideals. The paper argues that the adherents of these movements cannot be summarily dismissed as woolly-minded 'idealists' or simple-minded protesters. As the peace movements have organised and evolved since the beginning of the nineteenth century, they have had a positive impact on American ideas about peace and war. Direct influence on policy-makers might have been intermittent, but it has not been insubstantial. Furthermore, the peace advocates have had an enduring role in the American political system as the oldest sustained reform movement in the country, and they have had an essential role by providing a lasting forum for the advancement of alternative definitions of the American national interest.

A wide reading in legal theory and scholarship is the principal asset which James Piscatori contributes to his analysis of the American approach to the regulation of war and the use of force. He notes with approval that American theorists have been characterised by diversity of thought and flexibility of approach on the problem of what law should do about war and peace. Although apparently rather esoteric, the doctrines and categories which he examines have occasionally surfaced in the public consciousness in the evaluation of specific wars, when the assumptions which the theorists made clear and the goals which they advanced seemed relevant in shaping reactions to immediate and deadly problems. This was most notable in the long and painful debate about the Vietnam War.

In a closely related field, that of the ethical dimension in thinking about international relations, Kenneth Thompson points out that Americans have been prone both to exaggerate the scope and overstate the limitations of ethical thinking on war and peace. After expounding and criticising the oversimplified approaches of various cynics, utopians, and ideologists, he then outlines the thought of four distinguished exponents and representatives of more intricate and pluralistic moral outlooks, namely Reinhold Niebuhr, Hans J. Morgenthau, Walter Lippmann, and George F. Kennan. He concludes that the pluralistic approach to moral reasoning represented by these four men is more soundly based and is a more hopeful approach to thinking about war and peace and morality than the monistic approaches which have tended to prevail in American thinking.

Catherine Kelleher brings a political scientist's background to her examination of the shifting institutional balance between the Executive and Congress on the often bitter question of warmaking and peacemaking powers. She examines the historical and psychological context within which these debates have taken place, the specific issues which have arisen, and the efficacy and viability of the alternatives which have been proposed for power-sharing and constraint. These issues are no less important today than in the past, for 'who will guard the guards?' will always be a central problem in a democratic society, particularly one as powerful as the United States. She concludes that the American penchant for organisational answers to such questions will not be sufficient. The ultimate answer remains the health and vigilance of the American political community, which gives its policy-makers their education, which selects them, and which sets both the limits and the guidelines for their exercise of power.

In the final chapter Inis Claude looks at the American penchant for organisational solutions in another arena, namely the attempt to bring order to the international system. He argues that the American concern for international institutions has been a long and constructive one, beginning in the nineteenth century. From this perspective it is evident that the rejection of the League of

Nations should properly be regarded as an aberration in American attitudes to the institutionalising of international practices, while the enthusiastic participation in the United Nations represented not so much a revolution in attitudes but a return, albeit with greater intensity and scope than ever before, to well-established American predispositions. The paper concludes by discussing the development of thinking in recent years, the result of which is to show Americans being more confused and uncertain than at any other time in the last thirty, or even perhaps the last sixty years, about international organisation and the role that the United States can and should play.

Together, these essays attempt to find some order and pattern in the great diversity of American attitudes towards peace and war. In addition, they are a reminder of the extent to which American thought has both evolved from and enriched western thinking generally about these vital issues. Such complex themes cannot be easily summarised: indeed, the common themes to which most of the authors refer suggest variety rather than uniformity. They refer to the considerable difficulty of generalising about what constitutes *American* thinking about anything, to the many paradoxes in American attitudes, to the many pendulums in the American experience, to the complexity of American reality when set against its stereotypes, and to the difficulty of judging the U.S. either because of the persistence of clichés, the absence of well-established standards of judgement, or the confusion of American rhetoric. But if this complex subject refuses to fall into simple patterns, the essays in this book do clarify its overall shape and do scratch some definite lines through the tangle of experience and myth, deed and word, reality and image.

American Strategy: The Myths Revisited

Ken Booth

For the first 199 years of their 200 year history, Americans could claim that they had never lost a war: it is ironic therefore that they have almost always managed to be on the losing side of arguments about the character and competence of their strategy. For the United States, Corneille's aphorism has a tormenting pertinence: 'To win without risk is to triumph without glory.'

In the course of this essay use will be made of a convenient fiction, *American Strategic Man*, in order to focus the bundle of inter-related ideas which make up the popular image of the American way of war. It will be the contention of this essay that these ideas are largely myths, mistakes, or misconceptions, arising out of a general lack of awareness of American military history, an absence of sophisticated appreciations of the nature of strategy, and the recurrence and self-interest of various groups of myth-makers. These myth-makers cannot be isolated as single individuals or groups: they have included intellectuals and anti-intellectuals, Republicans and Democrats, military practitioners and civilians, the political left and right, and governmental insiders and out-siders. They have been ably abetted by numerous foreign commentators. The resulting myths widely pervade the literature on American strategy and foreign policy, and are consequently the staple diet of students.[1] This essay seeks to identify and re-examine some of the more important aspects of contemporary conventional wisdom. The discussion leads to the conclusion that the well-established image of *American Strategic Man*—everybody's favourite bad guy—is very misleading. It will be seen that to the extent a peculiar American way of strategy exists, it has been both very different and very much more complex than its reputation suggests.

According to conventional wisdom, *American Strategic Man* is made up of the following bundle of characteristics: Americans did not think seriously about strategy before World War II; American strategy has been characterised by overthink in the last twenty years; Americans do not know when they are threatened; Americans believe that peace is the normal pattern of relations between states; Americans have been reluctant in peacetime to think in terms of military power; Americans do not allow politics to intrude into war; Americans turn wars into crusades; Americans adopt a direct approach to strategy; the American way of war is overly technological; Americans are too belligerent in war; the American approach to strategy is to think in terms of absolutes. Before arguing that these propositions are misleading, several prefatory remarks need be made. Firstly, this reassessment is from a strategic perspective, which accepts that force has an established role in international politics. Other perspectives, particularly that of the pacifist, would provide a rather different critique of the American approach to strategy. Secondly, it is always necessary, when discussing *American* views about anything, to acknowledge the essential diversity of viewpoints. This essay is particularly concerned with the ideas of that group which R. A. Levine in *The Arms Debate* distinguished as the 'middle marginalists'.[2] Nevertheless, this in itself is a large group, made up of decision-makers, policy-planners, academic strategists, political scientists, diplomatic historians and others. For better or worse, it has been the group most responsible for American arms policies in the recent past. Furthermore, when thinking about the heterogeneity of American thinking it is also necessary to keep in mind the political processes relevant to the formulation of strategic doctrine. The practice of American strategy cannot be discussed apart from the 'bureaucractics' of the problem. Throughout its military history, what has emerged from the American policy process and has been edified by the grand name 'strategy' has often been a very hammered-out article, a make-shift thing, a diktat, a compromise, or any of the other multifarious outcomes produced by decision-making organisations. To adapt an old aphorism: strategy is a camel produced by a government charged with designing a war-horse. Thirdly, in criticising the established image of *American Strategic Man*, this essay is not claiming that the characteristics are inappropriate in all instances and for every individual; it is not claiming that American strategic thinking has avoided fallacies such as ethnocentrism, or that American strategic practice has not been guilty of excesses or has not suffered from avoidable failure. Rather, the aim of the essay is to restore the balance in the study of American strategy. In the following sections of the essay, the various images making up *American Strategic Man* will be examined in turn. By showing the weaknesses of the conventional wisdom, the basis will be established for developing a more sophisticated understanding of this complex phenomenon.

American Theorising About Strategy

(a) *Americans did not think seriously about strategy before World War II.*

The idea that Americans did not think seriously about strategy before World War II is based on two assumptions. The first is that the United States usually lacked a coherent national strategy for the employment of force. The second is that Americans did not write or think about strategy in any systematic way. These assumptions are based on a mixture of misconception and historical inaccuracy.

Until the Cold War the United States certainly lacked what has since been labelled a 'national security policy', involving the framing of coherent objectives, and their pursuit by the coordination of the military and non-military instruments of statecraft. But this was true also of other countries, until the arrival of the interwar dictatorships with their 'total strategy'.[3] For most countries strategy has been a neglected subject and has been conceptually divorced from political intercourse. Even so, the divorce has by no means been complete in all areas of U.S. activity: in the Caribbean diplomacy and the military instrument have always been close. But the main point is that the habit of judging U.S. strategy in terms of what we now understand as 'national security policy' is to distort what actually happened, by forcing the past into a modern conceptual framework :[4] such a framework was not appropriate for any of the Great Powers of the nineteenth century.

The reputation of American writing about 'strategy' has suffered from a similar misrepresentation. Those who now dismiss the written contribution of earlier generations of American military writers do so in terms of the exceptional standards of the so-called 'Golden Age' of contemporary strategic theorising in the 1950s and 1960s, a uniquely fertile period when strategic studies saw a hundred publishers bloom. Not only does this implicit standard distort the way 'strategy' was approached in the past, but it also seriously underestimates the amount of writing about military affairs which did take place in the United States. A pernicious influence in this respect has been Edward Mead Earle's well-worn textbook, the so-called *Makers of Modern Strategy*.[5] No other work has so greatly hindered the study of American strategic thinking. Since the only significant American thinkers identified in this book are Alexander Hamilton, Alfred Thayer Mahan, and William ('Billy') Mitchell, and since this book represents for most students in the last twenty years the sum total of their background reading into strategic history, the myth of America as a strategic innocent has been fostered and reinforced through the book's innumerable reprintings. The reality is somewhat different.

Throughout most of U.S. history, there has been a steady flow of military writing. Most of this work is now unknown or ignored; in its time, however, it played its part in the development of the thinking of those interested in or responsible for military policy. Typical titles were *Elements of Military Art and Science* (published in 1846), *Modern Warfare: Its Science and Art* (1860), *The Influence of Sea Power Upon History*, 1660–1783 (1890), *Principles of Strategy* (1894), *Elements of Strategy* (1906), *The Fundamentals of Military Strategy* (1928), and *Strategy* (1928). There were many more.[6] These titles are almost interchangeable with those of the works of pre-eminent European theorists such as Ferdinand Foch, Sir Julian Corbett, or General Colmar von der Goltz. Instead, with the exception of Mahan's famous work, these books were written by relatively unacknowledged American writers, namely H. Wager Halleck, E. B. Hunt, John Bigelow, G. J. Fiebeger, Oliver Prescott Robinson, and George J. Meyers. If it be argued that most of this early writing was narrow and technical rather than theoretical or philosophical, or that it was 'tactical' rather than 'strategic', then the same could be said about most contemporary British, French, or German military writing. And if it be argued that the United States failed to produce an original military philosopher, then the same could be said about all other countries—even including Germany after the death of the first and last Clausewitz in 1831.

The traditional American approach to strategic thinking shared more characteristics with its European counterparts than is usually thought. As in other countries, there was a succession of individuals writing books and articles about the military problems of the day. As in other countries these writers were mainly military professionals. As in other countries they approached their subjects from a technical or historical standpoint, as distinct from a theoretical one. As in other countries strategy was neglected as an object of study: military leaders were not 'educated' in it. As in other countries, soldiers were not expected to be scholars. And as has often happened in military history, soldiers with a scholarly bent proved to be less than effective practitioners. True to type, Henry Wager Halleck, who wrote *Elements of Military Art and Science*, the first American book on the principles of strategy (but 'strategy' very narrowly defined) proved himself to be a rather pedantic and undistinguished commander in the field.

The conclusion we must draw is that while previous generations of Americans were rarely at the forefront of strategic thinking, the United States was not a backwater, and indeed in some areas of military life produced first rate reformers and thinkers such as Rear Admiral Stephen B. Luce and Major General Emory Upton. The point is that most American military writers, like those everywhere, have been no more than averagely competent, but, unlike some of their European counterparts, have lacked academic discoverers and publicists. The evidence clearly shows that the image of the United States as a slumbering strategic Snow White until the belated arrival of the Prince, in the shape of Bernard Brodie[7] and his academic cohorts, is a patently false one.

(b) *American strategy in the last twenty years has been characterised by 'overthink'.*

The superficial image of *American Strategic Man* is that within half a generation he swung from 'underthink' to 'overthink'.

It is now commonly argued that there has been too much theorising by American strategists in the last twenty years.

The accusation of 'overthink', as one critic has noted, is completely misplaced. Just as one cannot be too healthy, one can hardly think too much or too well.[8] However, the real problem with strategic thinking, as with weapons procurement, is not only 'how much is enough?' but also 'have we got the right kind?'. In answer to the latter question, we are all liable to complain that there has been too much of the wrong kind, for there are numerous schools of thought about what constitutes the most valid approach to strategy. One professor's sophisticated strategic theorising is sometimes another professor's dehumanised nightmare.

The United States, to its credit, has supported a more vigorous and extensive arms debate than any other country. Inevitably, parts of this debate have attracted strong criticism. The increasingly prominent civilian strategists have sometimes been criticised by military professionals because of their inadequate practical experience, and they have been criticised by the radical community and others on the basis of their methodology, approach, and scholarly conduct. Some of the criticism has been well directed. On the other hand the attack has sometimes contained an element of anti-intellectualism. One has sometimes heard it suggested (with varying degrees of humour) that if the RAND Corporation, the Hudson Institute and the whole think-tank industry were eliminated—reminiscent of Stalin's proposal for the German General Staff—then many strategic problems would be eliminated with them. Whatever grain of truth there may be in this argument, it is heavily outweighed by the palpable fact that the use and threat of military force will continue to exercise the attention of governments for the foreseeable future. Strategy will continue to be a deadly business, demanding considerable attention from those responsible for or interested in the security of nations. And academic strategists will remain one of the few defences against the complete domination of military thinking by the professional specialists in violence.

Always quantitatively, and usually qualitatively, Americans have been at the forefront of contemporary strategic theorising. The war-peace establishment[9] in the United States has been the home of a marvellous catholicity of standpoints and methodologies. However bizarre, unwordly or inhuman some aspects of this debate may appear, taken as a whole it brings to mind the comment of a representative of an underdeveloped country, when he said that he would *welcome* America's industrial pollution problem. A democrat is likely to have the same paradoxical feeling about America's lively arms debate: some of it might offend, but with all its vitality it is significantly preferable to the underdevelopment, stagnation, neglect, or official orthodoxy which passes for defence thinking in other countries.

American Strategy in 'Peacetime'

(c) *Americans do not know when they are threatened.*

Americans have often been criticised for not being clear about their strategic interests, and for lacking a sense of urgency and proper timing in their dealing with threatening situations. These criticisms are overdrawn, and are usually based on the conviction which hindsight confers. In general, U.S. history reveals a reasonable appreciation of the strategic environment by those responsible for U.S. security, and a consistent pattern of rational responsiveness.

From the perspective of the Cold War, with all its alarms, there is a tendency to exaggerate the 'free security'[10] of the United States in earlier periods. In practice, however, Americans perceived a range of threats, from the fantastic to the possible, during this long period. Perhaps it is true that nineteenth-century Americans had as much security as men can expect in a world of sovereign states: nonetheless, there were alarms and they were taken seriously.[11] Indeed, Americans in the nineteenth century did perceive many military dangers, both real and imaginary.[12] The use of this fact to argue that nineteenth-century Americans felt almost as troubled as those in our own times[13] has more force if we remember that 'security' is a subjective concept: what is tolerable security for the modern generation would have been intolerable for those brought up in calmer times. As the world has become a more threatened place, man's sensitivity to cataclysmic possibilities has become blunted. Although objectively nineteenth-century Americans were not as threatened as today, subjectively they may have felt a greater sense of danger than we now think reasonable.

The so-called 'belated' entry of the United States into two world wars is often used as evidence to show that Americans have never been sure of their strategic interests. But what is the standard for determining whether the U.S. entries in 1917 and 1941 were 'belated'? The implicit standards, 1914 and 1939, are Eurocentric. There is little reason to suppose that an earlier entry would have been to the advantage of the United States: indeed, some have argued that the U.S. interventions were not belated enough.[14] In addition, Eurocentric perspectives diminish the significance of Latin America in U.S. outlooks. In terms of U.S. priorities, Latin America has had a significance which has been generally ignored by Europeans. *American Strategic Man* has usually been confident of his interests in the Western Hemisphere, and has been very sensitive to challenges. Like others, however, his sense of priority has diminished with distance from the homeland.

Critics have argued that with a more coherent national strategy Americans would not have been 'caught out', and would have been more successful. Perhaps sometimes more through luck than judgement, the American experience confounds such views. More often than not the critics have been inflamed by contemporary issues and have been searching for scapegoats. Furthermore, one might ask whether those states with a more coherent national strategy—those with a keener sense of threat and a longer tradition of foreign policy—have met their challenges more rationally and effectively. The evidence is not conclusive. It is but one step from having a highly developed sense of threat to engaging in pre-emptive strategies, as was illustrated by the momentum of the Schlieffen Plan. Similarly, the strategic thinking of those states with well-established lists of so-called 'vital interests' can easily become inflexible, as was illustrated by the frame of mind which led Britain to the Suez débâcle in 1956.

More than any other great power, the United States could always afford to be undersensitive about threats. The alternative pathway has led to trouble. When U.S. policy-makers did adopt a more urgent outlook, when they did inject a greater degree of strategic thinking into their policy-making, and when they did believe that they knew what were their 'vital interests', the outcome was the falling domino concept and the strategy of defending San Francisco on the Mekong. Given the geopolitical situation and interests of the United States, strategic hypersensitivity can be more damaging than strategic quietism. In nuclear planning military vigour can be ultimately disastrous. As Thomas Schelling has explained, military planning which encourages haste encourages war.[15] History suggests that the United States has less to fear from undersensitivity and deliberation than from attempting to overcompensate for quietism.

(d) *Americans believe that 'peace' is the normal pattern of relations between states.*

The alleged American belief that 'peace' is the normal pattern of relations between states has attracted great criticism from American strategists: 'No idea could be more dangerous' was Kissinger's comment.[16] According to such critics the conceptual polarisation of peace and war has made the United States vulnerable to those societies seeing conflict as the central theme of politics, whether the prevailing condition was temporarily one of peace or war.

In a narrow sense, peace is the norm in a state's foreign relations. Wars are short and intermittent and an absence of fighting is the prevailing condition. Peace meaning the absence of war has been the characteristic condition of American foreign relations. That some Americans had no higher hopes than this can be seen in the persistent debate about the best way of organising the country's military forces.[17] The absence of war was never taken to mean a 'positive peace': periodic alarms, crises, and expeditions were reminders of this. Certainly many Americans, like liberals elsewhere, hoped for a more constructive definition of peace, and hoped for a harmony of interests between the states in the system. But alongside this hope there was also an implicit and sometimes explicit recognition of the potential for conflict which existed as a result of the competitiveness of the Europeans. The fulsome rhetoric of peace in American public life must not be allowed to obscure the realistic appraisals which invariably accompanied it. Bringing the boys back home was never synonymous with radical support for general and comprehensive disarmament.

Belief in a harmony of interests which does not exist, and expecting peace by wishing, can lay countries open to those activists who conceive all politics in terms of brutal struggle. Historically, this is certainly true, but there are also grave dangers from the opposite philosophy, which sees war as 'normal'. The behaviour of societies with a high expectation of military conflict is likely to provoke and intensify such phenomena as arms races, preventive wars, high militarisation, and the finding of one's credibility always on the line. For a country in the position of the United States the idea that peace was normal made much sense as long as at least a skeleton of reasonable military preparedness was preserved. This has always been the case, with the possible exception of the interwar years. Peace was the normal expectation during the long era of 'isolated security', while in a thermonuclear context there is no alternative to 'peaceful coexistence'. Kissinger's criticism of the American approach should be completely reversed. For the United States, especially in the nuclear context, there is no more dangerous idea than to argue that peace is not normal.

(e) *Americans have been reluctant in peacetime to think in terms of military power.*

The view that Americans have been reluctant in peacetime to think in terms of military power was more relevant to American behaviour before the Cold War than since: with some justification it has sometimes been argued that the military perspective has been the dominant outlook of U.S. administrations in the last thirty years. The general criticism rests upon two propositions. The first is that, in Walter Lippmann's phrase, Americans have been 'too pacific in peace' and so have tended to abdicate the running of international politics in favour of those ready, willing, and able to use force. The second is the view that Americans have failed to make positive use in the diplomatic arena of whatever military assets they have possessed.

The allegation that Americans have been 'too pacific' is an example of a commentator learning the lessons of the last peace, in this case a post-World War II commentator generalising from the 'locust years' leading up to Pearl Harbor. From a strategic viewpoint there could obviously be little excuse for the failure of the United States, potentially the most powerful military power on earth, to deter direct attack by another state, Japan, which was significantly weaker in all the indices of power. This lack of authority was immediately underlined by Hitler's 'gratuitous' declaration of war.[18] This vulnerability was significant experience in U.S. strategic history, but it was exceptional. In general, those responsible for U.S. security have not been *so* pacific that American rights have been trampled on, or *so* incompetent in dealing in the currency of military power that they have been either profligate or swindled.

Inevitably, a degree of improvisation is necessary at the outbreak of any war. Accepting this rider, we might conclude that professional preparedness by the American military services has on most occasions been sufficient for the task in hand: their record is certainly no worse that those of their European counterparts. Furthermore, critics should recognise that until the arrival of inter-continental delivery systems American strategists were able to luxuriate in the advantages of a long haul strategy: critics should not assess historic America in terms of the instant responses and ready resources which characterise the strategic postures of a superpower in a world of inter-continental weapons systems and 'permeable' states. By the more leisurely standards of the day, the U.S. services responded well to their two greatest tests. The preparedness campaigns associated with Leonard Wood before 1917 (plus the coincidence of the Mexican War) enabled the United States to get the boys 'over there' in large enough numbers and with relative ease. A generation later, the quality of the training in the U.S. war colleges and the quality of thinking by military planners was such that adequate doctrinal frameworks were established in peacetime for total war across two continents. One could hardly ask for more from Army and Navy contingency planners.[19] Furthermore, the allegation that Americans have been 'too pacific' suggests a commitment to disarmament which has never been there in practice, though rhetoric has been plentiful. In fact, the switch to an arms control policy in the 1960s can been seen as a rejection of disarmament as an apparent ideal. For American leaders, like those of other states, disarmament policy has merely been a continuation of strategy by a reduction of military means.

The argument that U.S. leaders failed to translate relative military power into appreciable political advantage in the nuclear age has some validity. However, this is not a case of Americans being 'too pacific' or of their being strategically incompetent. As a background to this argument one must consider the difficulties in the modern period of transforming base military metal into diplomatic gold against a power like the Soviet Union, which was able to provide a range of counter-deterrents. Furthermore, all comments about this problem should stress that the period of 'peacetime' American strategic paramountcy coincided with the decline in the utility of the most powerful weapons. Military force was not as usable: its costs increased and the value of its achievable objectives waned. However, utility in non-use remained, and American strategists gave the theory and practice of deterrence a novel significance. In addition, the record of postwar crises suggests that the practice of the 'diplomacy of violence' by the United States has been generally clever, and generally more politically productive than that of its main adversary. Because it was impossible to know Soviet intentions, but at the same time because one would know only too well if deterrence failed, the overinsurance which was manifest in such ideas as 'overthink' and 'overkill' were understandable, if sometimes wasteful, predispositions on the part of those responsible for American national security.

Latin America is the clinching argument against those who view Americans as being reluctant to think in terms of military power, either out of principle or naïvety. In such countries as Mexico, Venezuela, Haiti, Puerto Rico, Cuba, the Dominion Republic, Honduras, or Nicaragua intervention or attempted military manipulation has been a regular characteristic of U.S. behaviour. In Latin America the U.S. military instrument has been characteristically used in a controlled and purposeful way. Perhaps the most interesting case in this respect, given his pacifistic and idealistic reputation, was Woodrow Wilson. Wilson had many sides: despite his reputation as an 'idealist', he was certainly not neglectful of the actual world of politics through which he had to move. His policy in the western hemisphere exemplified this. Arthur S. Link has described Wilson's perception, his sense of ultimate reality, and his consciousness of power as 'higher realism',[20] but still *realism*. Woodrow Wilson personifies the fact that the predominantly Eurocentric generalisations about American strategy have little relevance in the western hemisphere, traditionally the priority area of U.S. military interest. Indeed, in Latin America the U.S. has used force and the threat of force in ways which are more reminiscent of a protection racketeer than of the archetypal idealistic, impulsive, and absolutist *American Strategic Man* described at the start of this essay. From a Eurocentric perspective the continent of Latin America has always been regarded as insignificant. However, all generalisations about American strategy should be read with Latin America as a footnote.

American Strategy in War

(f) *Americans do not allow politics to intrude into war.*

No criticism of American strategy has been stronger than the allegation that Americans do not let politics intrude into wars. In particular, it is often argued that in their restless drive for ('military') victory Americans have obscured the real ('political') purpose of the business of war.

Several important examples, most recently from Indo-China, certainly show that U.S. leaders have not always been able to turn military activity into political success. However, to argue that they failed at least implies that they *tried*, but perhaps were hindered by faulty strategies or overly ambitious aims. Such mistakes are not peculiarly American. On the whole American leaders in the last two hundred years have been conscious of the need to let politics affect the way they prosecute their wars. Unfortunately for them, circumstantial factors have often intervened and prevented success: as Clausewitz rightly put it. 'War is movement in a resistant medium'.

The nineteenth century offers illustrations of a number of campaigns carried out with a political eye. Of particular interest were Winfield Scott's campaign in Mexico in 1846, and President Lincoln's attempt at the start of the Civil War to develop a moderate strategy which would help reconciliation (a posture which was judiciously supported by Major General McClellan). The Civil War itself is a classical example of war as movement in a resistant medium. No matter the sophistication of Lincoln's initial disposition, the war inexorably pushed to its bitter extremes. In a war in which neither side will compromise or surrender, there is no substitute for victory on the battlefield. Between political aspiration and successful military practice there is not only the fog of war: there are also its quicksands, tempests, chasms and every other conceivable climatic and geographic simile. As

Lincoln candidly admitted in 1864: 'I claim not to have controlled events, but confess plainly that events have controlled me'.

The idea that the U.S. military establishment has traditionally failed to see war in terms of politics would seem well supported by the career of Admiral Bradley Fiske. Fiske entered the Navy in the 1870s, and he participated in the development of war plans during the Taft era. However, he later confessed that it had not been until he heard a lecture by the President of the Naval War College in 1903 that he encountered the idea that war might be an instrument of politics. Until that moment he claimed never to have had any clear idea 'connected with war except that of fighting'.[21] Against the impression which such a story tends to create (confirming prejudices about the American approach) several comments are pertinent. Firstly, the responsibilities and perspectives of military contingency planners are both different and narrower than those of political decision-makers. Secondly, Fiske and many of his fellow officers were in the process of having their eyes opened to the wider possibilities by the writings of Alfred T. Mahan. And thirdly, and perhaps most important, it is necessary to recognise that there is nothing specifically *American* about Fiske's experience. Until very recently, for the military establishments of all countries, war *was* synonymous with the arts and science of fighting: strategy as such was always both a neglected and a highly reserved activity. The point was famously made by a German commander at about the same time that Fiske was having his eyes opened. The commander concerned told an associate: 'His Majesty keeps only one strategist, and neither you nor I is that man'.[22] At that moment the 'only one strategist' was von Schlieffen, the Chief of the General Staff. Paradoxical as it may now seem, the study of strategy and participation in strategic decision-making has not been professionally relevant for any military establishment until quite recently.

Those who have characterised the American approach to strategy as non-political have often dwelt upon the happenings of World War II. Some British participants and commentators, hurt by their own declining influence, disappointed in the aftermath of the war, and desperate to believe that their approach would have made a securer post-war world, have always been prominent amongst such critics of U.S. policy. Much of this criticism of U.S. policy grew out of Anglo-American differences of opinion concerning the best strategy to adopt for the Mediterranean theatre and the final campaign in north-west Europe.

As time has passed, studies of the campaigns have increasingly recognised that the American contribution was generally much more sensible and political than its British critics have alleged. In the Mediterranean, for example, it can be argued that it was not that the U.S. approach was 'non-political', but that Roosevelt had rather different priorities to those of the arch British nationalist, Winston Churchill. (It is worth mentioning in passing that in the pursuit of his goals Churchill showed much of the impatience which has been said to characterise the *American* approach to war. But this should cause no surprise: after all, Churchill was half-American.) Concerning Churchill's plans for the Balkans, military historians now accept that the Prime Minister's sense of military practicality did not match the worthiness of his political aspirations: in the event, American caution in the Balkans on military grounds was as justified as British caution had been in face of U.S. ambitions for an early cross-Channel invasion. Furthermore, while the British seem to have worried about the implications of the Soviet military advance earlier than their American colleagues, it is not obvious that a much tougher line against Stalin would have made for a more stable post-war world. In any case, tendencies towards a tougher line were checked by the conviction amongst the western leaders that continued cooperation with the Soviet Union would be necessary for a satisfactory post-war system. However, if impressing or deterring Stalin was the main criterion for a good strategy in the terminal campaigns, then the American leadership was not neglectful, if one accepts only a portion of the revisionist critique of U.S. policy. Even traditional interpretations show, if they do not stress, that U.S. planners like General Wedemeyer (Chief of the Policy and Strategy Group of the Operations Division of the War Department General Staff) did recognise the growing Soviet problem: the American desire to cross north-western Europe into the German heartland was as politically inspired as Churchill's aspirations for a new but successful Gallipoli on the periphery. In their planning for the final push to Berlin the arguments in favour of the American case seem solid. As the campaign was being planned, General Eisenhower told his Chief of Staff that he would 'cheerfully' readjust his plans for a broad push if taking Berlin was regarded as supremely important.[23]

For once, however, the western allies were not fascinated by the prospect of 'liberating' a capital. The broad front strategy made sense politically in terms of the ideas developing about zones of occupation; there would be little advantage to be gained from pressing into territory subsequently to be surrendered to the Soviet Union. Militarily, Eisenhower's broad front strategy made sense in terms of such principles of war as security, mass, simplicity, and co-operation. Logistically, it was entirely rational. And it surmounted the most important test of all: it succeeded. Montgomery's idea for a narrow thrust entailed many military risks, and for dubious political advantages. Furthermore, Montgomery himself was not the best commander for such a bold strike. About the unaccustomed panache which resulted in the disaster at Arnhem, Cornelius Ryan has written a best-seller called *A Bridge Too Far*: had Montgomery been given his head, and allowed to undertake a narrow thrust for Berlin, there is every chance that this best-seller would have been followed up by a sad sequel, *A Capital Too Far*.

American strategy in World War II has been compared unfavourably not only with that of Britain, but also with that of the Soviet Union. However, it is easy to exaggerate the extent of Stalin's Clausewitzian inspiration while overlooking his rational responsiveness to the sheer force of circumstances. The losses he was prepared to suffer in order to take particular objectives in the terminal campaigns was only partly evidence of his urgency and sense of purpose; it also reflected different values about the lives of men and the determination of what constituted 'acceptable casualities'. Furthermore, Stalin's general attitude to war as an instrument of politics shared at least one feature with that of his American colleagues. At the end of the war Stalin stressed to his Yugoslavian comrades that each side imposed its own social system as far as its army had power to do so.[24] Translated into American, Stalin's words share the same inspiration as those of Douglas MacArthur when he expressed what is usually regarded as the standard American comment on war: 'There is no substitute for victory.'

Korea is another war about which it is often argued that the Americans conceived it too much in terms of military victory, and not sufficiently in terms of political aims. This criticism is largely the result of the self-perpetuating analysis which results from the conventional image of *American Strategic Man*. Because this image rests on the assumption of an American preference for all-out war, commentators have focused obsessively on the activities of General MacArthur and especially his ideas about extending the war. By comparison, the attitudes of other representatives of the American military establishment have been overlooked: at least equal weight should be given to the fact that other commanders such as General Matthew Ridgeway (not to mention the Chairman of the Joint Chiefs, General Omar Bradley) approached their predicaments pragmatically and moderately, and adapted their thinking to the constraints set by the political leadership. MacArthur is certainly representative of some aspects of the American way of war, but the American military establishment is not simply the product of one mould. There has always been a Ridgeway for every MacArthur, just as there has been a McClellan for every Austerlitz—seeking Lee, a Bradley for every Patton, or a Spaatz for every LeMay. Korea undoubtedly created many great difficulties for U.S. strategy, but these should not be allowed to obscure either the learning or the achievement: and these were as much products of the American way of war as the melodrama surrounding MacArthur. While many have chosen to interpret the U.S. response to the Korean war in terms of confusion in face of a novel situation, one might as easily choose to be impressed by the speed and adaptability of the U.S. response to the exigencies of this first limited war of the nuclear age: and this adaptability was the more impressive because the war followed so quickly upon a total conflagration in which restraint of ends and means had been lacking. In general, the American military professionals operating in Korea were less dogmatic in their approach than many of the strategic commentators who subsequently wrote about the war, and who used its shaky foundations to build their sometimes outlandish structures of limited war theory.

The war in Vietnam was in part the product—a misapplication—of the limited war theories developed in the years after Korea. It was a war which for a long time will tarnish the image of American strategy. Whatever one might think of the justifications for the original U.S. military involvement in Vietnam, the subsequent relationship between war and politics was badly conceived and just as badly executed. The political aims were not achievable; the military strategy was not suitable; the tactics were flawed;

and the character of the war was such that it rapidly became unacceptable to large sections of domestic opinion. For these and other reasons, the war in Vietnam was a tragic exception in the American military experience.

(g) *Americans adopt a direct approach to strategy.*

This criticism has two main elements. The first is specific and technical: from this viewpoint the American way of war is contrasted with the 'indirect approach' formulated by B. H. Liddell Hart.[25] The second criticism is more general: from this perspective American strategy in war is said to be calculated to achieve military victory by the most direct means possible.

In Liddell Hart's terms, most American military campaigns have been 'direct'. But so have those of all other military powers: the so-called direct approach was the normal form of strategy in almost all the nearly 300 ancient and modern campaigns which Liddell Hart examined. Thus if one adopts Liddell Hart's perspective, the American approach is far from unique. Furthermore, if Americans as people are characterised by 'high ideals and low cunning', as the novelist Saul Bellow has suggested, then they would seem much better equipped for the business of strategy than their reputation would suggest: Liddell Hart argued that an understanding of strategic decision-making at the highest levels was synonymous with a proper sense of morality, while success at the lower levels depended upon the possession of such attributes as skill in deception. If high ideals and low cunning are the essence of the activity therefore, Americans would seem well fitted to play the role of strategist's strategist.

Indirect as well as direct approaches have been features of the campaigns of *American Strategic Man*. U.S. military history is full of the juxtaposition of both types. There have been 'direct approach' men (such as Hooker, Lee, or Eisenhower), but there have also been 'indirect approach' men (such as Washington, Greene, or Scott). Sherman's campaign in particular received considerable attention from Liddell Hart, because of its value in illustrating the characteristics and benefits of the indirect approach. In addition, Admiral Nimitz's principle of 'hitting 'em where they ain't' is a perfect reflection of the spirit of Liddell Hart's indirect approach, even if it lacks the British historian's literary style. *American Strategic Man* has always been multifaceted. This characteristic is embodied in Ulysses S. Grant. How should he be judged? Should his reputation rest on the war of manoeuvre which he wanted to fight, or on the war of attrition which he had to fight? Should he be judged primarily in terms of the deadlocked war of mass in the battlefields of Virginia, or in terms of the clever strategy and policy of reconciliation in the campaign for Vicksburg? Both parts of Grant are aspects of the American way of war, but because of the pervasiveness of the stereotyped image, and a general unfamiliarity with U.S. military history, the conventional wisdom thinks only of the Grant who presided over the killing ground in Virginia.

The epitome of America's alleged 'direct approach' to war is summed up for many commentators by MacArthur's words: 'There is no substitute for victory.' These words have been strongly criticised by the strategic intelligentsia, in part no doubt merely because the infamous MacArthur uttered them. Nevertheless, regardless of their source, they do have an important validity in the theory and practice of strategy.

There is room for at least some doubt about MacArthur's precise meaning.[26] If he meant that military victory was synonymous with a satisfactory peace then he was clearly foolish: the aftermath of two total wars and two unconditional surrenders should have taught him differently. On the other hand, if he meant that victory was preferable to any alternative merely because of the satisfaction it gave, this may be true for some survivors of war, but it is a crude outlook in the absence of any discussion of whether the price paid and the results which were obtained were justifiable. But most important of all, if MacArthur's argument was essentially that military victory gave a degree of control over the international environment which is never possible with alternatives—defeat, surrender, compromise or truce—then there can be little to criticise in his logic. And if the logic of this position is admitted, then one cannot argue with MacArthur on grounds of principle, but only over costs in particular cases. Furthermore, there is a strong argument that MacArthur's famous principle (if not his actual prescribed policy) was later vindicated by the experience of the Korean War itself. If it eventually took the threat of nuclear weapons to end the stalling of the government of the Chinese People's Republic in the truce negotiations,[27] it would seem apparent that the Chinese leaders did indeed live by the aphorism that power rolls out of the barrel of a gun. That being so, it can be legitimately argued that it was a 'blunder' on the part of the U.S. leadership when it chose not to continue the offensive of June 1951, when the Chinese forces were in disarray, for the purpose of gathering bargaining chips for an eventual settlement.[28] Military victory and a direct approach were eschewed by the American leaders: the very professional new commander of the Army, Lieutenant General James Van Fleet, had to withhold. Ironically, the man who could have offered a military victory on acceptable terms abstained from the un-American political interventionism of MacArthur, who could only offer victory on unacceptable terms. During the two years of the negotiations leading to Eisenhower's nuclear threat and the truce, over 12,000 Americans died in Korea: had the Americans used the advance for bargaining purposes, and then agreed to withdraw to the eventual truce lines, the war would have ended more satisfactorily. There would have been no substitute for the relatively easy victory which seemed within grasp in the summer of 1951.

(h) *The American way of war is overly technological.*
The general argument that the United States has always adopted a highly technological approach to war contains a variety of nuances. Firstly there is the implication that high technology warfare is particularly inhuman. Secondly, there is sometimes a guilt feeling caused by the belief that while manpower might be saved by firepower, political goals have been sacrificed by the indiscriminate character of most modern weapons. And thirdly, there is a frequently expressed belief that at least until the mid-1950s the main American contribution to strategic history was in technical innovation rather than in doctrinal development.

The problem of morality and warfare, of which high technology warfare is but one variant, is a notoriously difficult one. From a non-dogmatic viewpoint it might be argued that the only sense in which Americans have been 'culpable' has been because their ostensible standards have been 'higher'. By most standards American behaviour in war has rarely been wicked. With a handful of notable exceptions, the American way of war has not been seen as outrageous by the majority of international society. If this is accepted as a legitimate standard, then the American record over two hundred years is not unforgivable. Vietnam stands out as a particularly hurtful exception and warning.

Since governments have always regarded their primary responsibility to lie in saving their own troops rather than those of their enemies, the American preference for firepower over manpower is easily understood on a human level. But this preference has been met by a range of reactions, including some guilt feelings that Americans have left others to do the 'real' fighting and the belief that such a preference has usually been politically counterproductive. If guilt-feelings have to be assuaged, history records enough occasions in American military history to show that the country's leaders, when necessary, have not been squeamish about suffering terrible losses, while American soldiers have sometimes shown a determination to slog it out, and if necessary die, as well as the next citizen warrior. In terms of casualties per square mile, some of the battles for the Pacific Islands in World War II compared with those of the Western Front in the Great War. If technical superiority can overcome the need for Tarawas or Sommes, who will forego them? Technical superiority itself is not sufficient cause for guilt feelings: it is only deserving of blame if it is badly rather than well used, or if it is uncontrolled rather than controlled. In the last thirty years controlling the output of military research and development has been particularly difficult for both superpowers. The pressure to modernise has been intense. While Americans have been at the forefront of the urge to modernise and to perfect the machines of deterrence and death, they have also been at the forefront of the embryonic attempt to grapple with the increasing complexities of strategic arms limitation.

Those who accept that war is an unavoidable cruelty, a tragic dilemma, are drawn to the doctrine of contextual morality. If from this perspective a particular war is declared to be justifiable, as a lesser evil, the problem then becomes one of examining the cost-effectiveness of the instruments employed. By this standard there have been relatively few failures in the U.S. record. The strategic bombing campaign in World War II was wasteful in some respects, but this must be set against its experimental character. In terms of both cost-effectiveness and morality, the campaign executed by the U.S. air forces has been vindicated to a greater extent than that of the Royal Air Force. In terms of cost-effectiveness, as in other respects, Vietnam proved to be an exception in the American military experience: technological superiority was used in a strategically dysfunctional way.

In war, as in other aspects of life, it has always been tempting for foreigners to relegate Americans to the fashionably inferior category of 'doers' rather than 'thinkers'. The evidence from strategic history is much more mixed than this cliché about the great 'Can Do' society might suggest.

Without doubt, the innovative and improvising skill of U.S. society has made a major contribution to military history. However, there have been many important occasions when the 'Can Do' society has followed military leads set elsewhere. This is true of the post-war period (with ICBMs and missile-firing submarines) as well as earlier. Parallel with this mixed picture of technical accomplishment is a picture of doctrinal accomplishment which, as was suggested earlier, has been far more productive than the conventional image suggests. An interesting—some would say surprising—further illustration of this is provided by the U.S. Marine Corps. Throughout the inter-war years its planning sections produced a stream of doctrinal development, such that little improvisation was necessary when the Pacific War began. If not being surprised is one test of a strategic doctrine, the USMC proved that it had met its peacetime responsibilities to the full.

In the nuclear age, concern with high technology warfare is readily understandable. Never have science and strategy been such close or deadly companions. Scientifically, the United States felt that it could not afford to be out of date, lest it fall significantly behind its adversary. This sense of urgency answers the criticism that Americans have confused strategy with the maximum development of power. Certainly the United States has 'over-insured', but in this respect has been little different from the Soviet Union: on the other hand 'sufficiency' is an American concept, first enunciated in the mid-1950s. Equally, the argument that Americans 'seek refuge' in technology away from the 'hard' problems of strategy is scarcely supportable in the light of the extensive debating of strategic issues in the last twenty years. The image of *American Strategic Man* as being nine-tenths technology and one-tenth brain never has been valid, and is certainly not valid in the contemporary period.

The Extremism of the American Approach to Strategy

(i) *Americans are too belligerent in war.*

The criticism that Americans have been 'too belligerent' is applicable to limited campaigns rather than the whole military experience. Against the image of the march through Georgia, the raid on Dresden, or the bomb on Nagasaki must be set those episodes where military behaviour has been carefully limited, as in the interventions in Latin America, the phoney wars before 1917 and 1941, or the manipulation of military power since 1945. Some campaigns have undoubtedly shown a high degree of belligerency, but few would deem those 'excessive' in the circumstances. The final push across Europe in 1944–45 or the island-hopping across the Pacific would fall into this category. War often puts a high premium on extremes of aggressive spirit, and it is not unusual in such circumstances that nations will be profligate with enemy lives if they believe that it will contribute to the saving of their own. Extreme belligerency is sometimes rational from a strategic perspective.

The Indian Wars of the nineteenth century are often taken to typify an American tendency towards excessive bellicosity. However, as terrible as this story now reads, there is little in it which suggests that American society was especially violent in its treatment of so-called 'primitive peoples' in terms of the standards of the day. The Indian Wars occurred at a time when warfare was regarded as a normal means of settling clashes of interest, and when the act of war contained few reprehensible connotations. In fact, just the opposite was often the case. Furthermore, fighting between the Indians and the white settlers had been characterised by 'no quarter' well before the establishment of the American Republic. A century later the annihilation drives against the Indian nations seem inexcusably brutal, and often unnecessary. But in their historical context they were not exceptional. In the same era that the U.S. cavalry was ensuring, through annihilation, that the Indian threat was controlled, Imperial Germany carried out 'genocide tactics' and an 'extermination strategy' against the Hereros and Hottentots in south-west Africa, while the agents of the expanding British Empire gloried over the heaps of 'fuzzy wuzzy' slaughtered by small groups of brave men with very superior technology. In the age of imperialism, whether that process was salt-water or continental, war had a terrible utility.

In the mid-twentieth century, strategic bombing has been generally regarded as the prime illustration of excessive belligerency. There were some raids in World War II where vengeance rather than victory seems to have been the aim, but those who were not there should not be surprised if men grow angry in war. The strategic bombing campaign in that war is generally criticised in terms of cost-effectivness rather than 'excessive belligerency', but both these criticisms have been levelled against the campaign in Vietnam: in the latter case strategic bombing was seen to be both militarily ineffective and politically counterproductive. There were those, however, who argued that the bombing campaign in Indo-China was not *too* belligerent, but on the contrary was *not belligerent enough*. The proponents of this attitude argued that the United States failed to impose its will on its enemy because it did not push the war to the point at which it was unbearable for the North Vietnamese. This prescription had a deadly logic, based on Sherman's view that 'War is cruelty, and you cannot refine it', but logic is not everything in strategy. Bellicose as many of them were, the majority of Americans in the Johnson era were not prepared to accept the political and moral implications of a Sherman with B-52s marauding over Indo-China.

(j) *The American approach is to think in terms of absolutes.*

Whether or not American decision-makers have actually thought in terms of absolutes, the rhetoric of politicians is replete with the dichotomies between good and bad, red and dead, liberty and death. As the critics of U.S. policy have frequently pointed out, international politics is hardly ever amenable to such simple distinctions.

So far, this essay has argued that several aspects of the allegedly extremist character of the American way of war have been misconceived. It has been argued that both the military short-sightedness of the 1930s and the military excesses of the limited war in Vietnam were exceptions. Generally, America has neither been too pacific nor too belligerent. Two further episodes which are usually put forward as evidence of the American insistence on absolutes deserve attention. They are to be discussed not in terms of their being exceptions, but in terms of their being rational and reasonable policies, despite their reputation. The episodes are the hot war policy of unconditional surrender and the cold war policy of massive retaliation.

The critics of unconditional surrender have added little to our understanding of World War II. Both the weight of evidence and an imaginative appreciation of the exigencies of the time suggest that the criticisms of unconditional surrender seem almost entirely unjustified, unless, that is, one had an excessive faith in the German opposition to Hitler or unless one would have favoured changing sides and forming an alliance with Nazi Germany against Soviet Russia. The effect of the doctrine on the length of the war was probably marginal: if Goebbels had wanted a propaganda ploy he would certainly have invented one. But in any case the length of the war was not the main criterion, save for those whose lives were lost, in comparison with determining whether unconditional surrender was a preferable policy to a negotiated settlement with the highly ambitious and aggressive leaders of Nazi Germany and Imperial Japan. Few critics of unconditional surrender try to identify precise peace terms which would have been mutually acceptable to the peoples and governments concerned, would have shortened the war, and would have promised a more stable post-war order. Taking all the circumstances into account, the strategy of unconditional surrender was both effective and necessary. It was effective because it helped to keep the 'strange alliance' together in difficult times. It was necessary because aggressors who proclaim 'no capitulation' and 'New Orders' leave little alternative for those they attack.

Many myths have grown up around the so-called doctrine of massive retaliation. It is hardly surprising. In the doctrine and its creator, John Foster Dulles, we see the perfect scapegoat for critics of the American way of war: massive retaliation was apparently a marriage between an unsympathetic and moralising character and an extremist strategic posture. With the perspective of twenty years it is clearer that both the doctrine and the man have been badly misrepresented: the image in the popular mind is almost entirely fictitious.

In his strategic pronouncements Dulles generally did not say or mean what his critics have subsequently alleged. The apparent extremism of 'massive retaliation' is a product of the critics rather than of Dulles himself. It has frequently been argued that Dulles lost all sense of selectivity and flexibility, and that because of what was regarded as the all-or-nothing character of the threat, the United States would be left with no alternative but to choose between Armageddon or surrender. Consequently, it was argued that American threats carried no credibility. This picture is very misleading. From his writings both before and after his 'massive retaliation' speech in January 1954, it is evident that Dulles had a far more sophisticated view of the Soviet threat and of U.S. military policy than his critics have allowed. In his own mind his speech was not absolutist. On a number of occasions Dulles had stressed that reliance should not be placed on any single form of warfare, and that retaliation should include all forms of counter-attack with maximum flexibility. Not only did the critics choose to avoid a rounded picture of Dulles,[29] but they were equally wrong in their allegation that the doctrine lacked credibility. All that is known about Soviet defence policy in the second half of the 1950s suggests that its planners were greatly perturbed by the possibility of surprise attack,[30] although of course massive retalia-tion had this effect only in the relatively short period until Soviet strategic forces reached maturity. However, adversary reactions were only one element, and perhaps not the most important in Dulles' calculations. In his speech of January 1954 he was also trying to sell the 'new look' defence policy (with its prolonged burdens) to a public already weary of the effort demanded by the Korean War. But all he raised was a howl of domestic criticism. The irony of the massive retaliation episode, therefore, is that while Dulles terrified his enemies, he failed to impress his friends.

Massive retaliation deserves several additional comments. Firstly, 'nuclearmania' (as Khrushchev's critics called his shift from a conventional to a nuclear emphasis) was the order of the day. Following Eisenhower's 'new look' in 1953, the British version came in 1957 and the Soviet version in 1960. Dulles was merely a man of his time. He was also a man of his administration: while critics have focused their hostility on the Secretary of State, he was largely reflecting the views and interests of the administration as a whole, including those of the foremost American military pro-fessional of his day, General (then President) Eisenhower. Secondly, despite all the talk of flexibility in the Kennedy-McNamara era, when the eyeball-to-eyeball confrontation arose on 22 October 1962 President Kennedy's threat of a 'full retaliatory response' to any attack was pure massive retaliation (or rather than 'massive retaliation' of New Frontier demonology). Significantly, Kennedy's threat did not lead to inaction or surrender, but in fact led to what many commentators consider to be classical crisis control. Furthermore, none doubt that Kennedy's threat of massive retaliation lacked credibility. Certainly Khrushchev appeared impressed. Equally significant is the fact that the instruments of U.S. flexibility were the sort of local forces which Dulles had always said were necessary: the ships and tactics employed were the products of Eisenhower's berated defence policy. Indeed, against the argument that massive retaliation produced 'rigidity' in U.S. policy during the Eisenhower period must be set recent research findings which show that the mid-1950s represented the beginning of a period in which the United States frequently and increasingly (until 1966) used its armed forces for 'political objectives'.[31] Finally, those western European critics who have attacked Dulles for his alleged insistence on absolutes should be reminded that an almost absolute reliance on deterrence has been the preference of their governments, in the face of U.S. pressures for increased war-fighting forces.

(k) *Americans turn wars into crusades.*

One aspect of the absolutist image of the American way of war is the view that Americans turn wars into crusades. Amongst the implications of this implied criticism is the belief that when wars become crusades they cease to be rational and controllable. While it is certainly true that the United States has sometimes failed to achieve its objective in war, its strategy has only rarely been open to being described as irrational or uncontrolled. Another implication is the 'realist' belief that 'idealistic' motives should play no part in war. From this perspective, wars should be about something called 'national interests' as opposed to ideas of good and evil: wars which are 'necessary' are justifiable (indeed they are required) but 'just' wars should be avoided. This dichotomy fails to appreciate that the definition of 'necessary' is as subjective and as value-laden as is the definition of what is 'just'. Other misunderstandings arising out of this criticism have been caused by the semantic debasement which the word 'crusade' has suffered in the mouths of Americans: every war tends to be couched in the rhetoric of good and evil, and be described as a 'crusade'. With such a loose definition, the whole period since the French Revolution might be characterised as the Period of the Modern Crusades: from this perspective the American approach is merely one national manifestation of a highly ideological era.

Undoubtedly there has been a 'crusading' element in the wars in which the United States has engaged since it came to world power. It is important, however, to see this facet of American behaviour as part of the dynamics of each war. In view of the role of the Hearst press in the Spanish-American War, it might be argued that what this shows is that some Americans turn newspaper crusades into wars, which then turn Americans into newspaper readers. About the Great War twenty years later it is apparent that it did not require the United States to turn it into a crusade. The increasingly embittered Europeans had already done that themselves: God had been kept busy by both sides almost from the outset. Although American rhetoric added its own distinctive flavour after 1917, it was the British and French who initially turned the war into a crusade for the Americans. Allied propaganda before 1917, aimed at mobilising support in the United States, was full of atrocity stories and caricatures of the Beastly Hun, and it portrayed the war as a struggle between Civilisation and Barbarism. A generation later the crusading element in World War II requires neither explanation nor apology: if Adolf Hitler and his regime were not the embodiments of evil, then that word has no meaning. Few are likely to disagree with Taylor's conclusion that despite all the terrible suffering involved, it was fundamentally a 'good war'.[32] Even so, it was balance of power considerations rather than crusading spirit which initially impelled the U.S. entry into the war in Europe. But the other factors did play their part in the vigorous prosecution of the war. As with the original Crusades, far-reaching human activity is best generated by a mixture of basic self-interest and a sense of righteousness.

It is impossible to deny a crusading element in the American approach to war, with its evident sense of mission and associated moralising language. But Americans should not be judged too much on their rhetoric. The crusading element is not just a matter of ends: it is also concerned with means. In particular it is related to the fact that modern war demands sustained organised enthusiasm. Some find it necessary to turn wars into crusades, others do almost the opposite: in 1941 Stalin turned an ostensible communist crusade into a Great Patriotic War. Leaders have to do what is necessary to energise and mobilise their peoples to accept the horrors of modern war. Thus even if what is good for General Motors is good for American workers, those workers will not take up arms and fight 'foreign wars' on behalf of an industrial company. A higher call is needed. Modern wars have to be nationalised, even in the citadel of free enterprise. Once a conflict becomes 'Mr Truman's War' or 'Mr Johnson's War' it is too late. Americans cannot stand private enterprise in this area of life, and presidents know it. Wars have therefore to be given at least the trappings of crusades. As it happens, 'packaging' has been an activity in which Americans have always been skilled. Rather than simply asserting that Americans turn wars into crusades, therefore, it is at least equally important to add that crusades turn Americans into warriors.

Rethinking American Strategic Man

Several important themes have run through this essay: they are the problem of the degree of peculiarity in the American approach to strategy, the problem caused by the persistence of myths in obstructing our better understanding, the problem of determining detailed causation in American strategic history, and the problem of developing appropriate analytical criteria for assessing American behaviour. One's attitude towards these problems will have a fundamental impact on one's image of *American Strategic Man*.

1. *The problem of peculiarity.* On logical grounds it would be impossible to deny the existence of an American way of war. All nations have their own traditions and styles; the United States is no exception. However, the study of comparative strategic history minimises some of that sense of American peculiarity which has led to an over-emphasis on American cultural characteristics.[33] Some characteristics which have been thought to be peculiarly American have in fact been shared with other great powers. Strategy sometimes has its own iron laws. It is commonplace, for example, to note that the existence of nuclear weapons imposes a certain common rationality on their possessors. But universal

patterns can be seen in other aspects of U.S. strategic history. It is interesting to see, for example, that at the very beginning of the Republic, American strategy was analogous to that of all revolutionary movements which have to engage in strategy with limited resources. The American revolutionaries played in the same military drama as the Bolsheviks a century-and-a-half later, when Trotsky played George Washington's role, Tukachevskii played Nathanael Greene's role, and Frunze took the part of John C. Calhoun.

2. *The problem of the myths*. An accurate image of *American Strategic Man* is important not only for its own sake, but also because a false image contributes to bad history and may contribute to bad strategy. To the extent that the myths form the implicit or explicit frameworks of students, teachers, citizens, and officials, so they have become self-perpetuating. Strongly held myths obliterate a student's sensitivity to the 'facts' of American strategic history. The myths have both discouraged the study of American strategic history, and contributed to its being misread. Strongly held myths may also be significant in a practical sense, in that they might affect the outlooks of those concerned with policy-making. Those with access to power who believe the conventional image to be both true and undesirable might be led into overcompensating for what are seen as the old faults. In this respect one might speculate about the errors of the 'best and brightest' in the 1960s, a group which felt themselves to be New Men, created to redress the imbalances of the Old. In particular, one must consider the outlook of Henry Kissinger, who has accepted the conventional image of *American Strategic Man* but who at the same time has been one of its major critics.[34] It is too early to determine the extent to which his political behaviour has been a reaction against what he considered to be the mistakes revealed by his academic analyses, but his style gives plenty of scope for speculation.

3. *The problem of causation*. A close examination of American strategic history shows that important features of the American way of war cannot satisfactorily be explained by sweeping references to cultural characteristics ('deep traits in the American experience'). Better explanations often lie in the concatenation of accidental factors. War has often been shaped less by esoteric strategic thinking than by simple logistical possibilities. Furthermore, what are called 'strategies' are often determined as much

by internal as external considerations. Domestic politics play a crucial role: U.S. Presidents, like Janus, have to look two ways.[35] Throughout American history, public opinion has had an impact on the conduct of war which has not been fully recognised. In particular, public opinion has been critical in explaining the urge to keep up the momentum until victory has been secured. As George C. Marshall put it: 'a democracy cannot fight a Seven Years War'. This is especially true for a democracy which has been nationally secure and geographically isolated, and for whom nearly all wars have been 'over there', both physically and psychologically.

Inevitably the way a country attempts to adapt to war will be affected by such characteristics of its society as its level of technology, its administrative efficiency, its political unity, or the intensity of its sense of purpose. Thus in trying to explain American strategy, the characteristics of American society cannot be avoided: they are necessary for the completion of the jigsaw but in themselves they are not sufficient. The 'belligerency' of American behaviour can be explained partly in terms of the degree of violence which characterises some aspects of American society, the racist feelings which undoubtedly exist, and the moralistic outlooks which pervade many aspects of life. At the same time, however, American leaders have often been sensitive to the feeling that democracies cannot fight long wars and that Americans love peace: this has produced an urgency to 'get the darn thing over'. Thus the 'belligerency' which might be manifest in the American way of war can be explained by other than the *violent* traits in American society: it can also be explained by the American reluctance to fight in foreign wars, by the widespread desire for peace, and by the low threshold of war weariness. American 'society' can therefore explain external belligerence in terms of both American tolerance of violence and American intolerance of war. The peculiar characteristics of American society can explain both the getting into and the getting out of Vietnam. 'American society' explains almost everything, and therefore explains very little.

4. *The problem of analytical criteria.* It is evident that we lack appropriate standards for assessing American strategy. The thinking of most commentators is structured by distinctively Eurocentric perspectives, and especially those of continental Europe. These perspectives also inform many American outlooks, no doubt

because of the substantial role which those with recent European backgrounds have had in shaping our thinking on the subject. This pervasive Eurocentric perspective means that the American way of war has been a victim of inappropriate criteria. Continental European strategic criteria (developed from within a milieu of relatively equal and closely interacting powers, with strategies of necessity, and with traditional enemies just across a river-line or range of mountains) have not been appropriate for a country such as the United States which has been unique in terms of its relative power, remoteness, traditional security, industrial potential, choice, and (more latterly) its world-wide responsibilities and multiplicity of relationships. In terms of Stanley Hoffmann's analogy,[36] the problem becomes one of attempting to judge Gulliver's behaviour in a world of Lilliputians. From the perspective of a Gulliver, perhaps one should regard any arrogance of power or myths of omnipotence as behavioural norms. Instead therefore of berating Americans for sometimes behaving in an imperious way—for Gullivers will be Gullivers—perhaps we should be praising them for the general steadiness of their moderation.

Eurocentric perspectives and priorities have meant that some aspects of American strategic history have been misconceived, and that other features have been undervalued. In particular, Europeans have tended to undervalue the vitality of the American arms debate, the avoidance (with the exception of Vietnam) of costly and tragic errors, the good record of civilian control over the military, and the seriousness of the attempt to bring sophisticated planning into strategic affairs ('not because the future is predictable, but because it is not'). One notable element in American strategic thinking has been the frequent consciousness of the desirability of preventing the military instrument from shaping the political will. Although American leaders have by no means always been successful in their efforts, there is no similar consciousness evident in the traditional outlooks of other great military powers. This consciousness of the 'law of the instrument' runs through American military planning, from Jefferson's gunboat fleet, through the 1890 Naval Act and President Wilson's cancelling of fleet deployments and contingency planning in 1913, to congressional opposition to Fast Deployment Logistic Ships in the late 1960s. Senator Richard Russell expressed this fear best. He said: 'If Americans have the capability to go anywhere and do anything, we will always be going somewhere and doing something.' This historic consciousness of American power, choice, and responsibility is an important mark of Gulliver's self-restraint.

*   *   *

This essay has attempted to demonstrate that to the extent an American approach to strategy exists, it has been both very different and very much more complex than it has usually been portrayed, and that it has contained rather more positive features than many commentators have seen or cared to admit. Indeed, the argument of this essay suggests that that which has been pernicious in the American way of war is not that which is peculiar, while that which has been peculiar is not that which has been pernicious. Furthermore, from a perspective of two hundred years Vietnam can be seen not as typical of the American way of war, but as an aberration—a limited war that was lost. But Vietnam, like the many other episodes mentioned in the paper, reflect characteristics which are distinctively American. They are all the more American because of their complexity and diversity. The important point is that we should not accept any single image of *American Strategic Man* but several.[37] History, as opposed to the search for bad guys, demands it.

Notes

1. *American Strategic Man* as described below is a convenient fiction, but care has been taken to ensure that he is not a 'straw man'. Opinion-sampling and a wide range of literature show that he is very much alive and kicking (or more usually being kicked). See, *inter alia*, such standard works as Stephen E. Ambrose, *Rise To Globalism. American Foreign Policy* 1938–1970 (Harmondsworth: Penguin Books, 1971); Stanley Hoffmann, *Gulliver's Troubles, or the Setting of American Foreign Policy* (New York: McGraw-Hill Book Company, 1968); Henry A. Kissinger, *Nuclear Weapons and Foreign Policy* (New York: Harper, 1957); John W. Spanier, *American Foreign Policy Since World War II* (London: Nelson, 4th Edition, 1972); Russell F. Weigley, *The American Way of War. A History of United States Military Strategy and Policy* (New York: Macmillan, 1973). These books are given as representative because of their widespread use. Furthermore, far from being the worst of their type, they are the best.
2. R. A. Levine, *The Arms Debate* (Cambridge, Mass.: Harvard University Press, 1963).
3. The phrase is Correlli Barnett's: see his *Strategy and Society* (Manchester: Manchester University Press, 1974).

4. A notable exception is Richard D. Challener, *Admirals, Generals, and American Foreign Policy* 1898–1914 (Princeton, N. J.: Princeton University Press, 1973). See the Introduction.

5. Edward Mead Earle, *Makers of Modern Strategy; Military Thought from Machiavelli to Hitler* (Princeton, N. J.: Princeton University Press, first published 1941).

6. By far the most useful introduction to the evolution of American strategic thinking is Weigley, *op. cit.*

7. There is some room for dispute about the proper claimant for the role of the key strategic pioneer of the nuclear era. Bernard Brodie's strong claim is well substantiated in James E. King's *The New Strategy* (forthcoming), the first extensive intellectual history of strategy in the nuclear age. The mantle of 'Prince Charming' is, however, more popularly (and superficially) given to Henry Kissinger, whose book *Nuclear Weapons and Foreign Policy* was an early (but not *the* earliest) contribution marking the beginning of the 'golden age' of contemporary strategic theorising. As King has pointed out, however, Kissinger's book *was* the first best-seller in the field of nuclear strategy.

8. Harry L. Coles, 'Strategic Studies Since 1945: the era of overthink', *Military Review*, April 1973, pp. 3–16.

9. A. Herzog, *The War-Peace Establishment* (New York: Harper Row, 1965). This was a journalist's account of the spectrum of American thinking about national security in a most lively period.

10. The phrase is that of C. Vann Woodward, 'The Age of Reinterpretation', *American Historical Review*, LXVI (1960), pp. 1–19. The term is applied to the period before World War II.

11. See, for example, Thomas A. Bailey, *A Diplomatic History of the American People* (New York: Meredith Corporation, Eighth Edition, 1969). A substantial account of the activism of U.S. diplomacy in mid-century ('neutral, not isolationist') is presented by Alan Dowty, *The Limits of American Isolation: The United States and the Crimean War*, (New York: New York University Press, 1971).

12. William Goetzmann, *When the Eagle Screamed: The Romantic Horizon in American Diplomacy*, 1800–1860 (New York: Wiley, 1966).

13. *Ibid.*

14. Of particular interest, since it deals with the American entry into what is almost universally regarded as a justifiable war, is Bruce M. Russett's *No Clear and Present Danger. A Skeptical View of the U.S. Entry into World War II* (New York: Harper & Row, 1972).

15. Thomas C. Schelling, *Arms And Influence* (New Haven: Yale University Press, 1966), pp. 221–32.

16. Kissinger, *op. cit.*, p. 428.

17. See, for example, Walter Millis, *Arms and Men: A Study in American Military History* (New York: Putnam, 1956), *passim.*

18. A. J. P. Taylor's phrase. See his *English History* 1914–1945 (Oxford University Press, 1965), p. 532.

19. Weigley, *op. cit.*, p. 267.

20. Arthur S. Link, 'The Higher Realism of Woodrow Wilson', *Journal of*

Presbyterian History, XLI, No. 1, March 1963, pp. 4–13. Reprinted in John Braeman (Ed.), *Wilson* (Englewood Cliffs, N. J. Prentice Hall Inc., 1972), pp. 157–66.

21. Challener, *op. cit.*, pp. 14–15.
22. Walter Gorlitz, *The German General Staff: Its History and Structure 1657–1945* (London: Hollis and Carter, 1953), pp. 53, 134.
23. Quoted by Weigley, *op. cit.*, p. 353.
24. M. Djilas, *Conversations with Stalin* (Harmondsworth: Penguin Books, 1963), p. 90.
25. B. H. Liddell Hart, *Strategy: The Indirect Approach* (London: Faber, 1967).
26. See the discussion by Bernard Brodie, *War and Politics* (London: Cassell, 1973), pp. 4, 70–91. Brodie's view is that MacArthur did not have a sophisticated understanding of his phrase.
27. Dwight D. Eisenhower, *The White House Years: Mandate for Change*, 1953–1956 (London: Heinemann, 1963), pp. 178–81 is a discreet account of the episode.
28. See Brodie's argument, *op. cit.*, pp. 91–106.
29. For a sympathetic view of Dulles, see Michael A. Guhin, *John Foster Dulles: A Statesman and his Time* (New York: Columbia University Press, 1972). A different view is presented by Townsend Hoopes, *The Devil and John Foster Dulles* (Boston: Little, Brown, 1973).
30. e.g. T. W. Wolfe, *Soviet Military Theory: An Additional Source of Insight into its Development* (The RAND Corporation, P-2358, November, 1965).
31. Barry M. Blechman and Stephen S. Kaplan, *The Use of the Armed Forces as a Political Instrument* (Washington: The Brookings Institutions, 1976).
32. A. J. P. Taylor, *The Second World War* (Harmondsworth: Penguin Books, 1976), p. 234.
33. For a classification of different approaches see John Shy's important article, 'The American Military Experience: History and Learning', *The Journal of Interdisciplinary History*, Vol. I, February 1971, pp. 205–28.
34. Kissinger, *op. cit.*, especially Chapter 12.
35. See Samuel P. Huntington, *The Common Defense: Strategic Programs in National Politics* (New York: Columbia University Press, 1961).
36. Stanley Hoffmann, *op. cit.*
37. This comment follows the conclusion of David M. Potter, in 'The Quest for the National Character' (first published in 1962), reprinted in *History and American Society, Essays of David M. Potter* (London: Oxford University Press, 1973), ed. Don E. Fehrenbacher.

Alliances: Tradition and Change in American Views of Foreign Military Entanglements

Harvey Starr

Introduction[1]

The focus of this paper will be the apparently simple question, 'why do nations enter into alliances?', and how the answers apply to the foreign policy experience of the United States. The 'apparently' suggests that both the question and the answers are not as simple, or simplistic, as many observers have thought. The concept and practice of alliance are basic to the study and practice of international relations. Such basic concepts are rarely neat or easily explained; this is even more so when considered in the light of two hundred years of foreign policy during which politics and the international environment have changed in manifold ways.

In the following discussion, the selection of alliances as one of many foreign policy instruments will be discussed as a function of (i) changing American power within a relatively constant framework of national myth and rhetoric regarding America's self-image; (ii) a set of basic security interests regarding the Western Hemisphere; and (iii) a unilateral approach to foreign affairs characterised by broad swings in American foreign policy moods.

Why Do Nations Ally?

A discussion of 'foreign military entanglements' must focus on alliances. Alliances are but one form of interstate co-operation.

'Alignment' can be defined as two or more nations acting similarly towards some third object. 'Coalitions' are groups of nations exhibiting co-operative behaviour with common attitudes or approaches, and which may be formal or informal. Despite numerous conceptions of what alliances are,[2] definitions generally share two characteristics, namely that alliances are formalized by written agreements, and that they refer to war, security, and military affairs. Alliance, then, involves the collaboration of nations, generally for specified and limited periods, in regard to some mutually perceived security problem.

Given the necessity for common interests in relation to an outside threat, it is natural to find that students of alliance stress *aggregation of power* as the central reason why nations ally. The power aggregation view is often linked to terms such as 'expedient' or 'realist'. Aggregation is concerned with opposing any military threat to a nation's national security interests, so that a nation will ally with any state that can help it offset the power of others. It is from this perspective that alliance becomes the linchpin of the 'balance of power'—where power is used to deter others, or to defeat them if deterrence fails.

However, aggregation may not be the only nor the prime reason for alliance, even in regard to power and deterrence. A number of other reasons have emerged from the history and literature of alliances. A second function of alliance is 'pre-emptive', when A allies with B to prevent the addition of B's power to A's enemy, C.[3] While concerned with power, the reason for alliance may therefore not be the simple addition of another's power to one's own. Similarly, alliance may also serve 'strategic' functions, where one state allies with another to obtain the use of its territory for explicitly military strategic purposes.

In regard to a deterrent or balancing function, alliances add *precision* to international politics. Alliances have been created in the past in order to clarify the political alignment of nations, and to do so in a mutual and formal manner through treaty obligations. Deterrence depends upon the credibility of the threat: alliances assist in this by drawing lines and making clear the areas of national interests. Credibility also rests upon capability, and here alliances permit the projection of weapons and forces. Furthermore, alliances which permit this projection also provide troops which act as 'tripwires'; this increases the interdependence of the allies.

All of these signal a nation's willingness to back up a deterrent threat with action.

In addition to these basic reasons for alliance, there exist a number of others which have less to do with aggregation or multilateral co-operative behaviour. These may include: domestic political considerations, such as improving national security and stability; the desire to organise relations among allies, including the control or restraint of allies' foreign activities; the wish to extend protection and a deterrent umbrella to weaker allies in in order to enlarge one's sphere of influence; and the hope of gaining such intangible benefits as prestige. Finally, alliances have been employed to legitimise a nation's interventionary activities.

Nations may also join alliances to receive specific economic, territorial, or political benefits. In collective goods language, an alliance may be a 'privileged' group with a 'large' member.[4] This is a partner who desires some benefit—deterrence or world stability, for example—to such a degree that it will bear all the costs to obtain the benefit. If this benefit has the properties of a collective good, then it must be provided to all members of the alliance if the large member provides the benefit for itself. In this case the other partners may see no need to participate in the alliance or pay its costs. In this situation the large member will be ready to provide side payments to the other partners in order to retain their commitment to the alliance. These side payments may take many forms and be reason enough for some nations to enter into an alliance.[5]

Alliances may serve to add precision to a nation's foreign affairs, and may be particularly useful in maintaining the credibility of a nation's threats and promises. But in addition to their benefits, they also involve costs. The very loss of independence of flexibility implied in joining an alliance has been identified as the major *cost* of alliances. In essence, alliances not only create commitments, but they also create opportunities for others to test those commitments. If this testing occurs, nations may be trapped or at least constrained in their choice of action by treaty commitments. The most feared trap is war. Critics argue that alliances act as 'conduits', spreading international conflict into previously unaffected regions through alliance commitments.[6] This may be true both of powerful nations, finding their credibility and prestige challenged if they fail to come to the aid of weaker allies, and of weak allies finding themselves drawn into the web of great power conflicts. Expedient policy makers have sometimes reacted to the costs of an alliance by disregarding the relevant obligations.

In the next section, which discusses the early foreign policy of the post-Revolution United States, some of these costs will be noted, and it will be seen that none of the reasons for an alliance policy discussed above were compelling to American policy makers of this period.

Early Expediency: The United States as a Weak State in a World of Powers[7]

The first of three foreign policy styles used by Hans Morgenthau to describe American foreign policy was called 'realistic', in that American policy makers thought and acted in terms of power and self interest.[8] The behaviour of the United States regarding the French alliance may be used to illustrate a realist appreciation of power and expediency. American goals were fairly straight-forward in 1778, to defeat the British and gain independence. The Americans and the French were able to form an alliance on the basis of mutual, anti-British interests. Aggregation of power, the most commonly cited reason for alliance, was the aim of American diplomacy.

The Franco-American alliance was a classic 'war-weld' alliance. With the conclusion of the war, mutuality of interests disappeared. For the Americans the ending of the war converted the alliance from a useful tool of foreign policy into a burden. Only the costs of commitment remained. When the French Revolution precipitated war on the European continent, the obligations entailed by the alliance added to the problems of Washington's first administration by apparently requiring American support for the French. Washington fashioned a compromise between the positions of Hamilton, his Secretary of the Treasury, and Jefferson, his Secretary of State. He decided not to honour the treaty (as Hamilton wished), but neither did he repudiate it (in accordance with Jefferson's wishes). He simply proclaimed neutrality, without attempting to obtain additional concessions from Britain (as Jefferson had urged). The interests of the United States were attended to, and the alliance was not.

The French Treaty is one piece of evidence to support the 'realist' characterisation of early American foreign policy. Washington's Farewell Address of September 1796 is another. As has been noted by a number of observers, Washington—in an address actually drafted by Hamilton—warned only against *permanent* alliances. Washington took the flexible approach that alliances might be 'good' or 'bad' only inasmuch as they served American interests. Alliances in themselves were not condemned. Such expediency of action continued into a second style of American foreign policy, which Morgenthau termed the 'ideological'. Exemplified by men such as Jefferson and John Quincy Adams, the ideological style saw policy makers *thinking* in terms of moral principles, but *acting* in terms of power.[9]

Clearly, the foreign policy of this period could be characterised as expedient: American statesmen did what was conceived to be in the nation's best interests with the appropriate foreign policy tools. They were also 'realist' in their concern with relative power. Making the realist inferential leap, we will simply assert that a nation's best interests are largely determined by that nation's 'power'. Through most of history, and certainly in the period under consideration, military capabilities have been particularly important determinants of that power. If a nation was weak in terms of military capabilities, it had to find other tools and policies by which it could adapt to its environment. During the Revolution an alliance was one such tool. Afterwards, alliances were not used. They are a matter of expediency, not principle.[10] Why did American attitudes change?

In the period up to approximately the Mexican-American War, the young, weak United States had no need to use alliance for aggregation of power. Geographically remote from the centres of international power, the United States had little incentive to join alliances, even after the War of 1812. At this point the United States did share mutual interests with Britain, but the precision and costs of an alliance were unnecessary. Instead, the United States took advantage of Britain's being a 'large member' in a two-member 'privileged' group: Britain was willing to bear all the costs of protecting the Western Hemisphere in order to maintain a European balance and to further its commercial interests. The United States was, in collective goods terms, a 'free rider', and did not need to pay the costs of joining an alliance and finding itself once again dominated by Britain. The United States simply benefited from the extraordinary security provided by British diplomacy and seapower.

Another possibility was aggregation with other small powers, such as the emerging Latin American nations. George Liska has observed that alliances between small states have not been very prominent, and have been unsuccessful in providing either external security or internal stability to small nations.[11] Would the promise of benefits or side payments of some kind have brought the United States into such an alliance? Theories of coalition formation and of the distribution of rewards and losses in war coalitions,[12] indicate that the various political and economic benefits that might accrue to alliance partners tend to go to those with greater military power. As a weak state, the promise of such benefits to the United States was small. Indeed with a continent to exploit there were few material side payments worth the costs of alliance commitment.

America's youth, weakness, and recent colonial status gave compelling arguments in favour of a policy of non-alliance. The new, weak, ex-colonial states of the post-World War II period share many common features with the young United States, and they have employed many of the same non-alignment arguments. All these nations were militarily weak. They emerged during periods of major power conflict, and ran the risk of being drawn into them. At the same time there existed a great power umbrella under which the weak nations could take a 'free ride'. The young United States had the British navy, while the post-war non-aligned nations had the American nuclear deterrent. Most importantly, all these nations were preoccupied with internal concerns.

These internal concerns began with a collective need to seek, establish, and assert a new and unique identity separate from their former colonial status. In the post-war world, ex-colonial countries found the possibility of being viewed as satellites or 'camp followers' degrading. A policy of non-alignment permits a nation to build an independent identity and to assert its autonomy as a sovereign international actor. An independent international stance is a manifestation of 'counterdependence', a psychological state in which an individual or group is changing a relationship of dependence and/or inferiority to one of equality.[13] The identity crises of counterdependence produce strong pressures on national leaders to follow independent policies and not to appear to be leading a nation back into a dependency relationship. The legitimacy and tenure of a new nation's leaders may rest upon the pursuit of independent, non-aligned policies. In the American experience, the clearest expression that a sense of independence was mandatory for a healthy self-image was provided by John Quincy Adams. In regard to the future Monroe Doctrine, he noted in his diary in November 1823 that he had advised President Monroe, 'It would be more candid, as well as more dignified, to avow our principles explicitly to Russia and France, than to come in as a cockboat in the wake of the British man-of-war.'[14]

Also of importance to new, weak states is the argument that non-alignment cuts the conduit that alliance supposedly provides for war. The conduit argument, for example, was one aspect of India's longstanding international feud with Pakistan in the post-war period. India criticised Pakistan for joining SEATO and CENTO, and bringing the Cold War and superpower nuclear rivalry onto the sub-continent. Similarly, America's policy of non-alliance in the nineteenth century was designed to keep European conflicts European. However, geographic position and the state of technology meant that the United States could more easily opt out of nineteenth century great power struggles than could the post-war non-aligned nations escape the Cold War.

Expediency was therefore the key to American behaviour. The desire to behave flexibly in foreign relations was the main determinant of American attitudes towards alliance policy. It was recognised that an alliance with one power might provoke another, whereas a policy of non-alliance would permit a greater freedom of action. Liska has outlined three basic motives for small powers to ally with major powers: security, stability, and status.[15] However, none of these motives applied to the United States during its period as an emergent, weak nation following the Revolution and the French alliance. Expediency was the essence of young America's policy of non-alliance. This policy, which is part of a continuing theme of unilateralism in U.S. foreign policy, came to be cloaked with a series of justifications based on the protection of America's unique domestic character. These justifications came to rigidify the early expedential non-alliance policy under the rhetoric and ideology of 'isolationism'.

Under the Cloak of 'Isolationism': Introversion, Extroversion and Unilateralism

It is rare to encounter a commentary on American foreign policy which does not include 'isolationism' as a major theme, factor, or process. If isolationism is a meaningful concept, America's failure to employ alliances is easily explained and one need proceed no further in regard to the question of United States 'military entanglements'. But isolation is not a very useful or meaningful concept. It is necessary to develop a more complex answer to the questions surrounding U.S. alliance policy in the period after the early years discussed above.

The isolationist mystique has served to obscure or cloak much of American foreign policy. However, strong arguments support the view that the mystique of insularity has been employed as a cover for both policies of introversion and various forms of extroversion.[16] Part of the problem of 'isolationism', of course, is conceptual and definitional. Different interpretations of its meaning have permitted Americans to oppose almost any United States activity in foreign affairs from participation in the International Red Cross to participation in the United Nations.

The most narrow interpretation of isolation is the rejection of entangling military alliances. The early American policy of avoiding such commitments led some to interpret isolationism more broadly as an 'instinct for maintaining one's independence'.[17] For many, freedom of action meant freedom from constraints imposed by the more powerful European states. Isolation was not only non-alliance with Europeans, but it also implied a refusal to take part regularly as a member of the European diplomatic system. While commercial interactions were acceptable, political interactions were regarded as dangerous, for political interactions, like alliances, could act as conduits to war.

What we find in many works is a definition of isolationism in European terms only. Interaction and interference with other areas were acceptable. Aloofness to foreign affairs was not part of this interpretation: 'In the American tradition, isolationism did not represent a passive attitude towards politics. Rather it was one aspect of America's aggressive territorial growth and its cultural and economic expansion. . . .'[18]

This activist interpretation of isolationist thought has encouraged a number of observers to conclude that the United States was never isolationist in any general sense of the term, but only in the narrowest sense of peacetime alliances. The critics of the term are reacting to its dual nature. They question the utility of a term which is presumed to indicate aloofness or withdrawal, but is also said to indicate both commercial interactions and diplomatic and military intervention in the affairs of non-European nations. This duality derives from an American self-image of moral and political unique-ness, or 'exceptionalism', which called for the protection of the singular American democratic experiment. This was to be achieved both through avoidance of European power politics and war, and a missionary expansionism in non-European areas.

The outlook of the United States was based on a particular logic of international relations. It was assumed that if a nation wished to avoid war it needed to avoid conflict situations with other possible participants. For the United States this meant the avoidance of political involvement with the European powers. It also meant paying special attention to avoiding military en-tanglement, particularly military alliances, since alliances were basic to the European balance of power system in which war was in acceptable mechanism of deterrence and defence. Thus, no alliance entanglements would mean no war, or at least minimise the probability of war.

At the same time America's separation from Europe and its unique self-image led to, and was justified by, a strong missionary zeal to remould the world in the American image. This globalist theme ('liberal reformism') was, in fact, a way to rationalise unilateralist security policy. Thus, we arrive at a point where isolationism has been found to evolve through a series of argu-ments into simply another way to characterise American national security policy, in both its passive and active forms. The periodic shifts in U.S. foreign policy between international activity and international quiescence can be analysed in terms of the cycles of introversion and extroversion developed by Frank Klingberg.[19] Throughout these cycles, whether they have been classified as introvert or extrovert, whether policy appears insular or inter-ventionary, the constant theme is that American behaviour can be demonstrated to be unilateralist.

Klingberg's thesis was that there existed a patterned 'mood' alternation in American history. He argued that there are two

broad moods in American foreign policy: (1) extroversion,
'... a nation's willingness to bring its influence to bear upon
other nations, to exert positive pressure ... outside its borders',
and (2) introversion, '... when America was unwilling to exert
much positive pressure upon other nations.'[20] Extroversion is a
period of expansion and the extension of influence, while introversion consists of consolidation and preparation.

Employing a variety of indicators both of American foreign
policy behaviour (e.g. treaties, wars, armed interventions, annexa-
tions, diplomatic warnings, naval budgets, content analysis of
Presidential messages), and of the 'popular mood' of Americans
(e.g. analyses of political party platforms and election results)
Klingberg delineated four periods of introversion averaging
almost twenty-one years each, and three periods of extroversion
averaging twenty-seven years each.

Table 1
Klingberg's Phases of Introversion and Extroversion

Introvert	Extrovert
1776–1798	1798–1824
1824–1844	1844–1871
1871–1891	1891–1919
1919–1940	1940–

Klingberg's last period of extroversion begins around 1940.
Twenty-seven years later we discover the 'beginning of the end'
in Vietnam, a deceleration process that picked up momentum
with the decision of Lyndon Johnson not to seek re-nomination
and the subsequent election of Richard Nixon.

Klingberg proposed several possible reasons for the shift from
introversion to extroversion, including lack of success during
introvert periods, a desire for activity and excitement, or simply
a desire for change. Whatever the reason, America's coalition
activity can be found exclusively during extrovert periods.
Between 1821–1967 the United States participated in a number of
informal war coalitions.[21] These include participation in the
Boxer Rebellion in 1900, World War I in 1917 (as an 'associated',
not an allied power), the Russian Intervention beginning in 1918,
and three coalitions involving some type of formal arrangements,

namely World War II, the Korean War, and Vietnam. America's extensive alliance network after World War II was cast abroad during an extrovert period, and began to be retrieved during the latest introvert phase.

Klingberg saw introvert periods arising from the need for rest after periods of strain and tension, and for consolidation after a period of expansion. The Vietnam War was just such a strain, occurring at the conclusion of America's most expansionary period.[22] The arrival in 1967–68 of an introvert phase also therefore conformed perfectly with Klingberg's earlier analysis.

Nixonian foreign policy, though worrisome to some observers fearful of a return to 'isolationism', may be viewed as a predicted period of introversion. While the 1950s were part of a period of extroversion which employed all the methods of expansion including alliances, the late 1960s began the consolidative reaction which could have been predicted on the basis of Klingberg's cycles. This period has witnessed the curtailment of American expansion, and the reactions to the problems and burdens resulting from an active and expansionist policy.

As with earlier periods, introverted foreign policy behaviour has been accompanied by a public mood of introversion. On both the élite and mass levels there is an uncertainty over future directions in foreign policy, and belief in the end of American 'exceptionalism'.[23] The Nixon doctrine and the Nixon-Kissinger foreign policy in general has been described as a policy of 'retrenchment without disengagement', as a way to 'lower the American profile'.[24] Nixonian caution reflected the use of more selective criteria for foreign commitments and intervention. On élite and mass levels America's role as leader of the 'Free World' was seen as too burdensome. The need, in a period of introversion, was to reduce the burdens of involvement without losing the confidence of allies or weakening the credibility of American commitments.[25] This trend continued into the Ford administration under the guidance of Henry Kissinger.

By employing the concepts of introversion and extroversion the fluctuations of American foreign policy can be assessed without resorting to the rhetoric of isolationism, or attempting to see all American behaviour as part of 'withdrawal' or 'insulation'. The unifying feature in American policy is not isolationism but 'unilateralism'. Unilateralism relates to the desire of nations to maintain independence or self-sufficiency in foreign affairs. This desire for autonomy can take the form of either withdrawal or intervention. In the nineteenth century it generally involved the setting of limits on American participation in international politics: in the twentieth century it has generally involved active participation in international politics, while ultimately always relying on America's own skill and strength, even when participating in alliances. It is apparent that unilateralism derives from the realist or expedient goal of flexibility and freedom of action. Such a unilateral policy seeks to achieve American interests with the most appropriate instruments for particular tasks. As will be seen below, policies of alliance and non-alliance are both entirely consistent with the unifying theme of the American desire to maintain independence and self-sufficiency in foreign affairs. The apparent paradox is explained by the special character of a superpower alliance, namely the idea of a 'large member'.

Hans Morgenthau provides guidance in the search for a basic set of American interests by arguing that American foreign policy has been 'consistent', 'simple and coherent'. It has continuously held as its goal the establishment and maintenance of hegemony in the Western Hemisphere.[26] The physical security of the United States was perceived to rest upon America's unrivalled dominance in the New World. This dominance could be threatened only by external, European, power. American policy, therefore, was designed to prevent conditions in Europe such that any one power or group of powers could pose a threat to American hemispheric dominance. The mechanism of that policy, despite the cloak of isolationism and exceptionalist rhetoric, was the balance of power. American policy sought to create and maintain a European balance without the commitments and loss of flexibility attendant with alliance. Although it conflicted with the logic of isolationism, war might also be part of this American balancing mechanism.

The Monroe Doctrine epitomises the successful pursuit of a balance of power policy while retaining the flexibility and independence of a unilateral foreign policy. As noted, Anglo-American mutuality of interests permitted America to forego a formal alliance. The United States acted unilaterally and European powers were balanced off against each other in terms of British commercial interests, with the British navy opposing the possible recolonisation of Latin America by the continental powers. In addition, America established a 'doctrinal' claim to the whole hemisphere. Later corollaries by Presidents James Knox Polk and Theodore Roosevelt continued the unilateralist and hegemonial themes.

American power and interest may be seen as interrelated, with the expansion of one leading to the expansion of the other. Each extension of American power created new security interests to be protected and new areas in which to create balances against external threats. After 1898 the United States became a Pacific power. Thus the opportunity was created for American interests to be threatened not only in the New World but in the Pacific as well. As with the Monroe Doctrine, Hay's 'open door' notes of 1899 and 1900 were unilateral acts within the context of an informal Anglo-American alignment, aimed at balancing the power of the European states active in China.

This balancing theme can be drawn through World War I, World War II, and into the post-war period where changes in the worldwide distribution of power have affected America's choice of foreign policy instruments. In the earliest years of American foreign policy the United States achieved 'balance' through an informal coalition with Britain. The benefits to a young and weak nation of avoiding alliances were noted above. As the United States developed into a major power it found itself participating in informal war coalitions with the European powers to achieve a balance, as in World War I, and in a wartime alliance for the same purpose in World War II. Balance could be obtained only by American military participation in European conflicts.

With the conclusion of World War II the United States emerged as a 'superpower' in a bipolar world. America once again resorted to a policy of unilateral balancing. The Truman Doctrine, which set in motion a policy of containment to balance the Soviet threat to Europe, was consistent with the traditional policy of seeking balance in Europe in order to preserve the security of the Western Hemisphere. However, it has also been argued that the end of World War II brought about a 'revolution' in American foreign policy. [27] This would not be the case if the American alliance system could be demonstrated to be a unilateral instrument of American policy aimed at 'balancing' Soviet power.

The Superpower Alliance System

The utilisation of peacetime military alliances as instruments of American foreign policy coincided with a major change in America's power position relative to the international system. Emerging from World War II in what Klingberg would argue was a period of extroversion, the United States was no longer simply a major power, but a 'superpower' with 'vital' interests which were perceived as global. This global concern derived from the nature of the international system which had been transformed from multipolarity to bipolarity by World War II. The bipolar structure encouraged a zero-sum view of the world, such that triumphs by the opposing superpower were automatically seen as losses to the United States. A realist view of the world concluded that the United States was the only nation with the economic and military capabilities to balance the Soviet Union — to deter it from expansion or to defeat it in war.

By the end of World War II the United States had achieved a relative power position unsurpassed in its history. Consequently, the need to structure an international order to meet this expansion of power, and the need to deal with the concomitant growth of interests, was greater than ever before. America was an 'imperial' state, which according to George Liska is '. . . a state that combines the characteristics of a great power, which, being a world power and a globally paramount state, becomes automatically a power primarily responsible for shaping and maintaining a necessary modicum of world order . . .'[28] For the first time since the French Treaty, America's power position suggested the utility of formal alliances. As noted above, alliances may be employed to structure a world environment favourable to a nation's values and security interests,[29] but America's post-war alliances were to be different, in that their focus was not upon aggregation of power, but upon a variety of other functions which made them instruments of a predominantly unilateral policy.

Alliances may serve to add precision to international politics, and in so doing draw the sorts of clear lines that add credibility to deterrent threats. This was a common theme in America's post-war alliances: they were a response to a perceived Soviet threat, and were established to deter Soviet aggression. NATO had been created for essentially these reasons in 1949, and the logic of using alliances for precision was brought home to American policy makers by the Korean War. One lesson that Americans, particularly Dulles, drew from the North Korean attack was that the United States had to make it absolutely clear to the Communists precisely where it would resist Communist expansion, and so try to prevent future Korean-like miscalculations on the part of potential enemies.

Returning to previously discussed concepts, we note that American alliances served 'strategic' functions. The strategic role is essentially a unilateral one, with the United States actively using the territory of its allies for various strategic purposes—for the creation of a deterrence system, and the distribution of the actual physical means of deterrence. These purposes were to be achieved through the alliance functions of balancing and denial. American alliances were 'preemptive' in that America did not want the Soviet Union to augment its power or enhance its strategic position in the alliance areas. By allying with these nations, they were being denied to the Soviets.

Denial may be seen as a component of the 'balancing' function of alliances. Balance here is not meant in the cooperative, aggregation of power sense, where allies pool military capabilities in opposition to some enemy. Rather, it denotes denial of areas to the opponent. In addition, America's alliance system provided America with the opportunity to bring American power to bear against Soviet power, and to do so outside the Western Hemisphere. This notion of countervailing American power, employed at every possible point of Soviet pressure, was the official interpretation of Kennan's logic of containment ('the adroit and vigilant application of counter-force at a series of continually shifting geographical and political points . . .').[30]

The United States attempted to achieve containment by the projection of American power across geographic space through a variety of multilateral and bilateral treaties. The United States entered into 'collective defence arrangements' with forty-two nations in the post-war period. These included allies in the four multilateral treaties—the Rio Pact (1947), NATO (1949), ANZUS (1951), and SEATO (1954)—and bilateral treaties with the Philippines (1951), South Korea (1953), Taiwan (1954), and Japan (1960). The United States also promoted the formation of the Baghdad Pact in 1955; it co-operated informally in its activities, but never formally joined. This group became CENTO in 1959 after the withdrawal of Iraq.

The collective defence system indicated the extent of American extroversion and was a feature of American policy aiming at an acceptable world order. The alliances also demonstrated the enormous disparity of power between the United States and its 'partners'. Because of the extent of this predominance, America was left with significant freedom of action. Initially at least, America's alliances were neither constraints nor burdens, while they served a range of useful functions.

As noted earlier, a structure of international order may be strengthened through the control of one's allies, and the control of relations among allies. The United States has attempted to follow this policy in regard to Taiwan; its NATO allies (especially in the 1956 Suez affair), and its allies in general over such issues as the recognition of Communist China, or trade with Cuba. A related aspect of control concerns American interest in the domestic politics of allied governments. It has sometimes been argued that the United States sought allies not to augment power, but to use its military and economic aid to support friendly governments and to forestall revolution within the countries concerned. Support for this argument is provided by U.S. policy in Latin America, and in the American relationship with various South Vietnamese governments.

A final control function of alliances is in their use to legitimise unilateral American actions around the world, and to legitimise the American global presence. In an attempt to resemble, at least superficially, the moralistic and virtuous American self-image, alliances provide the impression of multilateralism in American foreign policy. Some situations perceived as threats to American security interests have been reacted to unilaterally, but have sometimes been presented to the world and the American people as multilateral, regional responses. This has been attempted most often in Latin America; the intervention in the Dominican Republic in 1965 was a notable example. The control of allies has simply been one aspect of an overriding American foreign policy goal, namely the establishment and maintenance of a world order amenable to American security interests, particularly dominance in the Western Hemisphere.

Deterring the Soviet Union has been a central feature of U.S.

alliance policy since World War II. Deterrence is a non-competitive benefit with collective good features. One feature of a collective good is 'jointness of supply', which means that if some good or benefit is provided to any one member of some group, all the group members are provided with it at no extra cost, and with no subtraction from the amount of the good available to others. A second characteristic is 'nonexclusiveness', meaning it is not possible to exclude group members who do not pay for a good from enjoying the benefits of that good. Deterrence may be seen as a 'mixed' good, one with some collective properties.[31] In that the United States acted as a 'large member' in a privileged group, American post-war alliance policy rested on the United States wanting deterrence to such an extent that it willingly and necessarily provided deterrence to its allies and others. In this case American policy was still unilateral but, because the goal sought had collective properties, its allies also benefited from the extended deterrence.

America's role as a large member may be demonstrated in several ways. In addition to dominating its allies in economic and military power, America's interests were global while her allies' were local or regional. Also relevant is the wheel analogy employed by Wolfers, in which the United States was seen at the hub and each ally was seen at the end of a spoke. Only the United States was connected with all of the spokes and was concerned with the entire wheel.[32] A somewhat different conception of the large member is that of a leader or 'entrepreneur', whose specialised role is to bring about the provision of collective goods.[33] NATO, for example, is distinguished from many past alliances in that such an entrepreneur—the United States—is a member.[34]

In summary, American alliances established during the late 1940s and 1950s can be seen as instruments of a unilateral policy. In general, they were not attempts to augment or aggregate power. These alliances served to deny the Soviet Union areas of expansion, while providing strategic locations for the projection of American power. Several deterrent functions were performed: they provided locations for American "tripwires", and they added precision and credibility to American commitments. The alliances were also used to legitimise American global involvement, and to aid in the general goal of international order by the control of American allies.

The most recent change in the role of America's alliance policy took place in the late 1960s, and resulted from a shift in the relative power of the United States, which in turn was a consequence of the Soviet achievement of strategic nuclear parity. This development has substantially altered American security needs. In particular it has intensified the realisation that international order requires policies that will lead to the moderation of tensions and the reduction of conflicts that might lead to mutual nuclear destruction. While America's alliances remained in the background, helping to clarify commitments, the task of attending to them was subordinated to the Nixon/Kissinger policy of dealing directly and unilaterally with the Soviet Union and the People's Republic of China. This change of emphasis in U.S. policy was a manifestation of the initial stages of a new introvert period which followed a war perceived as partially caused and defined by alliances. Vietnam was also a war which clearly indicated the limits of American global power.

Given these changing circumstances, and the styles of Nixon and Kissinger, it is not surprising that the American view of a 'stable structure of peace' called for Bismarckian flexibility in diplomacy. Brzezinski has observed that the Bismarckian balance was based on 'movement and flexibility, on taking by surprise both friends and enemies alike'.[35] Flexibility in diplomacy, then, was seen as a more useful foreign policy tool than alliances, and consequently alliances assumed a much lower priority in Nixon-Kissinger policy.[36] America's détente policy, its 'surprise diplomacy' in regard to China, and its monetary policy of the early 1970s, all indicate a unilateral policy of flexibility towards both allies and opponents.

Of the three basic components of Nixonian foreign policy, 'partnership' was quite clearly subordinate to 'negotiation' and 'strength'. In addition to the Nixon Doctrine, American ties to Taiwan and Japan were lessened, SEATO began the process of dismantlement, and the 'Year of Europe' never came to fruition. In 1969 Nixon even announced a 'low-profile' policy for Latin America. With no subsequent change in America's relative power in international relations (although a number of military and political figures attempted to argue that the trend was towards American *inferiority* to the Soviet Union), the alliance policy of the Ford Administration did not differ substantially from its predecessor.

Isolationism is the usual response to questions about America's historical experience with alliances. However, it has been demonstrated in this essay that the theme of American foreign policy through both periods of introversion and extroversion has been one of unilateralism and expediency. Consequently, U.S. leaders have employed the tools of foreign policy most appropriate for their perceptions of the country's basic balance of power security interests. Alliances are but one such tool. Those statesmen who have tended to invoke isolationism or anti-communism when confronted with explaining U.S. alliance policy have been too simplistic. By setting out the many possible purposes and uses of alliances in the light of general international relations theories, it has been possible to arrive at a more sophisticated understanding of why alliances were or were not employed during the first two hundred years of the American Republic.

Notes

1. Support for this research was granted by the Center for International Policy Studies, Indiana University, under Grant 750–0514 from the Ford Foundation.
2. Several different conceptions of alliances are: as techniques of statecraft, as international organisations, as regulating mechanisms in the balance of power. See Ole R. Holsti, P. Terrence Hopmann, and John D. Sullivan, *Unity and Disintegration in International Alliances: Comparative Studies* (New York: John Wiley and Sons, 1973), p. 3.
3. Edwin H. Fedder, 'The Concept of Alliance', *International Studies Quarterly*, Vol. XII, No. 1, 1968, p. 67. Here, Fedder develops the idea of three functions of alliance—augmentative, preemptive and strategic.
4. Mancur Olson, *The Logic of Collective Action* (New York: Schocken, 1971 revised edition), pp. 49–50.
5. These side payments could include direct economic or military aid, favourable trade agreements, specific political positions (possibly reflected in voting positions in international organisations), territorial or sphere of influence transfers, and so forth.
6. See Ole R. Holsti, 'Alliance and Coalition Diplomacy', in James N. Rosenau, Kenneth W. Thompson and Gavin Boyd (eds.), *World Politics* (New York: Free Press, 1976), p. 367.
7. I have freely revised the title of Marshall Singer's book, *Weak States in a World of Powers* (New York: Free Press, 1972).
8. See Hans J. Morgenthau, *In Defense of the National Interest* (New York: Knopf, 1951). On p. 18 Morgenthau quotes Hamilton's question: 'Must a nation subordinate its security, its happiness, nay its very existence to the

respect for treaty obligations . . .' and records Hamilton's negative answer.

9. The third style was the 'moralistic'—thinking *and* acting in terms of moral principles in the manner of Woodrow Wilson.

10. Hans J. Morgenthau, *Politics Among Nations* (New York: Knopf, 1973 fifth edition), p. 181.

11. George Liska, *Alliances and the Third World* (Baltimore: Johns Hopkins Press, 1968), p. 50.

12. Harvey Starr, *War Coalitions* (Lexington, Mass.: D. C. Heath, 1972).

13. Marshall Singer, *op. cit.*, p. 42.

14. Quoted in Richard Hofstadter (Ed.), *Great Issues in American History*, Vol. I (New York: Vintage Books, 1958), p. 243.

15. Liska, *op. cit.*, p. 50.

16. To be discussed in more detail below.

17. Robert H. Puckett, *America Faces the World: Isolationist Ideology in American Foreign Policy* (New York: MSS Information Corporation, 1972), p. 13. Below, the same idea will be labelled 'unilateralism', omitting both the isolationist rhetoric and the isolationist connotation of insularity or withdrawal.

18. Paul Seabury, *Power, Freedom and Diplomacy* (New York: Random House, 1963), p. 47.

19. Frank L. Klingberg, 'The Historical Alternation of Moods in American Foreign Policy', *World Politics*, Vol. IV, No. 2, 1952, pp. 239–273.

20. *Ibid.*, p. 239.

21. Starr, *op. cit.*, see Appendix A.

22. Laurence L. Whetten has observed: 'In the final analysis Vietnam is likely to be an American parallel to the Boer War for Britain and Algeria for France. These were manifestations of retrenchment within empires and the contraction of the outer limits of influence abroad . . .' See *Contemporary American Foreign Policy* (Lexington, Mass.: D. C. Heath, 1974), p. 59.

23. See Daniel Bell, 'The End of American Exceptionalism', *The Public Interest*, Vol. XLI, No. 2, 1975, pp. 193–224.

24. Robert E. Osgood, 'Introduction: The Nixon Doctrine and Strategy', in Robert E. Osgood, et. al., *Retreat From Empire?* (Baltimore: Johns Hopkins Press, 1973), p. 3.

25. The Nixon Doctrine, first enunciated on Guam in 1969, included three major points: (1) the United States would keep all its treaty commitments; (2) the United States would provide a nuclear shield for allied nations threatened by another nuclear power, or for nations 'whose survival we consider vital to our security and the security of the region as a whole'; (3) in cases of conventional aggression the United States would furnish military and economic aid when requested, 'But we shall look to the nation directly threatened to assume the primary responsibility of providing the manpower for its defense'. See *United States Foreign Policy, 1969–1970: A Report of the Secretary of State* (Washington, D.C.: U.S. Government Printing Office, Department of State Publication 8575, 1971), p. 36.

26. See Morgenthau, *op. cit.*; also *A New Foreign Policy for the United States* (New York: Praeger, 1969).

27. See, for example, Kenneth N. Waltz, *Foreign Policy and Democratic Politics* (Boston: Little, Brown, 1967), p. 77; and John G. Stoessinger, *The Might of Nations* (New York: Random House, 1973, fourth edition), p. 147.

28. George Liska, *Imperial America* (Baltimore: John Hopkins Press, 1967), p. 10.

29. *Ibid.*, p. 3. Liska also notes that, 'Alliances are the *institutional link* between the politics of the balance of power and the politics of preponderance or empire' (emphasis added). See *Alliances and the Third World, op. cit.*, p. 23.

30. "X" (George F. Kennan), 'The Sources of Soviet Conduct', *Foreign Affairs*, Vol. XXV, No. 4, 1947, p. 574.

31. See Bruce M. Russett and Harvey Starr, 'Alliances and the Price of Primacy', in Bruce M. Russett, *What Price Vigilance? The Burdens of National Defense* (New Haven: Yale University Press, 1970), pp. 94–95.

32. Arnold Wolfers (Ed.), *Alliance Policy in the Cold War* (Baltimore: Johns Hopkins Press, 1959), p. 7.

33. See, Norman Frohlich, Joe A. Oppenheimer and Oran A. Young, *Political Leadership and Collective Goods* (Princeton, N. J.: Princeton University Press, 1971).

34. See, Edward L. Morse, 'Core-Periphery Relations and the Bargaining Structure in NATO', paper prepared for the Annual Meeting of the American Science Association, New Orleans, September 1973, pp. 15–16.

35. Zbigniew Brzezinski, 'United States Foreign Policy: The Search for Focus', *Foreign Affairs*, Vol. LI, No. 4, 1973, p. 715.

36. John G. Stoessinger records Kissinger saying, in a moment of exasperation and anger, that he 'didn't care what happened to NATO.' See, *Henry Kissinger: The Anguish of Power* (New York: W. W. Norton, 1976), pp. 219–20.

Changing Conceptions of War in the United States

Anatol Rapoport

It is hardly necessary to point out that in a complex society a wide range of conceptions will be found regarding any phenomenon, including war. This is especially true of American society, where emerging conceptions are an amalgam of many inputs and where the absence of an officially sanctioned religion or philosophy has created a potentially limitless freedom of opinion. For these reasons it may seem at first thought impossible to say anything at all about 'American' thinking on any issue, in particular on war and peace. Nevertheless, there are certain themes related to these issues that have been given particular emphasis in various sectors of the American social environment. To the extent that these emphases reflect some specifics of American historical experience, an overview of the corresponding currents of thought may help form an impression of how Americans, representing different sectors of society, have thought about war and peace and, perhaps, how their thinking was influenced by their historical experience.

In assessing American conceptions of war, we shall be referring to four different milieus. One will be the American public at large. That is, we shall be examining conceptions of war as they are reflected in the mass media, in school books, in political speeches, etc. Next, we shall look at conceptions of war in the so called 'peace research community'. This comprises only some dozens of individuals scattered in universities or organised in peace research institutes. The thinking of these people deserves attention, not because of any significant influence that they may have either on public opinion or on the formulation of policies but simply because like other scholars of international relations, they are the people most concerned in their professional capacity with the 'causes' of war, that is, with factors that contribute to or detract from the likely occurrence of war. Thirdly, we shall be referring to the American war establishment, the military and its auxiliary institutions. This vast and powerful sector of American society is also professionally concerned with war, not directly with its causes, to be sure, as these are understood in a scientific or philosophical context, but in ways that have contributed to the formulation of thinking about the causes of war. The fourth sector of American society we shall be considering comprises the so-called peace movement and certain political circles that view this movement with varying degrees of sympathy and understanding.

In order to examine systematically a direction in thinking about the causes of war, we must first clarify in our own mind how causes are conceived. Although the notion of 'cause' is deeply ingrained in man's conception of the world, it is not usually associated with all phenomena, at least not in the same degree. For example, events that occur with great regularity and moreover are immune to human intervention do not as a rule evoke speculation about causes, except perhaps in the minds of philosophers. Among these are, for example, such regularly occurring natural phenomena as the alternation of seasons. On the other hand, irregularly occurring events, especially natural disasters, do instigate assignment of causes, indeed in a way that makes it possible to think about preventing such events. For instance, in primitive societies this is done by various appeals to deities who supposedly control them, by magic, and so on.

At times wars have also been classed with natural disasters, especially by people periodically subjected to conquest or slaughter by invaders in search of living space, booty, or slaves. In the Bible, wars are often depicted as punishment meted out by God for transgressions. However, when war became institutionalised as an instrument of state policy, used for explicit political goals, causes of wars became increasingly conceived teleologically in terms of intended consequences rather than in terms of antecedent determinants. The epitome of this voluntaristic approach to war is Clausewitz's treatise *On War*. This view takes for granted the traditional European nation-state system as the matrix of historical events.

It is sometimes said, with some justification I believe, that the European state system came into being at the close of the Thirty Years' War. The provisions of the Treaty of Westphalia implicitly recognised what today we call the nation state as a sovereign body, giving birth to the notion of 'national interest'. The nation has remained a key concept in both the theory and the practice of international relations. In both theory and practice, national interests are put at the centre of attention. The prefix 'real' in *Realpolitik* refers both to the presumed objectivity with which the workings of the international system are described and to the hegemony of practical considerations governing the formulation and implementation of national policy.

In *Realpolitik*, the international system is pictured as a Hobbesian world dominated by a war of all against all, where, however, the states rather than human individuals play the rôle of social atoms. Each state seeks to extend its domain, its power, or its influence, and each state is a potential obstacle to the strivings of others, thus a generator of frustrations in its neighbours. Politics is conceived as a game of strategy (to use contemporary fashionable terminology) with territory, power, or influence as stakes. War, to cite Clausewitz's immortal aphorism, is the continuation of politics by other means.

In tracing the roots of American thinking about the causes of war, the basic fact about American history must be kept in mind: America, in declaring its independence, broke away from the European nation-state system.

In the eighteenth century, most European states were absolute or near-absolute monarchies. What we call today national interest was then identified with the personal ambitions of princes. In breaking away from the European state system, the United States broke also with the monarchical system, thus freeing itself, so it seemed, from the necessity of constant manoeuvring in the international power game with or without resort to organised violence, the predominant preoccupation of European potentates and statesmen.

Clearly a most important factor that made the break real was geographical isolation. America was simply too far away to be kept within the European war system. This does not mean in any way that war as an organised activity disappeared from American experience. There was a vast continent to conquer, and conquest by violence, at time verging on genocide, continued throughout the first century of the new republic. In American history books, this conquest is usually pictured as 'the conquest of the frontier', sometimes as the 'Indian Wars'. But this experience was quite unlike the European experiences with war, such as the Thirty Years' War or the Napoleonic Wars, which engulfed the whole continent and affected entire populations. The Indian Wars were not conceived as natural disasters, nor as manifestations of an angry deity, nor as collisions between ambitious rulers, as wars appeared to people who were directly and adversely affected by them in their daily lives. Nor did the Indian Wars appear as malfunctions of an otherwise smoothly functioning 'system', as international wars were to appear later to many 'peace researchers'. The Indian Wars were seen by the American public rather as mopping-up operations undertaken in the process of 'moving in' on an otherwise empty continent with the intent of appropriating and exploiting its vast resources that were there for the taking. To brood on the 'causes of wars' in this context would have seemed as inappropriate as to question the necessity of clearing away forests to make the land arable.

During this century of isolation, American involvement in major wars (as distinguished from campaigns against Indian tribes) was confined to three such wars, the war of 1812–14 with England, the war of 1846–48 with Mexico, and the Civil War of 1861–65.

None of these wars was connected in American thought with the idea of war as an episode in the on-going game of international power politics. The war of 1812 was elevated in school books to the status of the 'Second War of Independence'. The Civil War was interpreted by both sides as a war of survival. The Mexican War, although fought against a sovereign state, was regarded more as an incident in the conquest of the West.

Nevertheless, the Mexican War is distinguished as the first war in American experience in which its 'justice' and the 'causes' for which it was waged were seriously questioned. To be sure, the justification and the condemnation of that war were not unmixed with more mundane considerations. Its partisans were for the most part southerners, who sought to extend the slave system to the newly conquered territories. Its opponents were for the most part northerners who opposed the extension of the slave system for reasons that had little to do with compassion for the slaves. Nevertheless, as is often the case, the clash of interests was readily translated into matters of principle. The northerners argued that conquest was incompatible with the ideals on which American political philosophy was supposedly founded. The expansionist policy, however, prevailed. In its most explicit version, it was rationalised by the so-called Manifest Destiny.

The doctrine of Manifest Destiny is obviously the American version of a militant messianic idea, analogous to the idea that linked the Spanish conquests to spreading the word of Christ, pictured the British conquests as the White Man's Burden of civilising savages, and made Germans see themselves as *Kulturträger*. In the American version, the idea was expressed as a 'force of history' that was to bring the blessings of American-style liberty to regions into which the United States was 'destined' to expand. Already in 1789, Jedediah Morse, a Congregational minister of Boston, wrote in a book on *geography* (anticipating geopolitics of a later day): '... it is well known that empire has been travelling from east to west. Probably the last and broadest seat will be America ... the largest empire that ever existed'.[1]

Shortly after the vast Mexican territories were conquered, the Manifest Destiny was interpreted as a policy of using the growing power of the United States to regenerate mankind, for instance, to revive Mexico, which was declared to be '... in a state of suspended animation. She is in fact dead.... This American Republic is strong enough to do anything that requires strength. It is vital enough to inject life into the dead'.[2]

After victory over Spain at the end of the century, pronouncements of this sort reached euphoric levels, as exemplified by the following excerpt of senatorial oratory:

> We will not repudiate our duty. ... We will not abandon our opportunity in the Orient. We will not renounce our part in the mission of our race, trustee under God, of the civilization of the world. ... We will move forward in our work ... with gratitude ... and thanksgiving to Almighty God that He has marked us as His chosen people, henceforth to lead in the regeneration of the world. ...

Our largest trade henceforth must be with Asia. The Pacific is our ocean. The power that rules the Pacific ... is the power that rules the world. And, with the Philippines, that power is and will forever be the American Republic.[3]

American intervention in World War I was justified in less blatant terms, but the messianic idea is clearly revealed in the proclaimed American war aim, 'to make the world safe for democracy'. Conveniently, at the time of the intervention, monarchy was already overthrown in Russia; so the embarrassing question why one despotic regime should be supported against another was avoided at that time. (It could not be avoided at the time of American interventions in the 1950s and 1960s.)

Publicised 'causes' for which the United States waged war gave way to inquiries about the 'causes of wars' in the wake of the widespread disillusionment which followed World War I. In many quarters, by no means confined to radical circles, American involvement in the European war was seen in retrospect as a mistake, and the climate became favourable to a search for scapegoats. Accordingly, venal motives such as safeguarding investments (loans to Allied powers) and profit hunger, especially in munitions industries, assumed at least in the popular mind the role of the 'causes of war'.

An isolationist mood prevailed until the era of 'fascist aggressions' in the 1930s, when for the first time since the Civil War the survival of the United States in a world dominated by dictatorships became a seriously argued issue. This time a sharp struggle ensued between the isolationists and the interventionists. The former comprised largely the conservative Right, opposed to all of Roosevelt's policies, and the radical Right, where sympathies for Nazi Germany were harboured. As for the radical left, which in the 1930s was dominated by the Communist Party, it was strongly interventionist until August 1939, then strongly isolationist until June 1941, then again strongly interventionist and militantly 'patriotic' until the onset of the Cold War.

Ambivalence generates uncertainty, which, in turn, generates awareness or suspicion of external influences governing events. As long as war appeared to Americans either as a struggle for national survival or as incidental to a triumphant expansionist drive or as the implementation of a messianic idea, in short, as a voluntary act, there was no motivational basis for undertaking a systematic inquiry into externally generated causes of war. When attitudes toward war became ambivalent and especially when war came to be regarded in its global aspects, a motivational basis for such inquiries appeared.

The first systematic American study of war and of its possible causes was undertaken by Quincy Wright and his collaborators at the University of Chicago in the 1920s. His *A Study of War*[4] is a scholarly work which in some respects foreshadows later concern with the *war system* as a global danger, distinguished from threats of particular wars. This awareness was a consequence of the fact that after World War II, America was firmly plugged into global politics, apparently irreversibly. At first, however, the awareness of the global war system was confined largely to intellectual circles, which in the United States are practically co-extensive with academic circles. For example, *The Bulletin of Atomic Scientists* was started by a group of scientists, possibly spurred by a feeling of collective guilt about opening Pandora's Box. This journal always contains a picture of a clock at a few minutes before twelve. The meaning of that symbol was all too clear: time is running out for doing something to prevent a holocaust.

The role of the *Bulletin* has been that of informing at least a sector of the thinking public of the dangers generated by the unprecedented destructive power of new weaponry. Implicitly, therefore, attention was drawn away, at least partially, from the image of war as an act perpetrated by specific 'aggressors' to that of a war system, that is, the structural features of global politics that constitute a substrata of war.

Two new features of war introduced by atomic weapons forced themselves upon public awareness. The first embodied the realisation that the concept of 'victory' was reduced to an absurdity. The second was the novel idea of an 'accidental war', accidental not in the sense of being instigated by misunderstood political or diplomatic moves but in the sense of being triggered by a physically garbled signal in the megawar machine or some such event outside of political control. In this image, war appeared as an 'explosion' rather than a concerted national effort with well defined goals to be achieved by prowess coupled with virtue and determination.

These changes in the image of war led to three developments in the United States, which are the theme of this paper. One was the institutionalisation of so-called 'peace research'. Another was 'going public' on the part of the military establishment, as manifested in the large effort to justify its continued existence and growth in a world where general war in its traditional rôle as a convenient option of politics had become patently absurd. The third was the so-called 'peace movement', which was at least partially a reaction to the second.

A landmark in the institutionalisation of peace research was the founding of the Center for Conflict Resolution at the University of Michigan in 1956 and of the quarterly journal, *The Journal of Conflict Resolution*. The centre has since been dissolved, but it performed its priming function. There are now a great many peace studies centres in American colleges and universities. A directory of these centres, including descriptions of programmes, was recently compiled by M. Cummins and W. Wlodarski of the Peace Studies Center at the University of Dayton (Ohio). As of 1974, some 60 such centres are listed. Only some include substantive research programmes, but they do provide an institutionalised setting for peace research. Such a setting is of decisive importance, especially in the United States, where an academic career depends crucially on publication record, which, in turn, depends on opportunities for pursuing research within academically recognised programmes.

The Journal of Conflict Resolution survived and continues publication. Its volume was expanded, and it has a solid readership. From an overview of its contents, one can form a picture of what the 'mainstream' of peace research is like. Of some 1000 papers published in *The Journal of Conflict Resolution*, I have sampled some 250. Of these, the largest number, 60 or about 25%, deal with military policy, discussing subjects such as deterrence, arms control, and the like, including a few papers on the mathematical theories of arms races, following a tradition set by Lewis F. Richardson in the 1920s. The next largest number, about 20%, are devoted to social-psychological and sociological factors, presumably related to large scale social conflicts, including war. Next in frequency (about 14%) are papers on international relations, including some analyses of United Nations procedures and decisions. About the same number deal with applications of game theory, particularly experimental games. General conflict theory is represented in about 7% of the papers, research on violence and non-violent resistence in about 4%. The remaining papers are distributed among a large variety of topics, such as general methodology of peace research, economic and ideological factors in war, political geography and geopolitics, regional integration, field studies conducted in conflict areas, and quantitative indices of international tensions—a sort of political meteorology, another heritage of the Richardsonian tradition.

Predominantly, then, the mainstream of institutionalised peace research puts the 'causes of war' (and generally, of large scale social conflict) at the centre of attention. In a way, this emphasis reflects the above-mentioned change of the image of war in at least a sector of the American thinking public: from an image of war as a struggle for national survival or a conquest of the frontier or a carrier of democratic ideals, to an image of war as a malfunctioning of the international system or a neurotic outburst or a disturbance of an equilibrium. Not quite fitting into this scheme are some polemical articles, especially critiques of prevailing strategic thinking in the military establishment, and papers related to game theory and to experimental games. These represent another direction in peace research about which I shall say more below.

A very different transformation of the image of war took place within the vast military establishment which the United States acquired in the Cold War era. This establishment includes not only the military itself, as symbolised by the Pentagon, but also a huge industrial complex, a source of rich profits to entrepreneurs and stockholders and of income to managerial staffs, employees, and workers. It includes also an extensive network of research agencies, organised in special institutes and pervading the entire system of higher education.

I hold the opinion that the so-called instinct of self-preservation and a striving to grow characterises not only the familiar living organisms but also 'super-organisms', of which organisations, institutions, and nation states are examples. This view does not depend on any mystique. That is to say, I do not see the 'mind' of a super-organism as some disembodied spirit any more than I see the mind of a sentient being in this way. What I call the 'mind' of the latter is what presents itself to our observations as organised, apparently purposeful, modes of behaviour; for these are seen as *prima facie* evidence of a 'mind'. Now, an organised way of behaving may well be a result of stochastic interactions among the elements of a system with built-in statistical biases. As a simple example, consider a cloud driven by wind. From a distance, the cloud seems to exhibit directed behaviour—movement as a whole. Yet, if we look inside the cloud with sufficient resolving power, we do not see anything resembling motion in one direction. We see air and vapour molecules moving chaotically in all directions. What appears from a distance as gross motion is a result of statistical bias governing the innumerable collisions between these molecules. Similarly, in a large aggregate of people in a framework of a social structure, individuals may all act in accordance with their personal inclinations and may interact in a vast variety of ways. But biases associated with the social structure are imposed on these actions and interactions, as a result of which the aggregate, viewed as a system, appears to behave like an organism; that is, it appears to have goals that may be independent of the goals of the individuals who comprise it. At any rate, self-preserving responses of organisations and institutions and their tendencies to grow are commonly observed phenomena. In particular, the hypertrophy of the military-industrial-scientific complex in the super-power societies is a striking development of recent decades. It has become a painful concern to those who see its rôle in a broader context of history and prognosis, but a source of profound satisfaction (perhaps unconscious in many instances) to those whose careers and life styles have become bound up with it.

One circumstance is of crucial importance. The ideological underpinnings of the American military establishment (here I always use the phrase in the broad sense to include auxiliary institutions) are quite different from those of traditional military establishments. The latter were products of generations of 'militarism', wherein the military profession was endowed with attributes of nobility, a special sense of honour, traditional rituals, and gaudy dress. At the root of this outlook was a conception of war as an activity in which individual impulses, including the instinct of self-preservation, are suppressed by a commitment to discipline and by loyalty to a large super-organism, most typically a nation state. In the militarist tradition, the actualisation of the commitment was war and the climax of war was envisaged (as Clausewitz vividly stated) as the Battle, which in the heydays of European militarism was a pageant as much as a massacre.

ust War, a study in contemporary American doctri

PL U21.T8 Tucker, Robert W.

JZ6368.E74

U21.2

JZ6369 C48

BT736.2 O36S

KZ6369.J87

HV6432 E427

B105 W345 J87

U21.2 W34S

History Seminar - Library (Research)
(book on back a to c/d)

) Educational Psychology - article review
   Article Review

) Latin America

) Cultural Diversity - Project, cultural
                                    events

) PPR - Sign up

) Insurance

7) Get Rid of Baby Crap

In America, those flag-waving, drum-beating, trumpet-blowing, sword-swinging manifestations of the libido never took hold. The social prestige of the professional soldier had been low before World War II. In that war, it rose sharply, but traditional militarism with its trappings could not be grafted on the predominantly individualistic self-image prevalent in American society. Most Americans perceived war not as a road to glory but as a regrettable necessity to be discharged as quickly as possible, so that 'normal' occupations could be resumed.

Herein was the rub. 'Return to normalcy' meant reduction of the military machine to peace-time proportions. But this was no longer possible without dismantling the huge organism within an organism that it had become, without truncating the long tentacles that this organism had spread into almost all areas of American life. I believe it was an analogue of the instinct of self-preservation, of an élan vital (speaking poetically) that stimulated the intellectual sector of the war community to prodigious efforts directed at constructing a new apologia for war, that is, an effort directed toward putting the theory and the philosophy of war on an intellectually respectable basis. An extensive militarist literature was produced, surpassing at least in volume the analogous militarist literature of Imperial Germany, represented by the works of von Bülow, Clausewitz, Treitschke, Bernhardi, and others.

Like all variations of military philosophy, American contributions to it preserve the voluntaristic mode and so contain little thought on the 'causes' of wars, except in the context of discussions about what provocations by others might be considered to elicit what sort of 'postures' or 'responses' by the United States. For the most part, the literature represents efforts to restore war to a position of respectability in the nuclear age. Militarist literature addressed to the general reader in the United States has taken on the dimensions of a large public relations project.

Writings dealing directly with nuclear war were oriented toward explaining the 'realities' of this sort of war, as seen by the authors, not, it seems, in order to stress the absurdity of adopting nuclear war as an 'option' in the game of power politics, but on the contrary with the aim of allaying mass fear, which, as the war community saw it, paralysed the 'will' of the United States.

Nevertheless, the thrust of this approach was not toward minimising the destructive potential of nuclear weapons. Rather, a matter-of-fact tone was adopted, as if the aim were to accustom the public to the idea of 'living with' the prospect of a nuclear war.

On this theme, the writings of H. Kahn are revealing. In his book *On Thermonuclear War*,[5] Kahn describes the weaponry not only of World War III but also of World Wars IV through to VIII. To be sure, this nomenclature refers not to successive world wars but to the levels of nuclear weaponry in successive decades or half-decades of the nuclear arms race. However, whether intentionally or not, the terminology can be seen to have helped remove the 'paralysis' supposedly engendered by an automatically triggered fear reaction to 'World War III'. I suppose that when one has talked enough about World Wars IV, V, etc., World War III ceases to portend the end of everything.

The same theme pervades another of Kahn's books, *On Escalation*, published on the eve of the Vietnam War.[6] In that book, Kahn distinguishes 44 rungs of the so-called 'escalation ladder', ranging from preliminary manoeuvres and probings through crises to military actions of increasing scope and intensity. Already the tenth or twelfth rung of this 'ladder' involves nuclear exchanges, and there are over thirty additional levels, culminating in the so-called 'spasm', the all-out nuclear war of popular imagination, which Kahn calls with pornographic humour the 'wargasm'.

The escalation ladder was produced to show that in reality modern war is much more complex than its popular image and that its megatechnology, far from depriving war of all meaning, offers unlimited opportunities for the exercise of rationality and strategic skills, including intricate skills of diplomacy, where one can develop virtuosity in the exercise of intimidation, blackmail, bluff, and deceit.

The 'educational' value of this approach is stated explicitly in at least one passage. In addressing audiences (representing a wide cross-section of the public) Kahn made a practice of asking what, in their opinion, the President of the United States would or should do if a single nuclear bomb were dropped on New York without warning. In the early years of mutual nuclear threat, Kahn relates, the predominant response was that the President should order immediate massive retaliation on the Soviet Union.

More recently, however, presumably after exposure to the educational efforts of the war community, a marked change occurred. Instead of shock, a lively discussion was stimulated, enriched by searching sophisticated questions. Why was there only one bomb? Did the Russians intend to convey some message to us by destroying New York but no more? If so, what was it? If retaliation is in order, should it be carefully calibrated to the magnitude of the provocation and, if so, what is the appropriate level? Most people agree, Kahn writes, that the elimination of Moscow would be an excessively severe chastisement, because Moscow means more to the Russians than New York to Americans; that perhaps Leningrad and Kiev could be exacted as appropriate payment. If the Russians did not think so and 'removed' Philadelphia to even the score, should this, perhaps, be accepted as 'fair' and negotiations started?[7]

Kahn notes with satisfaction that Americans are learning to think intelligently about the 'unthinkable'. The style of other writings on the military and diplomatic problems of the nuclear age is not as bizarre as Kahn's, but their message is similar: war, although unpleasant, is a necessary and a respectable adjunct to foreign policy.

Already in the late 1950s, when it became apparent that 'massive retaliation' as a response by the United States to some mischief perpetrated by the Communists might have costly consequences and that for this reason threats of such retaliation might not be taken seriously, attention was turned to so-called 'limited war' or 'measured responses'. The idea was to make the punishment fit the crime. Small infringements or probings, so-called 'nibbling on the edges of the Free World', on the part of the Global Communist Conspiracy deserve a response tailored to the magnitude of the offence. The response to more serious provocations could be appropriately amplified. Besides the presumed opportunity offered by 'limited war' for 'controlling' the magnitude of military operations, a 'measured response', according to its protagonists, would enhance the 'credibility' of the United States. The threat of massive retaliation was self-defeating, because it could not be seriously believed that a student riot in Guatemala would unleash a nuclear attack on Moscow. Limited operations, on the other hand, could actually be carried out, restoring the correspondence between words and deeds. Finally, it was argued, the practice of limited war would carry less danger of a mobilised public opinion against the use of force by the United States in pursuit of its national interests. As it turned out, however, this ploy did not work. The mobilisation of public opinion against the 'limited war' in Vietnam was far more massive than that instigated by the balance of terror.

One other theme in American militarist literature deserves attention, namely, counter-insurgency. In a book on that subject, J. S. Pustay views revolutions in underdeveloped countries as a progressive disease infesting the world. He describes them as '... a cellular development of resistance against an incumbent political regime ... which expands from the initial stage of sub-version-infiltration through the initial stages of overt resistance by small armed bands and insurrection to final fruition in civil war.'[8] Pustay's recommendation is to deal with such processes by arresting them at the start: 'The sooner a Communist insurgency can be recognised and the earlier the counter-insurgency operations can begin in earnest, the greater will be the chance of success for the incumbent regime.'[9]

It should be noted that by an 'incumbent regime' Pustay does not necessarily mean one in power. For example, he cites the successful suppressions of Arbenz's government in Guatemala and of Mossadegh's government in Iran as victories for the 'incumbent régime'. Apparently, in Pustay's view, an 'incumbent régime' is any group (whether a régime or not, whether in power or not) that opposes social change unacceptable to the United States. An 'insurgent' group is one that attempts to promote such change regardless of its power or of its legitimacy.

To summarise the message of the sector of American militarist literature addressed to the general reader, it was that *Realpolitik* has finally become dominant in at least the thinking of the war community and that the restored and modernised image of war as a political instrument is being offered to the public as a way of coping with the nuclear age in a rational, mature, above all, responsible manner. The message is embodied in the following statement of the central problem facing United States decision makers: '... the problem is this: How can the United States utilise its military power as a rational and effective instrument of national policy?'[10]

It is against the background of what was seen as a concerted effort by the war community to 'sell' war to the American public that the American peace movement should be viewed. The reaction to James R. Newman's devastating review of Kahn's *On Thermonuclear War* in *Scientific American*[11] was virtually a declaration of war against the intellectuals coopted by the military establishment.

Of course, the peace movement comprised a public much wider than that consisting of intellectual or academic circles, especially after the war scares of 1961 (the Berlin crisis) and 1962 (the Cuban missile crisis). The core of this movement, however, was made up predominantly of intellectuals. They provided the movement with a number of basic orientations. Again the diversity and fluidity of American public opinion must be kept in mind. At no time was the movement unified by a specific ideology; nor did it ever have a specific political complexion. In one respect, however, it reflected a change in the American image of war and of its causes. Attention was turned toward the military establishment (in its broad sense) as a generator of war and, be it noted, not merely as an impersonal element in the dynamics of the international system, such as Richardson depicted in his theory of arms races, but a conscious actor with goals, interests and strategies, directed primarily toward the preservation and expansion of the war system. Whereas Richardson said of his arms race equations that they describe what is likely to happen if people do not stop to think, the writings of the American militarists revealed what is likely to happen when people do think in the framework of military mentality.

The intellectual core of the American peace movement provided a new dimension to peace research, which I call the anti-military counter-research. Here three directions are discernible. One represents efforts to call attention to the flaws and biases in the logic underlying war research on the level of strategy (as distinguished from tactics). Another represents efforts to obtain and especially to disseminate information about preparations for war and the waging of wars that would otherwise remain concealed from the public eye. The third is concerned with so-called civilian defence, not to be confused with civil defence. The latter has been promoted by the military establishment, primarily, one could surmise, for the purpose of keeping the idea of war at the forefront of public consciousness. Civilian defence, on the other hand, is based, for the most part, on the assumption that the military can no longer protect the population against enemy action in any meaningful sense. It is concerned with the mobilisation of a population for non-military resistance against invasion.[12]

Ironically, the impetus to a far-reaching critique of traditional militarily oriented strategic thinking came from a prominent theoretician of the 'new look' in nuclear age diplomacy, T. C. Schelling. In 1958, Schelling published an article in which the main thrust was directed against the hegemony of the zero-sum game model of conflict in military thought.[13] A two-person zero-sum game is one where the interests of the two players are diametrically opposed: the more one wins, the more the other loses in any outcome. Consequently, there can never be a coincidence of preferences of the two players with regard to the outcomes. Methods developed in the mathematical theory of games permit (in principle) a calculation of an optimal strategy in situations of this sort. The zero-sum model, therefore, is fully congenial to the military mind with a flair for a 'scientific' approach to problems of strategy or tactics. In the mind of the military, a potential enemy is always present. Moreover, it is taken for granted that whatever this enemy *can* do to gain an advantage, he *will* do, which is the assumption underlying the 'rational solution' of the zero-sum game. In fact, such games are now frequently included as exercises in textbooks on military science.

Schelling pointed out that in reality the interests even of opponents in military confrontations may partially coincide. This is even more often true in non-military confrontations between hostile states. For example, both may have a strong common interest in avoiding a devastating war in which both may be losers. Schelling, therefore, recommended that more attention be paid to a theory of non-zero-sum games as models of conflict with partially opposed and partially coincident interests of participants. In doing this, he opened the flood gates to research, the results of which, if properly understood, undermine the very foundations of conventional strategic thinking.

Consider the so-called Prisoner's Dilemma game, cited by Schelling. In the context of the international situation, the game can be taken as a simplified model of the problem of arms control. Assume that two states are engaged in an arms race, and that each prefers some arms control agreement to continuing the race.

The well known obstacle in the way of such an agreement is the difficulty or impossibility of enforcing it. In the absence of effective enforcement procedures, it is to the advantage of each side to continue the race, *regardless* of whether the other stops the escalation or not. For, if state X freezes its level of armaments, state Y can gain an advantage by increasing its level. If X continues the race, Y cannot afford to remain behind. It follows that it is in the interest of each state individually to continue the arms race. Nevertheless, it is to their collective advantage to stop it.

To accept the full consequence of this conclusion would mean to recognise that a collectively rational decision would confer a greater advantage on *both* states than the two individually rational decisions. Acting on this conclusion, however, would mean permitting collective interest to override individual interest. But if states did this, they would be, in effect, abandoning national interest as the principal guide to policy and with it the *raison d'être* of military establishments. Consequently, while discussions of non-zero-sum models of conflict situations are common in militarist literature[14], their full implications are seldom, if ever, pursued.

A new factor in such situations is the possibility of communication and bargaining, which is absent in conflicts with totally conflicting interests. Accordingly, attention in strategic analysis was directed toward techniques of communication and negotiation. As an example, consider a so-called eyeball-to-eyeball confrontation like the Cuban missile crisis. If one side stands firm, the other, being rational, must yield to avoid a nuclear catastrophe. Collective rationality dictates mutual accommodation. The possibility of communication, however, opens up more exciting opportunities. If one side can *convince* the other that it does not intend to yield, even better, that it *cannot* yield even if it wanted to do so, 'victory' is assured. On the other hand, if one side can make itself incapable of *receiving* any communication, it becomes immune to intimidation. It follows that both sides see an advantage in incapacitating themselves in one way or another. From a common sense point of view, the conclusion appears absurd, but strategies based on it have been seriously offered by strategic analysis espousing the 'new look' in international relations.

All these stratagems of gamesmanship (not to be confused

with game theory) contain a basic flaw. Namely, whatever one side learns, the other can learn. The situation is entirely analogous to the arms race, where in the long run no permanent advantage accrues to either side, and the only result is a waste of resources and aggravation of tensions.

Pointing out these flaws amounts to pointing out the inadequacy of individual rationality in a world of ever tightening interdependence. This has been a central theme in what I have called antimilitary counter-research.

A more direct attack on the hegemony of the U.S. military establishment was made via dissemination of suppressed or semi-suppressed information. In the early 1960s the military was mobilising its political resources to block an agreement between the United States and the Soviet Union on banning tests of nuclear weapons in the atmosphere. A citizen committee in St. Louis sponsored a large research project on the deposition of radioactive strontium 90 in children's teeth. Children were asked to donate their milk teeth, and hundreds of thousands were gathered. Afterward the teeth were put on display in jars together with explanations of how the by-products of atmospheric tests find their way into the bodies of children: an example of how respectable, fully objective scientific research can be coupled with political action. Needless to say, the publicity was an important input to public opinion, which eventually made the test ban agreement politically feasible.

An even greater impact was achieved by the publication of a body of information known as the *Pentagon Papers*. Ironically, the 'research' in this case (in the sense of compiling the information) was done by the military establishment itself, having been commissioned by the then Secretary of Defence, Robert McNamara. The *Pentagon Papers* revealed the military establishment to be a powerful interest group within the body politic and showed, moreover, that the interests of this group were like those of any institution driven by an appetite for power and built-in pressures for expansion. The materials contained information about how the Vietnam War was deliberately engineered and how the huge political influence of the military was used to keep it going when it became clear that the war served no interest except that of the military establishment and its auxiliaries.

Ordinarily, one does not think of journalistic writing as

'research', mainly because the methods of data gathering used by journalists do not resemble those used by bona fide 'researchers'. Also, journalists do not present their findings as 'supports of hypotheses' and generally do not use the paraphernalia of scientific investigation and theorising. There is no question, however, that the efforts of a conscientious journalist can contribute to bringing to light and spreading information that is often of vital importance to people affected by decisions outside their control. Thus the end-products of academic research and of diligent journalism may be closely related. In fact, the latter often contributes considerably more to public enlightenment than the former, being more readily accessible, more easily understood, and usually more directly related to vital issues.

Some excerpts will illustrate these efforts to provide an antidote to the formidable public relations campaign launched by the 'defence community', as the military and its civilian entourage calls itself. Fred J. Cook relates:

> In Tacoma, Washington, the owner of a shoe store fitted three small children for shoes. The father gave him a twenty-dollar bill, and when the proprietor handed back the change, the father presented a small card. It read: 'You have just done business with a Mount Ranier Ordnance Depot employee. How much money will you lose when the $14 million payroll goes to Utah? Write your Congressman, Senator, Governor, if you want to protest this move.[15]

This is only one incident, from which no generalisation is warranted. But the pervasiveness of political pressure by the military can be amply documented. That is the job of the social scientist. The journalist's job is to make the formidable political power acquired by the 'defence community' concrete and vivid.

Everyone knows that military megatechnology has developed a frightening momentum. But to hear a general depict this momentum as a triumphal march toward Utopia is to have an experience that no knowledge about abstract generalisations can impart. Paul Dickson quotes General William C. Westmoreland:

> On the battlefield of the future, enemy forces will be located, tracked and targeted almost instantaneously through the use of data links, computer assisted intelligence evaluation, and automated fire control. With the first round kill probabilities approach-

ing certainty, and with surveillance devices that can continually track the enemy, the need for large forces to fix the opposition physically will be less important. . . .

Hundreds of years were required to achieve the mobility of the armored division. A little over two decades later we had the air-mobile division. With cooperative effort, no more than 10 years should separate us from the automated battlefield.[16]

The euphoric tone of this projection into a bright future is, I submit, more disquieting than the sabre-rattling and the For-God-and-Country bathos of the old time military. To the general, the 'completely automated battlefield' represents a blessing of progress in quite the same way as the eradication of drudgery by technology and the conquest of disease by scientific medicine engendered the fondest hopes of the 'enlightened humanitarians' of the nineteenth century.

Or, as another example consider the matter-of-fact confidence of the military in the assured future of their profession:

Having long ago fought the war to end all wars, the U.S. Army today maintains within its vast framework a group of 170 civilian analysts and military officers who are creating and 'fighting' the wars to end all wars that may be fought in the 1990's. In addition, the staff of this outfit, the Institute of Land Combat, is picking the weapons that will orchestrate those wars . . .

The final work will be an analysis of the alternative future armies possible by 1990 and will cover the period 1990–1995. When this plan is delivered, the institute will go into a second five-year cycle in which work will begin on another such plan that will probably cover the period from 1996 to the year 2000.[17]

It takes a lot of digging, probing, and leg work to bring these activities to the light of day. Paul Dickson quotes one of his contacts at the Institute of Land Combat saying, 'We're not too excited about certain Senators reading about the institute and misinterpreting what it does'.

The misgivings were not unfounded. In 1969, under the sponsorship of members of Congress, a 'Congressional Conference on the Military Budget and National Priorities' was convened in Washington. The participants included people of all political complexions, scientists and scholars, as well as members of Congress. It took place when the war in Vietnam was still raging but when the futility and stupidity of the war (if not its shocking immorality) was already clear to perhaps a majority of the American public. American politics being what they are, only this change in the public image of the war could have induced a large group of professional politicians to lend their voices to a frontal attack on the military establishment. The conference was symptomatic of the recent radical change in the American image of war and of its causes. (At the risk of repetition, I must again qualify the statement by pointing out that the reference is always to the sector of the American public where questions about the nature of war and about its causes are raised at all.) War now appeared not as a means of national survival or a vehicle for the spread of American political ideals or as a disturbance in the international system, but as a process kept going either in an active or a dormant stage by a specific interest group, which in the minds of some became identified with a parasitic growth within the society. The enemy, in other words, was identified within the gates.

The Conference brought together people of very widely differing orientations. Some were outspoken enemies of the military establishment as such. Some were long time adherents of *Realpolitik*. They all agreed in regarding the military establishment as a Frankenstein monster or a genie released from the bottle or a parasite. The topics discussed included an analysis of the arms race with due emphasis on the absurdity of its 'logic'. (At that time, the big issue was the development of the new nuclear gadget, the so-called ABM (anti-ballistic missile) and the multiple warhead missile, both of which obviously presaged another round of escalation.) The monstrous inflation of the military budget was revealed, and the attendant neglect of pressing social needs was pointed out. The proponents of 'national security' as a first priority of the nation also joined in the denunciation of the military on the grounds that it was not really doing its job, since in no way was the security of the nation assured by what was seen to be the malignant growth of megadeath technology.

Most directly relevant to this account was the awareness by the participants of the changed national mood. Here are some remarks by Kenneth Galbraith, a prominent, politically active economist.

We are in a moment when a strong anti-establishment, anti-institutional, and primarily anti-bureacratic, anti-military mood is sweeping through the country much more rapidly than would have been possible as recently as ten years ago. This is partly because of an enormous number of people coming into the schools and high schools and universities, but also because of the large number of people who have been brought into our politics by (Eugene) McCarthy and McGovern and Robert Kennedy last year (1968). These people have a far greater receptivity to ideas such as those we are talking about than do most members of trade unions and political organizations and far greater than grain dealers and undertakers and other entrepreneurs who comprise the historic Republican rank and file. We have a responsive constituency running to millions in this country to the ideas we are discussing.[18]

These words were spoken eight years ago. Since then the war in Vietnam has ended. Clearly, that war more than the war scares of 1961 and 1962 fed the mood described by Galbraith. With the end of the war came an end to teach-ins and mass rallies and flights to Canada to escape the draft. There was also a dramatic reversal in the U.S.-China policy, and the rhetoric of détente with the Soviet Union has become commonplace and acceptable. For want of objective criteria of causality, it is impossible to say how much the anti-establishment, anti-military mood mentioned by Galbraith contributed to the final acknowledgment of defeat in Indo-china by the American power élite and to the change of posture toward the erstwhile enemies. At any rate, the storm has blown over. Freed from the threat of draft, the outraged young are no longer threatening to tear the society apart. On the other hand, the military establishment continues to fatten. The arms race, like inflation, has become a fixture in American life. The generation now grown to adulthood has never lived without it as they have never lived without airplanes or television. So what can we say now about the image of war and ideas about its causes in American thought?

The past images are irretrievably gone. The messianic idea is dead. The systemic idea has always been confined to academic circles. The public at large could not be gripped by it, because the untrained mind is concerned with causes only when it appears possible to exert some control over them. So it was with the fury concentrated against the military establishment when the war in

Indo-china was raging. The war was going badly and the military were revealed as the instigators of it and as a principal obstacle to disengagement. But to end that war appeared within the power of aroused public opinion. So the image of the military as the culprit was nurtured.

If this shift of focus were to persist, loyalties would be re-aligned. Institutionalised war would appear in a new light: as violence perpetrated by the combined global military establishment against humanity. The present arms race is the clearest harbinger of the next and possibly final spasm of global violence. But the arms race is not perceived directly by the senses. It can be perceived only intellectually, and even this is difficult, for who can tell the difference between a million and a trillion tons of TNT? At present, it seems unlikely that the changes in American perceptions of war, welcome as they must be to any enemy of organised violence, are sufficiently far-reaching to effect any significant dislocation in the globally instituted war system. I would not venture, however, any extrapolation into the clouded future.

Notes

1. Cited in Van Alstyne, R. W., *The Rising American Empire* (Oxford: Basil Blackwell, 1960), p. 69.
2. 'The Fate of Mexico' (no by-line), *U.S. Democratic Review*, May, 1858, 339.
3. Senator Albert J. Beveridge, quoted in Van Alstyne, *op. cit.*, p. 187. Source: Bartlett, R. J., *The Record of American Diplomacy*. 3rd edn. (New York: Knopf, 1956), pp. 385–388.
4. Chicago: University of Chicago Press, 1942.
5. Princeton: Princeton University Press, 1960.
6. New York: Praeger, 1965.
7. Kahn, H., *On Escalation* (New York: Praeger, 1969), pp. 185–86.
8. Pustay, J. S., *Counter-insurgency Warfare* (New York: The Free Press, 1965), p. 5.
9. *Ibid.*, p. 78. See also the section entitled 'A Proposal for a U.S. Counter-insurgency Support Establishment', pp. 171ff.
10. Osgood, R. E., *Limited War: The Challenge to American Strategy* (Chicago: University of Chicago Press, 1957), p. ix.
11. Newman, James R., review of *On Thermonuclear War* ((Princeton: Princeton U. P., 1961) by H. Kahn. *Scientific American*, 204, No. 3, March, 1961, pp. 197–200.
12. Cf. Sharp, G., 'Tyranny Could Not Quell Them: How Norway's Teachers Defeated Quisling During the Nazi Occupation and What It Means for Unarmed Defence Today'. Excerpts in Sibley, M., ed., *The Quiet Battle.* (Boston: Beacon Press, 1963), pp. 170–86; *The Politics of Nonviolent Action.* (Boston: Porter Sargeant, 1973.

13. Schelling, T. C., 'The Strategy of Conflict: Prospectus for a Re-orientation of Game Theory', *The Journal of Conflict Resolution*, Vol. 2, 1958, pp. 203–64.
14. Cf. Berkowitz, M. and Bock, P. G., eds., *American National Security* (New York: The Free Press, 1965), Part Three.
15. Cook, F. J., *The Warfare State* (New York: Collier Books, 1962), p. 192.
16. Dickson, P., *Think Tanks* (New York: Atheneum, 1971), p. 169.
17. *Ibid.*, p. 163.
18. *The Progressive*, June, 1969, p. 46.

Vigilant Ambivalence:
American Attitudes to Foreign Wars

Edmund Ions

The familiar caveat about attempts to generalise about American attitudes applies with peculiar force to foreign wars. We have to contend not only with two hundred years of change in the historical experiences of America, but also with fundamental changes in the international system of states as the thrust of new doctrines in the nineteenth and twentieth centuries challenged old orthodoxies. Again, while the American bicentennial of 1976 quite naturally reviewed the achievements of two centuries of independence, it is worth noting that some basic American attitudes derive from the original settlers. Thus, if we are discussing ideas and attitudes, as distinct from political forms, we must have in mind a tricentennial of American ideals, not simply the bicentennial of independence. Some of these ideals belong to the underlying logic and purpose of the American experience, and to ignore them would be tantamount to saying that the vigorous debates on the Constitution at the time of independence had only a passing connection with the experiences of the Colonial era.

The American Revolution was an assertion of political independence, but it was also an intellectual re-affirmation: that the European system was alien to Americans. The American experience has been not merely one of Republicanism but also of Federalism; the attempt, that is to say, to invite and persuade independently organised polities to come together by sacrificing important elements of sovereignty, in order to form a more powerful, if not a more perfect union. Having succeeded in that attempt by 1790, the American Republic was able to chart for itself a course whose eventual effects would be, in a literal sense, world shaking, once the benefits of union became allied to the ability to exploit the continent's vast natural resources.

Seeking a phrase or term which sums up, in historical retrospect, the American attitude towards foreign wars, I would suggest that it has been one of vigilant ambivalence. This basic attitude can be detected in incidents and occasions as far apart as Washington's Farewell Address in 1796 and Franklin Roosevelt's dealings with Churchill and Stalin at Yalta in 1945. It underpins the delayed entry of the United States in the two great wars of the twentieth century. It explains the fierce debates of the 1890s between expansionists such as Theodore Roosevelt, following the doctrines of Alfred Thayer Mahan, and those arguing that adventures abroad were no part of America's destiny, manifest or latent. The ambivalence continues today in the 1970s, in what is clearly a reassessment by President Carter's Administration, of *détente* and the personalised diplomacy of the Nixon-Kissinger era.

There is a convenient historical starting point for charting this American ambivalence in the diverging recommendations of Hamilton and Jefferson in the aftermath of the French Revolution. Initially, it will be recalled, most Americans welcomed the Revolution, but after the execution of Louis XVI in 1793, opinion began to divide. The divisions became even sharper when France declared war on Britain, Spain, and Holland. Alexander Hamilton's sympathies lay with Britain, Jefferson's with France, but both agreed on the wisdom of American neutrality in the conflict. Accordingly, Washington's proclamation of neutrality on 22 April 1793 becomes the first, most important statement of American attitudes towards conflicts overseas, and it is worth noting the sentiments injected into the statement by Washington. In his proclamation the President declared that:

> ... The duty and interest of the United States require that they should with good faith and sincerity adopt and pursue a conduct friendly and impartial toward the belligerent powers.[1]

Washington goes on to 'exhort and warn' the citizens of the United States 'carefully to avoid all acts and proceeding whatsoever which may in any manner tend to contravene such disposition'.

We may characterise such a national attitude as one of bene-volent neutrality, with malice towards none. The term 'neutrality' was to enter the vocabulary of international relations at a later date, but the essential spirit is there. Equally, however, there is an echo of that 'decent respect to the opinions of mankind' which informed the Declaration of Independence in 1776, and which provides in turn enduring clues to a genuine strain of idealism in American attitudes to the affairs of nations. It is a strain that becomes submerged in later decades, as idealism comes into conflict with self-interest, but it is worth noting that it never disappears entirely, even in the era of *Realpolitik*. It was present for instance in the austere morality of Woodrow Wilson at Paris in 1919, and in John F. Kennedy's Inaugural Address in 1961.

But nations, like individuals, discover the necessity for com-promises, even for some sacrifice of idealism as they grow older. The difference between American attitudes towards war or rumours of wars in the Europe of 1793, and the Europe of 1914 say, is that in the earlier period America had the luxury of a choice of attitudes. That luxury, self-evidently, can be attributed to distance, to the slowness of communications, and to the fact that the quarrels of Europe were not likely to extend to the new world in the foreseeable future. There was no question of a domino theory. What emerges from this is that whilst the logic of American history points towards built-in isolationist tendencies, the record shows that the new Republic could not depend on such a posture, and that this truth was increasingly forced upon it by external circumstance. It is here that the notion of a vigilant ambivalence takes root in the basic American attitude towards involvement in conflicts beyond its own borders. Idealism had to seek a com-promise with self interest in much the same way that George Washington's Farewell Address had to seek a compromise between the conflicting views of the President's advisers. There is a familiar but crucial passage in Washington's Address which bears upon the subject:

> The great rule of conduct for us in regard to foreign nations is, in extending our commercial relations to have with them as little *political* connection as possible. ... It is our true policy to steer clear of permanent alliances with any portion of the foreign world, so far, I mean, as we are at liberty to do it ... Taking care always to keep ourselves by suitable establishments on a

> respectable defensive posture, we may safely trust to temporary
> alliances for extraordinary emergencies.[2]

As early as 1796 idealism was attenuated by a degree of self-interest. There is also the recognition that the new Republic could not hope to avoid external obligations in protecting its interests. This realism was evident in an earlier Cabinet paper, by Alexander Hamilton, dated 15 September 1790:

> It is necessary then, to reflect, however painful the reflection, that gratitude is a duty, or sentiment, which between nations can rarely have any solid foundation . . . . .

The hard-headedness and the implicit pragmatism of Hamilton's observation can be detected in the utterances of many of his contemporaries in 1790. Needless to say, the experiences of the Revolution and the subsequent debates on the Federal Convention provided the crucible for national attitudes, in particular the recognition that the affairs of nations are not regulated by charity or piety but essentially by self-interest, even when cloaked by high-sounding rhetoric. For the Americans, as for every other nation, the most powerful attitudes to international conflict would result from the moulding influence of history itself. We can trace the process of adaptation and change in some episodes of the first half of the nineteenth century.

The purchase of Louisiana from France in 1803 was prompted by Jefferson's concern at the threat posed to national security by an alien power commanding the lower reaches of the Mississippi and thus the flow of American commerce. With the later incorporation of the Florida territory, the Americans were thus, within a decade, engaged in contestation with two European powers— France and Spain. The War of 1812 added a third, England. By 1823, Russian claims along the Pacific coast north of the 51st Parallel brought a fourth. These contestations, together with growing American fears of further European designs on Latin America, culminated in the Monroe Doctrine of 1823. That proclamation brought a fundamental and irreversible change to American attitudes to foreign affairs. But a decade earlier, the American victories in the war of 1812 deeply affected the psychology of the young nation in its attitude to war, at home or abroad.

The background to the war was the interference with American ships and sea lanes by the superior British naval forces, including blockade and the impressment of American seamen. Diplomatic channels were used in the 1810–11 period, but by November 1811, war fever was sweeping America, and a phrase that became a commonplace in our time, "War Hawks", entered the vocabulary. Although they were in a minority, the hawks were powerful in the Senate and then in the lower House too. Eventually, the war fever gained a convert in President Madison. The importance of Madison's War Message of 1812 is that Congress declared war on Britain. The significance of this should not be underestimated, bearing in mind that at this time American naval forces could not hope to match Britain's strength on the seas.

In the war that followed, the importance of General Andrew Jackson's victory at the Battle of New Orleans in 1815 was psychological and political, not merely military. Jackson later became President, and so takes his place in a remarkable line of ex-Generals who became Presidents of the Republic in its first century of development: Washington, William Harrison, Zachary Taylor, Franklin Pierce, Ulysses Grant; and we can add ex-Colonel Theodore Roosevelt, the Rough Rider of San Juan. The list became attenuated in our own time, until Dwight Eisenhower recovered the tradition, but it is worth noting that modern Presidential candidates still like to remind the voters of any war-time service they can claim. Thus the Presidency of the Republic has often been associated with those qualities of valour and patriotism brought out by war service. The tradition is of course not unique to the United States, and one could catalogue at length examples from other states and systems—from Churchill and de Gaulle to Nasser or Mao Tse-tung, or a dozen examples from the new nations of the Third World and the military juntas of Latin America. That ex-soldiers should assume the highest offices of the State, whether by peaceful, orthodox means, or alternatively by *coup d'état* is of course a witness to the fact that in times of national peril or emergency a nation looks instinctively for special sets of qualities in a new leader. Eisenhower's victory in 1952, it will be remembered, is very much associated with his famous statement that if elected, he would go to Korea, where American soldiers were being killed in a particularly bloody war. Thus what may be termed a sporadic martial tradition has persisted in the American Presidency.

We noted above that the Monroe Doctrine brought a fundamental shift in America's attitudes to events within its own
hemisphere. Two distinct elements can be discovered in President
Monroe's Message to Congress on 2 December 1823. The first,
and most important element is present in the passage:

> ... The American continents, by the free and independent
> condition which they have assumed and maintained, are hence-
> forth not to be considered as subjects for future colonization by
> any European powers.

The second element, which can be traced right through the
Message, is a re-affirmation of the original American posture in
relation to events abroad:

> ... In the wars of the European powers in matters relating to
> themselves we have never taken any part, nor does it comport
> with our policy to do so ... Our policy in regard to Europe
> is not to interfere in the internal concerns of any of its powers ...[3]

As we noted earlier, the two elements of American policy (non-
interference by Europe and non-interference in Europe) could be
combined in the age of sail, when it took weeks to travel between
the old world and the new. This became less possible when the
age of steam arrived and American diplomacy had to come to
terms with a shrinking world. But before speedier ocean travel
and the era of the steel navy, Americans had the bitter and maturing
experience of the Civil War of 1861–65. At the end of that terrible
struggle Americans could grasp, as few Europeans could grasp,
that war was no longer a matter of professional soldiers discharging
powder and shot on well-demarcated terrain; they knew that it
now involved pillage, devastation and death for the civilian
population as well. After 1865 then, Americans could have no
fond illusions about the romanticism of war.

The nineteenth century wrote another more peaceful chapter
of the American story, more extensive, more complex, yet possibly
more significant for American attitudes to foreign wars. Immigration transformed American society and culture. The massive
influx, from the waves of Irish and German immigrants in the
1830s and 1840s, to the Jewish, Slavic, and Mediterranean immigration of the 1880s and 1890s, was bound to have profound
effects on attitudes to events in Europe and elsewhere. This was

seen in 1915, and the opposition of German-Americans to Woodrow Wilson's developing diplomacy,[4] and can be seen today, in American support for Israel or in the support of Fenian organisations for Irish independence. By the end of the nineteenth century, so many national minorities existed in the United States that any conflagration abroad, large or small, was likely to engage the attention of at least one—and usually more than one—minority group.

Whereas some historians might argue that this would have a divisive influence, it is more likely that it had an opposite, broader effect, that of providing a form of social cement. Common sentiments and convictions towards the great issues of the time— religious toleration, the right to assemble, freedom of speech and opinion, individual liberty—came together in the common aspirations of the immigrants, now congregated in the cities or dispersed on homesteads across the continent.

Clearly, for the 1890s an urban gloss must be placed on Crèvecoeur's question of the previous century: 'What then is the American, this new man?' But the answer was, and still is, essentially as Crèvecoeur rendered it: the American is an amalgam of all the nations—belonging to all of them and to none of them at the same time. Translated in terms of a set of national interests, the effect of immigration was that isolationism could have no *permanent* place in the American mind, still less in American hearts. To argue the opposite is tantamount to saying that the first or second generation immigrants who formed the overwhelming majority of the American national stock by the 1890s had no interest in the culture, the language, or the nations from which they sprang.

American immigration is a vast, complex theme, and an already extensive literature has only begun to exploit the possibilities.[5] I can only touch on some aspects here. Two sorts of motives brought the immigrants to America: political and economic. Naturally the two were often mixed in the complex of reasons which alone could bring a European peasant to collect his family and set out on the hazardous journey across the Atlantic with no certainty—other than assurances in letters from brothers, sisters or cousins in the New World—that a land of opportunity was there.

As to the political motive, America has been the land of political exiles and a haven for the politically oppressed ever since the first expeditions of the Huguenots reached the shores of Florida in 1562. The Puritan exodus to Massachusetts after 1630, the Quakers in Pennsylvania, the Swiss Mennonites, and other sects from Europe arrived in America because of political persecution for their religious beliefs. In the nineteenth century, the German *Burschenshaften* refugees were driven out because of their liberalism in the 1817–20 period, whilst the 1848 revolutions brought the German 'Forty-Eighters' and later the notable visit of Louis Kossuth and a band of Hungarian exiles in December 1851. When Russian pogroms against the Jews began in earnest in the 1880s, there came that great influx which eventually would have such remarkable effects on the cultural and artistic life of New York, and on America generally. In the present century, political exiles from Mexico, from Russia after the revolution of 1917, from Italy after Mussolini's march on Rome in 1922, in greater numbers again from Hitler's Germany after 1933, and from Austria after the *Anschluss* in 1938, all belong in a tradition of political exile the effects of which are incalculable, but from which certain conclusions are justified.

The vital point is that America is now immigrant America and has been so for more than a century. When political liberties are in the balance, whether these be in Hungary in 1956, or Czechoslovakia in 1968, or Poland in 1971 — to take three examples — the American reaction goes well beyond the particular immigrant group in question. The white Anglo-Saxon Protestants are no more than a respectable minority group when seen from the perspectives of downtown Chicago or Detroit, Cleveland or Milwaukee, from Salt Lake City or Los Angeles. Threats to political liberty abroad affect Americans in a way that many Europeans may find it difficult to appreciate. If Europeans conclude that Americans sometimes carry patriotism, even bellicosity, to rather embarrassing lengths, they do well to remember that for the average American, the experiences of himself and his family across two or three generations are fundamentally different than those of the average European.

The second motive (and very often the dominant one) for the American immigrant was an economic one; the wish to better himself, and especially to escape the privations, and very often the destitution of, say, Ireland in the 1830s, or of Greece, Hungary or southern Italy in the 1880s. The dream of success, linked to an ethic of competition, in which the rewards came to those who worked hard, and who were prepared to take risks (whether this amounted to starting up a small business on borrowed capital, or going out west to farm or pan for gold) is too familiar to need any rehearsal here. What it bequeathed was an attitude of 'What I have, I hold'. The effects could be brutal. The American Indian met this doctrine in its extreme form—the extinction of an aboriginal culture in the name of the right of conquest and *force majeure*.

Europeans are understandably agnostic about the American tendency to speak of the 'American way of life' as though it were invested with some special virtue. The essence of the slogan is a defence of the materialist society, one in which success is measured by the acquisition of consumer goods. But it is also a society in which the privileges of class or birthright have not entered, as they did so conspicuously in the societies of the old world, until greater equality came to those societies in the post-1945 period. For the average American the blessings of American life have always been earned the hard way, whether we have in mind the farmers who tamed and tilled the wilderness of New England in the seventeenth century, the share croppers of the Mid-West in the nineteenth century, or the risk-takers of venture capitalism. Second and third generation wealth is a recent phenomenon in America. The heroes of Horatio Alger's stories were not born to the purple.

The two strains, political and economic, built into the immigrant story, compounded the ambivalence already installed in national attitudes in the seed-time of the Republic. They help to explain a curious amalgam of detachment and involvement at one and the same time. It is putting it much too strongly to say that today Americans have a love-hate relationship with Europe as a result or the two great wars into which they were drawn this century. The national attitude is more complex than that. There is a willingness to share the bounty of American wealth with others, in Europe and beyond, as the aid programmes continuously confirm. But there is equally, and surely justifiably, a conviction that if the new world has to intervene to repair the political and economic dislocations of the old (whether it be in wartime with lend-lease, or with Marshall Aid in the 1940s, or grain surpluses to Russia in the 1970s) then the American system is superior.

Attachment to the 'American way of life' is thus more than a mere political slogan. It is a fundamental set of beliefs which underpins an economic system. The American success story is the ultimate historical vindication of the individual immigrant's decision to leave behind the old world for the new. This sense of self-vindication, even where it exists in fugitive form, in the second or third generation immigrant, reinforces the basic ambivalence referred to above. Despite sentimental journeys to Ireland made by two American Presidents in turn—Kennedy and Nixon—to see the land of their forefathers, there was never any wish to return there. In a historical, but also in an important philosophical and ideological sense, the American turned his back on Europe. He is ready to concede his roots there, and more often than not he is proud of his roots in European culture. But for obvious psychological reasons he is not at all willing to concede that the transplant to new soil was a mistake, or that the transplanted stock is an inferior strain. On the contrary, the American believes, as self respect dictates, that the strain is more healthy, and certainly more vigorous. Where there is a positive commitment or a presence in Europe—in NATO, for instance—the motive is ultimate self-interest and the recognition of a shrinking world.

Europeans like to regard isolationism as a peculiarly American phenomenon, yet there is a significant and ironic European version which is worth pondering. It has consisted of a curious form of myopia: a reluctance or an inability to recognise that the United States has a much more important role to play in regulating the international system than any European state can claim. Although this realisation is now a commonplace in the nuclear age, when Europeans have no choice but to acknowledge American power, it is a comparatively recent concession.

It would have been surprising indeed if the preponderant wealth and power of industrialised America had not brought fundamental changes in its attitude towards conflicts and involvement overseas. This was evident by the end of the nineteenth century, when the United States was a world power. It was the mistake of European statesmen not to recognise this as early as they should have done. In retrospect, we can see that it ought to have been the cornerstone of Germany's diplomatic strategy in 1914 and again in 1939 to ensure that at all costs the enormous military and economic potential of the United States should be kept out of the European conflict, if it indeed could not be harnessed to Germany's war aims. In the event, American entry into the war was to prove decisive in the 1917–18 period, as it was in the 1941–45 period. It is idle to speculate on what might have happened if the over-riding strategy of the Axis powers had been to preserve American neutrality at all costs. But we know enough to recognise that once the immense potential of the American economy was placed on a war footing the 'arsenal of democracy' was a decisive factor in two world wars, leaving the final issue in little doubt when manpower was added to inexhaustible supplies of material.

Professor Marcus Cunliffe reminded us some years ago of the dangers of assuming that there are turning points or watersheds in the history of a nation.[6] Too often these are merely convenient devices imposed on events with the ease of hindsight in order to invest a particular decade, a period, even a century, with a sense of completeness or finality. Such exercises of convenience in-variably do violence to the continuum of history and run the risk of distorting the interpretation. That said and agreed, it seems to me nevertheless that the 1890s brought a profound change in American attitudes to events abroad. Theodore Roosevelt's description of the Spanish-American War in Cuba in 1898 as a 'splendid little war' was far removed from the cautious, self-justifying sentiments of the Monroe Doctrine in 1823. How do we account for the difference? The explanation goes well beyond Roosevelt's bellicosity.

In 1890, the United States census director reported that no more free land lay in the west. The American frontier had closed. Three years later, in 1893, the American historian Frederick Jackson Turner gave his seminal paper to the American Historical Asso-ciation, 'The Significance of the Frontier in American History'. The thesis was to be modified in later years, and it was to have its share of criticism among some of Turner's contemporaries, but it had a profound effect on a whole generation of historians because of its appeal and its plausibility. Turner was seeking the roots of the American national character. He wanted to answer the vital question: why are the Americans as they are? Turner found the explanation in the existence of a moving frontier, the constant availability of free land to the west. From the days of the earliest settlements, the Americans had always lived within easy reach of cheap land. Independence was there for the taking; complete freedom lay at the margin of settled land. In the long process of occupying the continent, Turner argued, the American mind and its attitudes to political and social institutions were shaped. This was the fundamental difference between the new world and the old.

In the third quarter of the nineteenth century, however, other complex strains were at work on the American mind. Social Darwinism appealed to some leading thinkers, and Richard Hofstadter has shown in a brilliant and penetrating study the way in which the doctrine was absorbed and utilised by the expansionists.[7] Such views also conspired with the doctrines of A.T. Mahan in his writings on the influence of sea power in history.[8] It only remained for Mahan to find some ready champions in American politics for his views to have a profound effect when the age of steam and steel finally displaced the age of sail. Mahan had his champions in Theodore Roosevelt, Senator Henry Cabot Lodge, and other expansionists in the U.S. Senate.[9]

The Monroe Doctrine was transformed into a much more positive assertion of American hegemony in the Venezuela Boundary dispute with Britain in 1895. That dispute ended by the two nations agreeing to arbitration, but the note from Secretary of State Olney to Salisbury in July 1895 was the best guide to the new temper of a continental power which was now actually flexing its muscles. '. . . Today the United States is practically sovereign on this continent, and its fiat is law upon the subjects to which it confines its interposition.' This was a far cry from the language of President Monroe's Message of 1823, and a universe away from Washington's Farewell Address.[10]

Without, therefore, indulging in any 'watershed' theories of history, it seems to me that the decade of the 1890s provides the key to America's interventionism and new diplomatic postures. The war with Spain in 1898 despatched a declining colonial power from Cuba. The resulting Treaty of Paris added Puerto Rico, Guam and the Philippines to American possessions. In 1904 President Theodore Roosevelt enunciated the Roosevelt Corollary to the Monroe Doctrine whereby America assumed the right to exercise an international police power if this were necessary to prevent European intervention in American spheres of interest. This was the doctrine used to justify intervention in Santo Domingo. Its historical significance was that the European powers did not challenge the American right to intervene.

Reviewing the decades on either side of the turn of the century, therefore, one sees both continuity and change in American attitudes. During those years, America was coming to terms with the possibilities but also with the responsibilities of power. It is putting it much too simply to say that the United States was merely replacing Spanish colonialism with American. Given the declining power of Spain and its inability to govern turbulent regions of Latin America and the Caribbean theatre, it became clear that a political vacuum existed in an area of vital strategic interest to the United States. One need only look at the location of Cuba on the map to grasp its significance. Talk of an Isthmian Canal between the two continents had gone on for more than half a century. The Clayton-Bulwer Treaty of 1850 between Britain and the United States proposed that neither of the two powers should obtain or maintain exclusive control of a canal but that both should guarantee its neutrality. Yet the Hay-Pauncefoote Treaty of 1901 gave the United States sole right of construction, maintenance and control. The treaty was itself a testimony to the changed relationships between the two maritime powers.

Thus another fundamental and irreversible change came into American attitudes during the 1890s. The change was due to two reasons, both closely connected. The first was that American self-interest now required, indeed dictated, a permanent concern with events abroad, especially where economic or political instability threatened. The second was that the United States could no longer avoid the responsibilities entailed by its immense economic power. Needless to say, in the age of imperialism self-interest became coincident with the search for markets. Trade followed the flag, but it was necessary first to plant the flag. The Roosevelt Corollary was an economic doctrine as much as a strategic one.

Given this new assertiveness, did the tradition of vigilant ambivalence become lost in a new, imperialist orthodoxy? Certainly it was diluted, but it was not entirely dispersed. We can gauge this by reviewing three instances of American external involvement during the present century. (1) In 1904, Theodore Roosevelt took care not to involve the United States in the Russo-Japanese war, even though America's Open Door policy with China was at issue when the Russians marched into Manchuria. In the event, Roosevelt mediated between the two belligerents and earned a Nobel Peace prize in 1906 for his work in bringing an end to hostilities. (2) From 1914 to 1916, Woodrow Wilson saw his role in relation to the European conflagration as a mediator between the two sides, and his diplomacy was entirely geared to that end. He saw his *essential* rôle as that of a peace-maker even after America entered the war in 1917. (3) On the outbreak of war in 1939, Franklin Roosevelt said to the American people, in his fireside chat of 3 September: 'This nation will remain a neutral nation'. He then promptly added a significant rider: 'But I cannot ask that every American remain neutral in thought as well'. One would be hard put to encapsulate the theme of vigilant ambivalence in crisper form.

The two parts of Roosevelt's statement accurately conveyed the new and inescapable logic of American's rôle in the face of international conflicts. A world power deludes itself if it assumes that it can claim the luxury of deciding for itself whether to remain completely neutral. This is not to say that its diplomacy may not be formulated so as to reduce to a minimum the likelihood of being drawn directly into a conflict. Self-interest usually dictates this, as for example in America's relations with its principal adversary during the Cold War period. Ever since the two super-powers came face to face in the Cuban missile crisis of 1962, prudence has dictated the politics of non-confrontation. National self-interest dictates this form since the prime lesson of the crisis of October 1962 was that once on the escalator of confrontation, it is a very difficult task—militarily and diplomatically—to get off it. As Arthur Schlesinger noted in his account of the crisis, President Kennedy 'had peered into the abyss and knew the potentiality of chaos'.[11] So had the Russians, needless to say, and since then we have witnessed that difficult, sometimes tortuous process in various theatres of the world by which the two super-powers attempt to ensure, through their client states, that their armed forces do not come face to face in direct confrontation with each other. The Soviet Union kept out of Vietnam. The United States kept out of Czechoslovakia. It is reasonable to assume that American policies will be governed by the politics of non-confrontation in the foreseeable future; so, too, will the policies of the Soviet Union. Neither super-power will seek checkmate. Both will ensure that the main adversary is left room for manoeuvre.

One cannot leave this topic without a discussion, if too brief, of the American involvement in Vietnam. The literature is now extensive. The hawks and the doves have had their say. A good deal more will be written on the war and many further morals will be drawn. Among the welter of lessons the most obvious, but still the most important one, is that American technology and superior fire power in the air, at sea, and on the ground, are no longer the deciding factor for certain types of engagement—most obviously for guerilla warfare. The United States may have to accept in future that there are conflicts where she cannot intervene success-fully because the strategy, tactics, and required logistics of the conflict make her technology a liability, not an asset. If the United States develops a capacity for a style of warfare quite different to the one she maintained in Vietnam and Korea, this may change.

The second lesson relates to the problem of engaging in an unpopular war abroad, when the justification for it is not accepted by a majority of the American people. The United States army was defeated in Vietnam: there is no avoiding this bald truth. The ultimate defeat was caused only partly by a long series of strategic and tactical reverses and a badly trained South Vietnamese army. There was a disintegration of morale in the American army, and a number of bitter lessons were learned. Among them was the realisation that a long drawn out war in support of a series of corrupt regimes inevitably loses the support of the American people. As the unavoidable brutality of war is portrayed on television screens night after night, the elected representatives of the people find it more and more difficult to justify the war. Eventually, the cost in blood and treasure becomes insupportable, and an American presence can no longer be sustained. Vietnam showed up the acute dilemma of maintaining public support for a contained but costly war in another part of the globe. It is a continuing problem for open societies with free access to the media and there is no obvious solution, whatever the rights or wrongs of a particular engagement.[12] The rôle of the media and mass communications presents new sets of problems, therefore, and America's 'Goldfish Bowl' democracy guarantees unique discomforts in this direction.

These are the areas in which the real problems for American involvement overseas now occur. They come down to the pro-blems of a democratic society which permits and institutionalises political opposition to every aspect of policy, domestic or foreign.

No democrat will wish to alter that basic and necessary condition of the open society. But it may be that democracies must begin to consider whether elements of bi-partisanship can be encouraged, if not institutionalised, in limited and well-defined areas of policy making.

The arguments for doing so apply with peculiar force to the United States because of its preponderance of military power. The argument is not purely self-regarding, still less unilateral in intent, for as every student of politics in the nuclear age readily appreciates, the real problems concern uncertainty in regard both to an adversary's intentions and beyond that to his will. Yet it must be recognised frankly that one of the elements of uncertainty in the strategic balance derives from that chief ornament of western democracy—institutionalised opposition, on a party basis, to current policies. Recent Presidential elections have demonstrated the exploitation of the defence issue, and it is clear that national security and defence spending will continue to be dominant issues in future elections. The effects can be bizarre when we consider, for instance, that in the 1960 Presidential election, John F. Kennedy, a Liberal-Democrat, made the missile gap the most effective part of his campaign against a retired general, Dwight Eisenhower. In the 1976 Presidential election, Ronald Reagan came very near to denying the Republican nomination to an incumbent President on the issue of national security. The point is that the electoral cycle injects into global politics deep uncertainties and the repeated promise of discontinuity. America's adversaries must therefore find it extremely difficult, to say the least, to predict the future, just as the cloak of secrecy in their own political systems injects a different kind of uncertainty. The result, on both sides, is to play safe: to stock-pile, to procrastinate, to posture, to develop new weapons systems, and to ensure maximum preparation for unexpected contingencies.

This global situation provides no argument for abandoning the regular process of organised opposition in western democracies. But it may provide an argument for, at the very least, mitigating it in carefully defined areas of policy relating to national security and defence spending. If, by elements of bi-partisanship, defence spending becomes less of a party issue, and accordingly is not 'up for grabs' by aspiring candidates for office—whether it be the Presidency or for the Congress—the external advantages of continuity may be more far reaching than present conventional wisdom allows us to perceive. If to the historical tradition of ambivalence we have traced here, we graft this further element of institutionalised uncertainty, it is then difficult to deny the possibility that these two factors may have an important bearing on the chances of some future war, arising out of an adversary's miscalculation of American intentions or will.

Notes

1. Henry S. Commager (Ed.) *Documents of American History* (6th Edn. New York: Appleton-Century-Crofts, 1958) I: 163.

2. *Ibid.*, I: 174.

3. *Ibid.*, I:236–7.

4. Cf., Edmund Ions, *James Bryce and American Democracy, 1870–1922* (London: Macmillan, 1968) chaps. 20, 21.

5. A valuable collection of reprints of scholarly monographs on immigration is now available from the Arno Press, in collaboration with the *New York Times*. See, for instance, Albert B. Faust, *The German Element in the United States* (2 vols., first published in 1909), Vol 2, chap. IV, 'Political Influence of the German Element in the United States' (New York: Arno Press, 1969). And see other studies in the series on Irish, Scotch-Irish, Italian, Czech, Russian, and Scandinavian immigrants. Series title, *The American Immigration Collection*.

6. Marcus Cunliffe, "American Watersheds" in Hennig Cohen, (Ed), *The American Experience* (Boston: Houghton Mifflin, 1968), pp. 366–80.

7. Richard Hofstadter, *Social Darwinism in American Thought* (Revised Edn, New York: Braziller 1959), chap. 9.

8. A. T. Mahan, *The Influence of Sea Power on History*, 1660–1783 (Boston: Little, Brown, 1890), and *Sea Power in its Relations to the War of* 1812 (2 vols., Boston: Little, Brown, 1905).

9. Julius W. Pratt, *Expansionists of* 1898 (Baltimore: Johns Hopkins Press, 1936).

10. See also President Cleveland's Message to Congress on the Venezuela Boundary Controversy, dated 17 December 1895. Britain had contended that the Americans were seeking to extend the Monroe doctrine to another hemisphere, that this was unacceptable, and inadmissible in international law. Cleveland declared, *inter alia*, 'The Monroe Doctrine finds its recognition in those principles of international law which are based upon the theory that every nation shall have its rights protected and its just claims enforced ... This Government is entirely confident that under the sanction of this doctrine we have clear rights and undoubted claims ...'. Commager, *op. cit.* II: 171. (If the legality of the Olney/Cleveland replies could be questioned, the new American confidence and assertiveness was not in doubt).

11. A. M. Schlesinger, Jr., *A Thousand Days: John F. Kennedy in the White House* (Boston: Houghton Mifflin, 1965), p. 725.

12. Edmund Ions, *Dissent in America: The Constraints on Foreign Policy*, Conflict Studies No. 18, London: Institute for the Study of Conflict, 1971).

The Existential Adventurer and War: Three Case Studies from American Fiction

Moorhead Wright

Most of the essays in this book are concerned with the large social and political developments which have shaped the American approach to the problems of war and peace. In this paper by contrast I intend to focus on the individual's experience of and reaction to war, taking for my raw material three fictional protagonists—Henry Fleming in Stephen Crane's *The Red Badge of Courage*, Frederic Henry in Ernest Hemingway's *A Farewell to Arms*, and Billy Pilgrim in Kurt Vonnegut's *Slaughterhouse Five*. The settings of these three novels are the three greatest wars which Americans have experienced—the Civil War, World War I, and World War II. Moreover, they form a kind of informal trilogy: Hemingway is known to have read and been influenced by *The Red Badge of Courage*, and the doomed Edgard Derby (a school teacher who is shot for picking up a teapot in the ruins of Dresden at the end of the war) reads Crane's novel at one point in *Slaughterhouse Five*.

My assumption is that human nature is the basis of politics and war, and that the novelist's main contribution lies in exploring this area. General theories of human nature are of course abundant, but many are too over-simplified either in the direction of praise (e.g. man the rational animal) or condemnation (e.g. man the sinner). They do not help to account for the tensions and paradoxes which characterise political and social life. For my purposes in this paper the most adequate conception of man's nature which I have found is that of the poet, W.H. Auden:

> Man is a history-making creature who can neither repeat his past nor leave it behind; at every moment he adds to and thereby modifies everything that had previously happened to him. Hence the difficulty of finding a single image which can stand as an adequate symbol for man's kind of existence. If we think of his ever-open future, then the natural image is of a single pilgrim walking along an unending road into hitherto unexplored country; if we think of his never forgettable past, then that natural image of a great crowded city, built in every style of architecture, in which the dead are as active citizens as the living ... Every man is both a citizen and a pilgrim ...[1]

On the whole the American consciousness has been dominated by the image of the road, and the European consciousness by the image of the city. America is archetypally the land of movement, frontiers, social mobility, and the open road; the recent success of Robert M. Pirsig's *Zen and the Art of Motorcycle Maintenance* testifies to the durability of this image. Europe, on the other hand, is the continent of great cities which form the centres of attraction or repulsion in the popular consciousness. The distinction is of course not as clear-cut as that, for the American consciousness has been formed by a curiously ambivalent attitude toward Europe. The United States had its origins in a rebellion against Europe and what it stood for, but Americans have often been drawn back to their European origins.

It is not surprising then that the American novelist's pre-occupation with the wandering pilgrim has its origins in European literature. For example, John Bunyan's *Pilgrim's Progress* is the explicit model on which E.E. Cummings based his *The Enormous Room*, a semi-fictional account of the author's imprisonment in France during World War I, and there are clear parallels in *Slaughterhouse Five*. But the pre-dominance of this type can only be explained in American terms, as did William Barrett in 1952.

> American fiction gives us a new kind of hero because the American himself is a new kind of man. Call him the existential adventurer, the character who seems always to operate on the margin of new and unlimited possibilities of experience; but you have also to recognize as the other side of this coin the fact that this hero has at his center something of a vacuum, for he too does not know who

he is, and there are no sustaining frames of tradition by which
he can easily define himself.[2]

Among the existential adventurers are Henry Fleming, Frederic
Henry and Billy Pilgrim.

In Stephen Crane's novel of the American Civil War, Henry
Fleming is a raw, untried country youth who seeks the romance
and glory of war but who finds that his romantic, chivalric preconceptions of battle are false. Soldiers and generals do not strike
heroic poses; the dead are not borne home triumphantly on their
shields but fester where they have fallen; and courage is not
a conscious emulation of an ideal mode of behaviour but a
temporary delirium produced by animal fury and social pride or
fear.

Crane's attempt to devalue the heroic in war stems in part
from a reaction against a literary and cultural tradition of idealized
courage and chivalry. But another major element in his desire to
reduce war to the commonplace arises from his casting of Fleming's
experiences in the form of a 'life' or initiation allegory. Henry
Fleming is the archetypal youth who leaves home unaware of
himself or the world. His participation in battle is his introduction
to life as for the first time he tests himself and his preconceptions
of experience against experience itself. He emerges at the end of
the battle not entirely self-perceptive or firm-willed, but rather
as one who has encountered some of the strengths and some of the
failings of himself and others. Crane implies that although Fleming
may again run from battle and although he will no doubt always
have the human inclination to rationalise his weaknesses, he is
at least no longer the innocent.

To Crane, therefore, war as an allegorical setting for the emergence of youth into knowledge embodies both the violence of
his initiation and the commonplaces of life which it reveals—
that men are controlled by the trivial, the accidental, the degrading-
ly unheroic, despite the preservation of such emblems of the
noble as a red badge (the bloody bandage covering a battle wound)
or captured flag. His image of life as an unheroic battle captures
in one ironic symbol his belief that we reveal character in violence
but that human character is predominantly fallible and self-
deceptive.

Furthermore, *The Red Badge of Courage* presents a vision of
man as a creature capable of advancing in some areas of knowledge

and power but forever imprisoned within the walls of certain inescapable human and social limitations. Crane suggests a parallel between Henry Fleming's 'will' and an animal's instinctive response to crisis or danger. He also presents Fleming's discovery that he is enclosed in a 'moving box' of 'tradition and law' even at those moments when he believes himself capable of rational decision and action; in other words the opinions and actions of other men control and direct him.

Despite these limitations and inadequacies, man is not painted in totally negative terms in *The Red Badge*. Something has happened to Fleming which Crane approves. Early in the novel Fleming feels at odds with his comrades. He is separated from them by doubts about his behaviour under fire and by the fear of their knowledge of his doubts. These doubts and fears isolate him from his fellows, and his isolation is intensified by his growing awareness that the repressive power of the 'moving box' of his regiment binds him to a group from which he now wishes to escape. Once in battle, however, Fleming becomes 'not a man but a member' as he is 'welded into a common personality which was dominated by a single desire'. This 'subtle battle brotherhood' replaces his earlier isolation, and in one sense the rest of the novel is devoted to Fleming's loss and recovery of his feeling of oneness with his fellows. After his initial success in battle, Henry loses this quality as he deserts his comrades and then wanders away from his regiment; he is most isolated from the regiment and from mankind occurs when he abandons the tattered soldier. After gaining a 'red badge' which symbolically reunites him with those soldiers who remained and fought, he returns to his regiment and participates successfully in the last stages of the battle. Here, as elsewhere, there is a deflating irony, for Henry's 'red badge' is not the result of a true battle wound but of an accidental blow on the head by a rifle in a scuffle with one of his fellow Union soldiers. But despite the tainted origin of this symbol of fraternity, its effect on Henry and his fellows is real and significant. He is accepted gladly when he returns, and in his renewed confidence and pride he finds strength and a kind of happiness. Crane believed that this feeling of trust and mutual confidence among men is essential. For Crane courage has primarily a social reality, a quality which exists not absolutely but by virtue of other men's opinions, it follows that the social unity born of a courageous fellowship may therefore be based on self-deception or on deception of others. He also demonstrates that this bond of fellowship may be destructive and oppressive when it restricts or determines individual choice, as in the 'moving box' of the regiment. Fleming, after all, at first stands fast because he is afraid of what his comrades will do or think, then runs because he feels that the rest of the regiment is deserting as well. But Crane also maintains that in social cohesion man gains both what little power of self-preservation he possesses and a gratifying and necessary sense of acceptance and acknowledgment difficult to attain otherwise. He attacks the conventional heroic ideal by showing that a man's actions in battle are usually determined by his imitation of the actions of others or by the group as a whole. But this presentation of the reality and power of the group also suggests the advantages possible in group unity and group action. Men struggle, and in their struggle they learn something about their limitations and capacities and something about the nature of their relations with their fellow men, and this knowledge is rewarding even though they never discover the full significance or direction of the campaign in which they are engaged.

A sharply contrasting image of war is presented through the eyes of Frederic Henry, the narrator and main protagonist of Hemingway's novel. He is a rootless American expatriate who drives an ambulance in the Italian army in World War I. He has neither patriotism nor hatred of the Austrians. In fact, the war and his involvement in it are as unreal experiences to him as anything else in his meaningless and unconnected life. 'Well, I knew I would not be killed. Not in this war. It did not have anything to do with me. It seemed no more dangerous to me myself than war in the movies'. Although he has had sexual experiences with many women, none of them has made any impact on his personality. In short, the self of the Frederic Henry which we meet at the beginning of the novel is practically non-existent.

This is revealed in his first reaction to the possibility of an affair with the British nurse, Catherine Barkley: 'I knew I did not love Catherine Barkley nor had any idea of loving her. This was a game, like bridge, in which you said things instead of playing cards. Like bridge you had to pretend you were playing for money or playing for some stakes. Nobody had mentioned what the stakes were. It was all right with me.'

In his incapacity to care he can, of course, play for any amount of stakes because he has nothing to lose. The wound he receives is the first lesson to him of what he stands to lose. The effect of the nearness of death and the horror of the wound, as well as the pain and the drip of the haemorrhaging corpse above him in the ambulance, are enough to indoctrinate that value of life which the fear of death must inevitably cause. But his friend the priest, visiting him in hospital, reminds him how far he still has to go: 'You do not see it (the war) ... even wounded you do not see it. I can tell.' The unheroic nature of Frederic Henry's wound—'blown up while we were eating cheese'—echoes the pseudo-wound of Henry Fleming.

The wound permits the consummation of the affair with Catherine during the four months or so of Henry's convalescence in a Milan hospital. Henry 'loves' Catherine in a superficial sense, worries about not having married her when he learns that she is pregnant, and certainly enjoys the island of pleasure and fulfilment which she creates for him in the midst of war.

Frederic returns to the front where he finds his two friends, the hard-working surgeon Rinaldi and the Priest, have fared badly under the strain of the summer offensives. Rinaldi fears that he has contracted syphilis, and the priest has become depressed in his faith by the action of the war. He had believed in some kind of miracle which would intercede and cause men to lay down their arms, but now he has begun to doubt his belief. Frederic joins the Caporetto retreat, during which he makes a vain attempt to save his ambulance crew and follow out his orders. He eventually jumps from a bridge into the river when caught in a police blockade in search of Italian army officers for summary execution as scapegoats for the military fiasco. Yet his actions still maintain the passive, moved-about quality that we observed in his character before his meeting with Catherine. He deserts at last, but only because he has been pushed to the wall. In his resolve to make his way back to Catherine there is a slight move closer to a mutual love relationship, but it should be noted that 'the separate peace' is made by Henry neither as an action through which he can rejoin his beloved, nor as an act of disillusionment with the ideals of war, which he never had to start with.

Moved by circumstances beyond his control, he accepts the consequences of his forced actions, among them the obligations of caring for Catherine. The game which Frederic had entered so casually some six months before has become a game which he cannot back out of, and the stakes are very high. In the escape with Catherine across the lake to Switzerland, the 'separate peace' has become a separate 'union', and the way is prepared for the fulfilment of Rinaldi's earlier prophesy that the 'caring' Henry would have a better time than he, but he would also suffer more remorse.

The interlude of Catherine's pregnancy in a chalet outside Montreux brings the separate 'union' to its culmination. They then go to the hospital where the baby is stillborn and Catherine dies from an inept Caesarian operation. Frederic Henry is left 'saying good-bye to a statue', which is all he has left of his gamble with love. In the rain, the persistent symbol of foreboding in the novel, he returns alone to his hotel, a winner who is taking nothing away from the gaming table but a 'self' vulnerable to the hurts of the world.

In the two novels we have discussed so far war is merely an episode, though a formative one, in the lives of its protagonists, presented to us as it was experienced by Henry Fleming and remembered by Frederic Henry. The conventions of narrative form are maintained. But with *Slaughterhouse Five* all this is changed. Here we have a 'New Novel' which works at several interconnected levels: (1) the novelist's experience as a POW during the Dresden fire bombing and his attempts to write a book about it; (2) the entire life of Billy Pilgrim, an archetypally American GI; (3) fragments of scholarly books on the Children's Crusade and a history of the Dresden bombing; (4) current events at the time of writing (1972), including brief allusions to Vietnam; and (5) a science fiction fantasy about the planet Tralfamadore. The device which connects most of them is the fact that Billy Pilgrim is a time-traveller—he has become 'unstuck in time'. From the novelist's point of view this enables him to juxtapose fragments of his story and the various levels without the constraints of strict chronology. From Billy Pilgrim's point of view, it enables him to see his whole life synoptically, including his own violent death in 1976. The fictional 'life' is thus in effect made to coincide with the time during which Billy Pilgrim was a prisoner of war, culminating in the bombing of Dresden.

As we have seen, Henry Fleming is a combat soldier who briefly deserts, returns to his regiment, and fights courageously, bearing in the latter stages the unit's flag through the perils of the battle. Frederic Henry is an ambulance driver who is wounded in his first exposure to enemy shelling in the Italian mountains, then later is caught up in a massive retreat, and deserts in what we would regard as entirely justifiable circumstances. Billy Pilgrim's role in World War II is even more marginal: he is a chaplain's assistant, 'a valet to a preacher' who joins an infantry regiment in December 1944 when it is in the process of being destroyed by the Germans in the Battle of the Bulge. 'Billy survived, but he was a dazed wanderer far behind the new German lines', with three others. Eventually he is taken prisoner, sent to the British compound in the centre of an extermination camp for Russian prisoners of war, and eventually to Dresden where he and 100 American POWs survive the Dresden fire-bombing only because they are housed in a cement block slaughterhouse.

Note how increasingly peripheral the protagonists are: soldier and flag-bearer, ambulance driver, and chaplain's assistant. This marginality of role is associated with a sense of futility on the part of the individuals in war. At the end of *The Red Badge of Courage* after a furious battle Henry's regiment calmly retraces its way back over the same ground that it has just fought so desperately to gain. Frederic Henry's only real act of war is to kill a deserting Italian army sergeant. As a chaplain's assistant Billy was 'powerless to harm the enemy or help his friends'. This powerlessness is carried to even greater extremes in the bizarre world of Joseph Heller's *Catch 22*, in which again the remedy is the flight of the idealist Yossarian to neutral Sweden.

Returning to Auden's symbols of the citizen and the pilgrim, we may associate each of these symbols with a complex of attitudes. The pilgrim represents the individual as self-discoverer, the citizen stands for the individual multiplied and conforming. Auden argues that man combines these two qualities, but modern war tends to force their separation. Henry Fleming was still able to reconcile them in the context of the American Civil War. His voyage of self-discovery brought him back from the wilderness to the social bonds of the fighting unit. But with the First World War we find Frederic Henry moving away from the war in various stages, eventually fleeing to neutral Switzerland. His self-discovery is largely negative in that he discovers what he is not by comparison with the priest and Rinaldi:

> Anger was washed away in the river along with any obligation . . .
> I wished them all the luck. They were the good ones, and the brave
> ones, and the calm ones and the sensible ones, and they deserved
> it. But it was not my show any more . . .

The withdrawal of Billy Pilgrim is even more extreme, as he escapes
to the science-fiction realm of Tralfamadore.

There are certainly indications that Billy has learned little about
himself, that he is the individual multiplied and confirming. For
example, the middle-age Billy attends a Lions Club meeting at
which a major in the Marines talks about the war in Vietnam:

> The major had been there on two separate tours of duty. He told
> of many terrible and many wonderful things he had seen. He was
> in favour of increased bombings, of bombing North Vietnam
> back into the Stone Age, if it refused to see reason. Billy was not
> moved to protest the bombing of North Vietnam, did not shudder
> about the hideous things he himself had seen bombing do. He
> was simply having lunch with the Lions Club, of which he was
> past president now.

Yet against this seeming insensitivity we must set the fact that
Billy is given to inexplicable bouts of weeping, as though his
distress had gone underground.

The existential adventurer is alternatively attracted and repelled
by war; that he has no sure bearings in the war context is probably
due to that absence of 'sustaining frames of tradition' referred to
by Barrett, and which are so evident for example in David Jones'
In Parenthesis. In each novel there are powerful counter-attractions
to the fearsome engagement of war: the mysterious forest with
its religious overtones of *The Red Badge of Courage* in which Henry
Fleming wanders; the love idyll with Catherine in *A Farewell to
Arms*; and the science fiction uptopia of Tralfamadore in *Slaughterhouse Five*. Each of these romantic alternatives to the reality of war
is characteristic of the predominant cultural milieu of the epochs
in which each novel was written.

Although we have studied the nominal protagonists in these
novels, in a sense the real heroes are the novelists themselves.
Although Crane himself had not experienced war at the time he
wrote *The Red Badge of Courage*, one can clearly see in the novel a
self-exploration behind the novelist's portrayal of the young
recruit's psychological reaction to war. Frederic Henry's war

experiences closely parallel Hemingway's own war experiences, as Michael S. Reynolds has now copiously documented.[3] But in these two novels the author's *persona* at least
remains in the background and so it is plausible to classify them
as novels in the conventional sense; with *Slaughterhouse Five* we
enter a new realm where the autobiographical element is much
more explicit. The first chapter is an account of how Vonnegut
came to write the book and begins, 'All this happened, more or less.
The war parts, anyway, are more or less true.' And there are frequent autobiographical interjections, such as: 'That was I. That
was me. That was the author of this book.'

The logical culmination of the tendency of the author's *persona*
to take over the novel occurs in Norman Mailer's *The Armies
of the Night*, in which the writer's 'performance' in an anti-Vietnam
War demonstration in Washington in 1967 becomes the principal
subject matter. The blurring of the conventional distinctions between fact and fiction is heightened by the dual structure of the
book: 'History as a Novel' and 'The Novel as History'. Mailer
is in effect 'making' the history which is the subject of his novel,
and he is also commenting on the 'novelistic' nature of contemporary history. The danger here is that the existential adventurer
totters on the brink of self-parody, but it is to Mailer's credit that
he avoids this pitfall.

In the three novels we have been considering, the existential
adventurers are the survivors, but it is the victims who are the
most memorable characters in the novels: Jim Conklin, the 'tall
soldier' whose death is vividly described in *The Red Badge of
Courage*; Rinaldi and the Priest in *A Farewell to Arms*; and poor
old Edgar Derby in *Slaughterhouse Five*. It is these characters who
embody that ideal fusion of individuality and community which
may be the only positive by-product of war in human terms.

Notes

1. W. H. Auden, *The Dyer's Hand* (London: Faber & Faber, 1963), 278–279.
2. William Barrett, "Introspective America", *Confluence*, vol. I, No. 1, March
   1952, pp. 43–44.
3. Michael S. Reynolds, *Hemingway's First War: The Making of A Farewell
   to Arms*, (Princeton, N. J.: Princeton University Press, 1976).

More Than Dovish:
Movements and Ideals of Peace
in the United States

Charles Chatfield

The title of this paper is drawn from a story by Devere Allen, a journalist and pacifist who was both fascinated and disturbed by the peace societies with which he worked in the 1920s. They should have been sophisticated but were often naïve, he felt; they needed unity but were divided; they aspired to universal principles but yet were parochial. Allen etched his characterisation of them with natural whimsy:

> The Dove of Peace had hatched two fledglings in her nest, it seems. One she named Abolition-of-War and the other Abolition-of-Aggressive-War. The second bird seized the greater share of food and attention. While Abolition languished, Abolition-of-Aggressive-War grew strong and assertive, flying far from home in pursuit of his kind of peace.
>
> One evening, however, Abolition-of-Aggressive-War returned to the nest battered, exhausted, and whimpering with disillusionment. The Dove drew out his tale with difficulty.
>
> There had been a quarrel in the orchard, she learned. The wrens claimed as their own a hollow limb in which they had nested the year before, but the bluebirds had found the limb empty and had nested in it this year. Which were the aggressors could not readily be ascertained, and the wrens and bluebirds had turned the orchard into a war zone. At length the dovelet had persuaded the birds to agree to submit future disputes to a Bird Council but, as it turned out, no family of birds would accept

a judgment against it, and a new conflict had involved even more species. The young would-be peacemaker himself had been badly pecked, and his pride had been hurt. He had failed to keep the peace, he complained to the Dove, and added, "That's what comes of being an imposter."

The mother Dove was shocked. "Coo-ah! An Imposter?" she exclaimed.

The truth was, the youngster wailed, that he had not a drop of dove blood in his body. He had been dropped as an egg in the dove's nest, but he was really a little cuckoo. For generations the cuckoos had left their eggs in dove's nests, he admitted, and his family traits had always betrayed their hosts.

The Dove was perplexed. "Why haven't my ancestors learned something from their experience?" she demanded.

The young cuckoo replied, a trifle maliciously but infinitely wise, "It is because, after all, you have been only doves."[1]

Somewhat flightly, naïve, and self-annointed: Allen's image of our voluntary peace societies is provocative. It is also inadequate, as he knew. The naïveté, divisiveness, and narrowness that have accompanied the organisations and ideals of the American peace movement were inherent in the development of their attempt to achieve a broadly ranging public influence in the American political system.

The United States was conceived in the context of a public debate over the merits of war, and the first generation of its leaders faced questions of war and peace which were inseparable from domestic politics. By 1815 the nation had spawned organised associations of peace advocates. Henceforth, American thinking about peace was influenced not only by political or academic leaders by also by public movements. These organised peace advocates have espoused a wide range of programmes and ideals that constitute the oldest sustained reform movement in the American experience. Organised to influence public policy, they advanced various approaches to peace and they competed with one another for support. Their movement has provided a tenuous but enduring forum for the evolution of alternative definitions of foreign policy.

Organisations

Occasionally peace reform has generated movements of public opinion and influence on a scale as broad as neutralism in the 1930s or opposition to the war in Vietnam, but for the most part it has been a minority affair like most other reform programmes in American history. Occasionally anti-war protest has coincided with peace advocacy, but these expressions must be distinguished from one another because numerous peace advocates have supported or condoned wars to which there was organised opposition. Indeed, the movement achieved continuity through its organisation between wars. Its socialising role and its impact can be gauged in terms of political processes common to the American scene.

'Peace movement' denotes the congeries of persons who have identified themselves with the cause of peace and were variously labelled: absolute pacifists, whether religious or secular, non-resistant or liberal; internationalists, both conservatives interested in expanding influence without political commitments and liberals who support participation in international organisations and even collective security; anti-war socialists; and even isolationists. Like other broad reform movements in the United States, the peace movement has become a coalition of diverse constituencies— groups of persons each united by a distinctive point of view (absolute pacifism, world government, Marxist analysis) together with social characteristics (being Christians, women, professionals) and/or functional programmes (educating, lobbying).

The social and ideological characteristics of these groups inform the ethos of the movement and help to explain the kinds and limits of its influence. Since each group identifies its own programme with the 'true' national interest, it cultivates the support of particular segments of public opinion. Various constituent groups attract publics with quite inconsistent political outlooks and interests, so that the peace movement has formed an increasingly complex social infrastructure of voluntary associations through which foreign policy issues have been screened.

Beginning as a single-purpose, moralistic campaign early in the nineteenth century, the peace movement acquired diversified constituencies in the twentieth and became involved in the politics of coalition.

The Early Movement

In its first hundred years the peace movement grew beyond anything that could have been predicted from its original character.

Local organisations were initiated in 1815, and the national American Peace Society was founded in 1828. They were small, poverty-stricken groups united by religious and humanitarian morality. They had the support of no national leaders except John Quincy Adams and Charles Sumner. They enlisted only a few businessmen who spread their benevolence thinly. The early movement developed an arsenal of practical objections to warfare and framed various proposals for world confederation, international law, and arbitration; but nonetheless it was an essentially moral crusade.

Early peace advocates tried to infuse their ethos into the hostile environment of American society. Their broadsides contained an important element of eighteenth-century rationalism, together with a realistic assessment of the devastation of the Napoleonic wars. But their reasoning was moralistic and their morality was religious: 'The American Peace Society, being founded on the principle that all war is contrary to the spirit of the gospel, shall have for its object to illustrate the inconsistency of war with Christianity, to show its baleful influence on all the great interests of mankind, and to devise means for insuring universal and permanent peace.'[2] Man was created in the image of God, these crusaders preached, and he is capable of making free, ethical responses. Since man is accountable both as an individual and in society, governments should adapt their customs to a moral regimen. Since moral truth admits no qualification, and since war is a dire social custom rather than necessary human function, the disciples believed, warfare could be exorcised by an act of the moral will. Their purpose was to bring the society to the threshold of choice.

A handful of peace missionaries laboured ardently. They published tracts and journals, sponsored essay contests, and solicited petitions to Congress. They toured the country: William Ladd, robust former sea-captain who piloted the American Peace Society in the late 1830s, travelled over 1300 miles in 1835 alone. Elihu Burritt, the learned blacksmith of the movement, founded his League of Universal Brotherhood on a missionary trip to England, sponsored an anti-war pledge there, and organised exchanges of declarations of friendship between English and French towns and English and American workingmen.

The odds were against the disciples. They had neither money nor large memberships. Citing gospel chapter and verse, they got short shrift from organised Christianity, for which war represented the will of God. Decrying the rule of force, they were scarcely heard in a wilderness culture prone to violence. Pleading for internationalism, they made little sense to an isolated nation. Propagandising for peace, they seemed irrelevant to a society imbued with westward-conquering Manifest Destiny. Confident of the self-evident nature of moral truth, they were themselves confused and divided by the Civil War. Outside of Massachusetts they got little response.

Nor did they relate to the separate interests of other groups. Although they assumed that their message was universal, they studiously avoided commitments to reform groups that might embroil them in controversy. They perceived the destructive reality of war; but they naïvely assumed that their version of truth would be self-evident and compelling to others. They were, as Devere Allen wrote, only doves. They were a community without a polity: neither their ideals nor their organisation fitted them for influence in a society where advocates of change were fiercely competitive.

William Ladd revealed the problems of the whole early move-ment when in 1836 he wrote on the duty of females to promote the cause of peace. He believed that the world would respond to ethics the more it was christianised and civilised, and he thought that women could be agents of this process. What, then, could women do? They could pray, study the gospel, lead peaceful lives, educate children, distribute pamphlets and periodicals, join peace societies, and perhaps even write children's books.[3] Despite the fact that the feminist movement was in full swing, it never seemed to occur to Ladd that women might constitute an element with interests of their own to which the peace move-ment might be allied, or that they were capable of sharing decision. But by 1915 women had identified themselves as a distinct social group and were winning decision-making power in domestic affairs. When the Women's Peace Party was founded that year, its platform read, in part:

> ... we demand that our right to be consulted in the settlement of questions concerning not alone the life of individuals but of nations be recognised and respected.[4]

The Women's Peace Party was a measure of the diversification of of the peace movement in the twentieth century.

The Established Movement

The rise of diversified constituencies within the peace movement took place about the turn of the century. It was a concomitant of the emergence of professions in American society and of the nation's growing world rôle. Peace became a respectable vocation for influential lawyers, educators, clergymen, social workers, businessmen, and government leaders. The movement became established, both in the sense that it had a mature form of organisation and in the sense that it drew its support from the leadership class.

In the latter part of the nineteenth century arbitration attracted a good deal of political support, and some members of Congress joined the Interparliamentary Union. Americans already had contributed to international law, and in 1906 they organised the American Society of International Law. Early in the new century projects for a world court and international organisation drew support from political leaders, including State Department officers and Presidents William Howard Taft and Woodrow Wilson. University presidents and educators became increasingly prominent in peace societies, and some religious liberals saw the concern with peace as an opportunity for social leadership and church unity. Women active in the suffrage movement brought peace within the purview of their sex. Most symbolic of the new prestige of the movement, however, was the fact that leading businessmen joined it and endowed substantial peace foundations.

It was easy for contemporaries to mistake respectability for a general conversion to internationalism and peace. Quite to the contrary, as Roland Marchand has demonstrated, 'in nearly every case, the connecting link' between these constituencies and the peace movement 'was the perception of some new group of how certain configurations of international politics or attitudes toward international affairs would affect its crucial domestic concerns.'[5] This is not to suggest that peace advocates were insincere. Rather, they had a genuine attachment to peace programmes in so far as these reflected an extension of domestic and professional priorities. They represented diversified constituencies. Nonetheless, leading peace advocates early in this century shared a common ethos.[6] They insisted on the natural inequality of men and nations and assumed that a conflict of interests among them was natural. They trusted in formal arrangements to give rational direction to conflict and to resolve problems, thus valuing compulsory arbitration, negotiated arms limitation, international law, and a confederation of governments. Themselves the successful directors of large-scale organisations, they felt comfortable with the complex institutional arrangements predicated by an interdependent world. They sought order and control in an arena threatened with disruption by unchecked national interests. At the same time, they assumed that national sovereignty is the ultimate reality in international life, and they accepted the atomistic character of international relations as an inevitable consequence. Accordingly, they assumed that foreign policy should represent essentially national interests, although they preferred to supplement the ultimate sanction of force with negotiated agreements. They had few qualms in this regard, because they associated the sovereign nations in the West with rational society. World law and organisation were matters of practical adjustment to an interdependent world, and they would guarantee the stability of an international order dominated by the progressive, successful civilisation of the Atlantic community. Americans shared this ethos with many counterparts in England.

There was a minority viewpoint in the established peace movement which was not clearly articulated until 1914. There were some who sought a broader basis for morality than the national interest. But the core of an alternative ethos, human morality, was suffused by misty optimism and eclipsed by the pragmatic, progressive bent that made new international institutions seem so promising.

The established movement, for its part, identified itself so closely with the prevailing national interest that it could not challenge the drift of foreign policy even though it had greatly broadened the public base of policy analysis to include academic, business, professional and political groups. Only when international and domestic conditions conflicted with established perceptions and interests in World War I did new groups enter the movement, adding their own ethos and opening the modern phase of peace reform.

The Modern Movement

Increasingly the peace societies established before 1914 supported the Allied cause and then American intervention in the hope of influencing a peace settlement along internationalist lines.

Opponents of intervention and militarism forged new organisa-tions: the American Union Against Militarism, the Fellowship of Reconciliation (FOR), and the Women's Peace Party, all formed in 1915. New constituencies affiliated with these groups: social workers, reformers, anti-war socialists, social gospel ministers, and prominent women. Progressives all, they were accustomed to mobilising public opinion for various causes. They swung into action for peace. The American Union blunted Woodrow Wilson's 1916 preparedness programme with a vigorous public campaign. The Women's Peace Party cooperated with European women to promote mediation by neutral nations under American auspices and, when Wilson balked, through a commission of private persons. A liberal anti-war coalition was formed to oppose intervention. When war was declared, it cooperated with anti-war socialists in a campaign for liberal peace aims and freedom of debate. When that programme was frustrated by the crusading spirit of the war effort, a radical wing of the American Union formed the National Civil Liberties Bureau (subsequently the American Civil Liberties Union) to cooperate with the pacifist Fellowship of Reconciliation in defence of conscientious objectors. The American Friends Service Committee was formed in 1917 in order to promote active relief work abroad as an alternative form of service for Quaker conscientious objectors.

As the United States mobilised for war, the membership of these groups was reduced to a handful of pacifists who refused to sanction the war effort. They formed a tightly-knit community which combined absolute war resistance with an orientation to political reform. They were the nucleus of the broadly based, liberal pacifist wing of the peace movement which emerged from World War I.

These peace advocates rejected abstract moral theorems and institutional practicality in favour of what Jane Addams called 'cosmopolitan sympathy'. That is to say, they replaced the moral and institutional internationalism of the early and established peace movements with social impulses, a community orientation born of their own professional experiences. Their morality em-braced humanity and excluded organised violence. They became victims of militant patriotism during the war, and they concluded that warfare was but the most horrendous institution of a social system of exploitation that also had its peacetime victims. Warfare was the consummate form of arbitrary authority, of which all violence was an expression. That is what Randolph Bourne meant when he declared, 'War is the health of the State.'[7] War is a correlative of injustice, the wartime pacifists concluded, and peace is linked to justice.

This perception imbued the liberal pacifist wing of the modern peace movement. Leaders in pacifist organisations formed during World War I developed wide-ranging programmes for social amelioration at home and abroad in the following generation. Some of them became actively involved in the labour movement, socialism, and the struggle for black freedom. When civil rights groups became an important constituency of anti-war protest in the 1960s the movement had come full circle, because in the 1940s leadership for the non-violent Committee of Racial Equality had emerged from the peace campaigns of the FOR. Liberal pacifists aligned themselves with reform groups in the generation following 1918 both in the interest of social justice and in order to gain support for their foreign policy position. They also allied with non-resistant churches such as those of the Mennonites and the Brethren, whose traditional form of pacifism proscribed political involvement, in order to influence legislation regarding conscientious objection.

Meanwhile, many of the traditional internationalists had become more political also. Some had contributed to Wilsonian policy and remained committed to its vision of world order. Some had helped to form and popularise the League of Nations and had been enmeshed in the politics of its rejection. Like liberal pacifists, therefore, traditional internationalists emerged from World War I understanding the importance of public support for a progressive foreign policy.

Thus the modern peace movement acquired highly organised wings, each with a distinct orientation, each with diversified constituencies, and each motivated to seek public support for its positions. Both wings therefore became involved in the politics of coalition.

The Politics of Coalition

Reform groups necessarily form coalitions in order to have political influence. A coalition can gain access to specific civic interest, and ideological groups to the extent that it appears to represent a wide range of concerns and resources. The more inclusive a coalition becomes, however, the more difficult it becomes to satisfy the restricted tenets and programme demands of its various member groups. The greater its appeal to a broad public, the more it threatens its own distinct constituencies. Not surprisingly, coalitions of peace societies have been very tenuous. They have been weakened or shattered by lack of cooperation among peace groups, by a narrow definition of public interest, or by a loss of support from civic and interest groups outside the coalition. The tensions of coalition politics are the source of competitiveness, what some have called belligerence, in the organised peace movement since World War I when it acquired both diversified constituencies and a need for political support.

Internationalists failed to give foreign policy a clear direction in the 1920s, for example, because they could not engineer cooperation among their own constituent groups. After the failure to bring the United States into the League of Nations, two other programmes vied with one another: accession to the World Court and negotiation of a treaty outlawing war. It was widely understood that all three steps to international cooperation were related. The issue was, which would be politically viable? The key to effective coalition was held by the leader of the Senate Foreign Relations Committee, William E. Borah, who manoeuvred artfully to keep internationalists at bay and divided while retaining initiative for himself. Liberal pacifists and leaders in the League of Nations Non-Partisan Association drew up a sensible compromise programme, but it was scuttled. The better part of a decade was wasted in internecine controversy.

In the following decade a major coalition was attempted between the internationalist and pacifist wings of the movement. By 1932 leaders in both elements agreed on the desirability of a strong international organisation and forthright condemnation of aggression such as Japan was waging in Manchuria. They formalised their consensus in a National Peace Conference. Within a few years, however, the pacifists had grown sceptical of the League's ability to keep peace. Regarding it as an alliance in a continuing European power struggle, they took the initiative in securing new neutrality legislation. Meanwhile, internationlists clarified their commitment to collective security as well as to changes in the international system. At about the same time both wings opened campaigns for public support, but the pacifists out-manoeuvred their colleagues and gained control of the coalition through the Emergency Peace Campaign (1936–37). This half-million dollar campaign included a number of programmes common to both wings, but it was most effectively used to buttress neutralism. Internationalists withdrew before it ended, thus weakening its appeal. In its wake there emerged two competing coalitions: the internationalist Committee to Defend America by Aiding the Allies, and a Pacifist-Socialist Keep America Out of War Committee. Political controversy was severe in 1937–38, but public support for the Allies mounted after the outbreak of war in Europe. Subject to every kind of pressure, the anti-war coalition virtually collapsed in the months before 7 December 1941.

Internationalists cooperated during World War II in order to fashion a United Nations Organisation, but the pacifist coalition was limited largely to work on behalf of conscientious objectors. The two wings did work together briefly after the war to defeat a proposal for universal military training, but pacifists again became isolated as the policy of containment attracted liberal internationalist support. They failed to defeat peacetime conscription in 1948. Opposition to the Korean War was insignificant, and even the challenge to the nuclear arms race could not sustain a coalition until a thaw in the Cold War was occasioned by changes in Soviet leadership.

Then, in 1957, a small group of pacifists fashioned two organisations: the liberal and internationalist committee for a SANE Nuclear Policy and the radical pacifist Committee for Non-violent Action. The pair worked in tandem for a nuclear non-proliferation treaty, SANE trying to win support through traditional processes and CNVA sponsoring direct actions such as sailing into test zones or swimming out to Polaris submarines. Their programme was coordinated with campaigns in England and Germany. SANE was weakened by controversy over alleged communists in its ranks, but both groups survived to join a gathering coalition opposed to the war in Vietnam.

Opposition to the Vietnam War came from the FOR and American Friends Service Committee, which kept Americans in touch with Vietnamese peace groups, from the War Registers League,

SANE, and from new constituencies, including civil rights leaders, groups of academics, and Students for a Democratic Society.

The anti-war campaigns of the 1960s involved the largest coalitions in peace reform history, and they were marked by severe tensions. For example, the series of marches on Washington which attracted national media coverage drained vital resources from local groups and, therefore, weakened their ability to reach local public affiliates. This strategy of the centre was organised by the Mobilisation, and toward the end of the decade there was mounting resistance to it. A new coalition, the Moratorium, was formed in response to this pressure and in order to move potential supporters in Congress by going directly to their local constituencies. The Moratorium planned to coordinate periodic demonstrations on local levels, a strategy of the periphery. The two grand strategies conflicted when the Mobilisation scheduled its march of 15 November 1969, to coincide with a Moratorium demonstration. The latter gave way and exhausted its resources in behalf of the march. By the spring of 1970 both coalitions had largely dispersed.

There were related tensions in the movement: the issue of communists or persons advocating violence in anti-war campaigns; the choice between confronting the public dramatically or appealing to the electorate in conventional ways; and divisive questions about the terms of withdrawal, the extent of United States complicity, and the character of Vietnamese regimes. Controversy was minimised by holding to the single issue of ending the war.

The tensions of coalition politics should not obscure its importance. Coalition is a necessary strategy for public influence in the American political system, and it has produced results on a broad scale. A loose coalition of peace advocates muted the strident imperialism that followed the Spanish-American War. Another coalition delayed intervention in World War I, and then contributed to the internationalist foreign policy goals that ultimately sanctioned American entry. A coalition of pacifists and internationalists helped to rewrite neutrality policy in the 1930s and provided an arena for the debate over intervention in the European war. Internationalists cooperated with the State Department to fashion the Charter of the United Nations which they popularised. Subsequently they imbued even the Cold War with an internationalist ethos which made a later transition to détente plausible. A broad coalition marshalled support for nuclear arms limitation and arms control, and another provided the impetus and environment for reassessing the Vietnam commitment. Withdrawal from that war was mandated by popular opinion largely generated by the peace movement.

Innumerable specific policies reflect the influence of peace coalitions: arbitration treaties of the nineteenth-century; the First and Second Hague Conferences; the genesis of the World Court; the formation of the League of Nations and United Nations; popular sovereignty and human rights cases as foreign policy issues; accommodation to Latin America since the 1920s and to black Africa more recently; and a series of proposals to liberalise international economics and control the arms race. American peace groups financially sustained an international connection (and some European organisations) between the World Wars, and they maintained direct contact with League agencies when the government did not officially do so. They framed specific foreign aid programmes after World War II and intervened with the State Department on behalf of refugees. Domestically they won ever more liberal legislation for conscientious objectors and federal funding for international and peace education. Some peace groups adapted techniques of nonviolent action to both social justice and foreign policy.

The recurrence of war overshadowed such specific accomplishments in the minds of peace advocates who tended to measure their success or failure by their ultimate goals. That is why the little cuckoo in Devere Allen's story felt so disillusioned when he could not keep the peace. Jane Addams confessed that 'the pacifist in war time is literally starved of any gratification of that natural desire to have his own decisions justified by his fellows,' while internationalists in World War I naïvely valued their acceptance by men in power as a mark of influence.[8]

In a broader view, however, the function of peace reform is to test rather than to make foreign policy. Voluntary peace societies function in a federal system as agents through which alternative programmes and definitions of national interest are initiated and tested for public support. The politics of coalition make it necessary to test policy alternatives for support among the informed constituencies of the movement as well as within the general public.

Tension among diverse peace groups is a corollary of their significance. The free existence of principled dissent is, after all, assurance that foreign policy-making is consistent with democratic institutions, and the free competition of peace societies for public influence is an index of the adaptability of their policy views to a changing world.

Ideals

None of the antitheses in American culture is sharper than a strong attachment to law and peace, offset by frequent violence and war. The ambivalence is aptly caught in a political cartoon showing a lanky Uncle Sam balanced precariously, one foot upon a thundering war horse and the other on a flying dove of peace. Even the peace movement has been divided between pacifists altogether opposed to fighting and other reformers unwilling to give up the ultimate sanction. Nonetheless, peace advocates have reinforced American scepticism of military institutions and have explored the morality of power on both individual and social levels. From the two wings of the modern movement emerged both an ethos emphasising orderly change and an ethos stressing justice and non-violence—moralities of power that may become fused in the transnational orientation of contemporary peace reform.

Scepticism of Military Institutions

The support of large-scale military organisation in peacetime is a recent phenomenon in the United States, dating from World War II. For the most part, the nation has been sceptical of military institutions, although it never doubted the legitimacy of war itself. Thus Bruce Catton has written:

> ... a nation which did not especially like to think about war and which had very little use for military tradition and ritual turned out to be amazingly warlike when the test came. It detested war, but when the time came for thinking with the muscles and the viscera, war fitted as a glove fits the hand. It required the American to do with all of his might that which he did best anyway, and at the same moment it relieved him of the need to do any serious thinking about what was likely to come of it all.[9]

That was the problem, according to peace advocates: the American needed to think seriously about the outcome of war.

They began by attacking the idealisation of militarism in social philosophy, religion, and the arts. Washington astride Nelson, and Lee on Traveler: artistic images of martial glory in 'the noblest profession' gave way only to an alternative imagination that was evoked in satire, literary realism, and documentary media. The idealisation that war is the will of God was attacked by pacifists in their earliest tracts, and it was finally repudiated by major denominations reacting against the excesses of religious zeal in 1917–18. Another romanticism, widely accepted and epitomised in Ruskin's dictum that 'war is the foundation of all high virtues and faculties of man,' had been challenged in enlightenment thought but had been given a new sanction in the Darwinian metaphor of natural selection. David Starr Jordan, among others, argued that the 'harvest of thorns' is degradation, a kind of reverse selection. Even those who regard warfare as necessary today reflect Jordan's feeling that war is bad, 'only to be justified as the last resort of "mangled, murdered liberty", a terrible agony to be evoked only when all other acts of self-defence shall fail'.[10]

Peace reformers also reinforced a traditional distaste for military institutions as being antithetical to class and democratic interests. The argument from class has been less persuasive, historically, but it was a motivating idea for anti-war socialists in World War I and in the 1930s, and for Marxists in the New Left of the 1960s. More significant has been the argument from democratic values such as egalitarianism, moral responsibility, mobility and resistance to hierarchy, and individualism. In this spirit liberal pacifists sustained opposition to peacetime conscription which they pictured as a form of regimentation antithetical to individualism and voluntarism, and as an institution associated with totalitarianism and contrasted with the American Dream: the classic cartoon depicts an athletic but headless man—'the perfect soldier'.

Moreover, peace reformers contrasted militarism to traditional American institutions such as law and commercial relations. Contemporary spokesmen for multinational corporations echo the belief of businessmen early in the century that commerce is an integrating and peaceful force. John Bates Clark described the world as an 'economic organism,' a notion rooted in the Free

Trade internationalism of Cobden, Bright, and Bastiat. The exchange system of the global market place was seen as an alternative to war. Businessmen in the established peace movement also argued that freedom from the burden of armaments had given the nation a competitive advantage.

They were all the more ready to support the political institutions of an interdependent order: international law, arbitration, and some form of world organisation. Such programmes had been formally advanced in the United States since at least 1842, and they were explicitly valued as being consistent with American forms. The world was but the federal system writ large. Thus William Ladd added to his *Essay on a Congress of Nations* (1842) the original idea that the executive function should be separated from the judicial one. An obvious reference to the United States Constitution, Ladd's suggestion illustrates an underlying American preference for an international order which is an extension of their own national institutions. 'It was the dream of the fathers that . . . the American government and republican manhood should be co-extensive,' said David Starr Jordan in 1898.[11] He was warning that 'imperial democracy' is a contradiction in terms, and he asked, 'Shall our armies go where our institutions cannot?'

As the United States became more involved abroad, peace advocates extended their scepticism of the institution of war. At the same time, sociological and pragmatic distinctions became available to them. Liberal pacifist Kirby Page insisted that war should be judged not for its spirit or ideals but, rather, as a method.[12] The issue is what war does, he wrote; what is important is the process, not the event. This manner of thinking was strengthened by access to European sociology (notably Novocov and Kropotkin) and to British studies of imperialism (especially those of J. A. Hobson). It was confirmed by the post-World War I revisionism of historians such as Harry Elmer Barnes and by the elaborate research of James T. Shotwell for the Carnegie Endowment. By contrast, it had taken a profoundly idealistic spirit, blissfully ignorant of social processes, to enable Ralph Barton Perry to conclude during the war, 'It is then in keeping with the record of human progress that the last war should be the worst, —and the worst the last.'[13]

In retrospect the axiom seems facetious, for World War I was the awful first wave of a sustained global conflict that issued in a second. In the interlude searching analyses of the international system and war were made by leading peace advocates. They noted that military threat introduces rigidity into international relations. They concluded that the corollary to peace is equitable change which war, viewed as a social system, impedes. Their thinking was aptly expressed by John Foster Dulles in 1939. It is 'flexibility and not rigidity which creates lasting stability,' he wrote. In order to attain peace it is necessary to deal with the causes of war as well as with immediate crises, and for this purpose a 'flexible and balanced form of world society' is required.[14] Dulles reflected the common concern of modern peace reformers with the relationships of equity and order, peace and change in international affairs. By the time he wrote, however, the peace movement had again become divided over the issue of a specific war, despite that its leaders shared a common scepticism of military institutions.

Moralities of Peace

Moral thought in America has shifted from an absolutistic conception of truth to ethical relativism. There are important exceptions. The Quaker doctrine of the Inner Light which influenced many early peace advocates was highly individual and subjective while, on the other hand, doctrinaire morality persisted when it was given institutional support. But on the whole, the notion that truth is unequivocal and external to the conscience has evolved into the concept of alternative standards of morality.

In turn, there has developed a distinction between the moral precepts appropriate to individual choices and those characteristic of groups. This distinction, put most explicitly by Reinhold Niebuhr, has been influential. It is useful in this discussion because the peace movement has generated both moral standards on which individuals might base their dissent from war and social standards for collective policy.

Two broad standards for the exercise of national power have been counterposed within the twentieth-century peace movement, and they correspond roughly to its two wings: the traditional internationalists who organised the established movement and the liberal pacifists who organised during and after World War I. Both standards predicate an international context for the definition of American interests and both were formed in the spirit of William James in that they prefer open ended possibilities and the reconciliation of differences in the discovery of a common good. Each has, however, a distinct locus of attention: one is oriented to the prerequisites of international order, the other to the requirements of global justice.

Traditional internationalists evolved a morality for the responsible *use* of national power. It was described by Nicholas Murray Butler, head of the Division of Education and Intercourse of the Carnegie Endowment, as 'the international mind':

> ... that habit of thinking of foreign relations and business, and that habit of dealing with them, which regard the several nations of the civilised world as friendly and cooperative equals in aiding the progress of civilisation, in developing commerce and industry, and in spreading enlightenment and culture throughout the world.[15]

The prerequisite of progress, development, and enlightenment in that sense is stability. Indeed, the core of the internationalist ethos is order. Under its aegis internationalists supported the League of Nations and tried to strengthen it; in its service they transformed the League of Nations Association into a committee for collective security, helped to form the United Nations, and finally evolved the post-war combination of containing the Soviet Union while engineering cooperation within the western world. Order is not synonymous with the *status quo* in this view, although there have been conservatives who wished it were. Rather, collective security arrangements are justified in order to maintain a tenuous balance between dynamic, competing nations so that the institutions of an interdependent world can evolve incrementally. These institutions are the bulwark against arbitrary change, unpredictability, and insecurity. Orderly change itself has been a primary ideal, and its functional corollary has been the controlled application of national power.

The attention of most internationalists through the Cold War period was on 'the several nations of the civilised world as ... equals.' Without altogether neglecting the Third World, they acted as though the proper sphere of foreign policy was in the industrialised northern hemisphere. Not oblivious to social revolution, they acted as though the primary agents of development were established governments together with their agencies, international bodies. The traditional province of international relations is the process of resolving or containing disputes, and this reflects a normative view: world society would evolve through the agency of nation-states whose relationships should be governed according to rules and understandings that would ensure openness of competition or cooperation among them. In this respect, détente is an expression of the internationalist ethos, seemingly making it possible to measure the controlled application of national power in terms of the orderly evolution of the civilised world.

On the other hand, liberal pacifists evolved criteria for the responsible *goals* of national power. Their ethics derived not only from their anti-war sectarian origins but also from the ideals of the social gospel movement: the kingdom of God on earth as a measure of social institutions, the brotherhood of common humanity, and the integrity of individual life and choice. Their great object was the reconciliation of people, not the adjustment of conflicting interests. Sensitive to great disparities alienating classes and groups from one another, liberal pacifists placed great emphasis on social change. Indeed, a concern for social justice is at the core of the pacifist ethos.

It shares authority with a concern for peace. Viewed as the absense of war, peace was traditionally an end in itself for absolute pacifists. That was the inheritance of centuries of sectarian witness. In the context of their World War I experience and their post-war social action, however, liberal pacifists revised the connotations of peace. They came to accept the reality of conflict. They sought ethical forms of it. They eventually made a distinction between violent and non-violent conflict, one which was both moral and practical: arguing that the ends and means of social action are two facets of a single process and that the coherence of the process will determine its consequences, pacifists said that violence and war are inconsistent with the goals of justice and peace. Violence and war, they insisted, violate the lives and integrity of persons and reify arbitrary authority in society, thus buttressing injustice.

The locus of pacifist ethics was common humanity. Liberal pacifists would not attribute responsibility for war to any one nation; but, instead found all nations implicated. They refused to identify liberty and civilisation with any nations exclusively. Thus, John Haynes Holmes offered an alternative definition of the 'international mind':

> Wherever in any nation, as actually in all nations, men are weighted and broken with the yoke of tyranny, there the international mind would speak its sympathy and give its aid. Wherever men are struggling to break the shackles of political or economic bondage, there the international mind would declare and fight the war that is war. Wherever men are languishing in darkness, weeping in mute despair or striking in mad revolt, there the international mind would see its brethren, in their state of misery behold its country, and in their dreams of better days and happier peoples feel the impulse of its patriotism.[16]

The peoples of the world are interdependent in their struggles for a common humanity, according to the pacifists: the essential reality of international relations is transnational. Against that reality all policy should be measured. By that rule the mere cooperation of sovereign nations is inadequate.

Such ideals as these moralities of peace are abstracted from positions taken by leaders in the pacifist and internationalist constituencies; but in the war crises of the twentieth century it has been precisely the communities which have been divided from one another. The liberal, internationally concerned pacifist was part of a community united in principle by a common rejection of war. The internationalist active in peace organisations was related to a cosmopolitan establishment with diverse domestic and foreign priorities. In peacetime leaders in the two wings could cooperate, as they did in the 1920s and early 1930s; in wartime they were largely isolated from one another within their own communities. They were polarised, too, by their perspectives, the internationalists viewing the world as divided by two congeries of nation states and the pacifists preferring to see the world as divided between decision-makers and victims across all boundaries.

Each side brought its own ethos to the Vietnam War. Liberal internationalists reacted against it largely because they perceived that the controlled application of military power in Vietnam was illusory and futile, and that the attempt was weakening the nation's constructive influence for international order. Pacifists instinctively sided with the oppressed (on both sides) and against warfare (on both sides): they reacted against wanton, apparently arbitrary use of force and the misconception of social revolution in South East Asia. Both wings were anxious about the fate of American institutions, too, as they formed coalitions in opposition to the war.

Their uneasy cooperation was limited by the very single-issue orientation which had been the basis of any liaison and, hence, of public influence. This limited serious discussion within the peace movement about the terms of withdrawal or about the larger aspects of foreign policy.

With the end of the war, the *ad hoc* single-issue groups collapsed, leaving the established pacifist and internationalist societies, together with important new peace constituencies: a peace education and research community (notably the Institute for World Order, the Institute for Policy Studies, and the Consortium for Peace Research, Education and Development), nuclei of peace-minded individuals in political life, and recently-founded organisations with broad, liberal constituencies (such as the World Without War Council). Within these groups there emerged the discussion of long-range foreign policy issues which had been stifled during the war. New conceptual tools were at hand for the analysis of conflict and international systems, and for an integrative approach to social processes in a global context.

Transnational Orientation

There has always been a transnational orientation in the peace movement. Under its auspices transnational networks were formed, as individuals participated in international conferences and groups maintained contacts with peace societies abroad (as early as 1815 with the formation of the London Peace Society). Linkages were established through international peace societies: Elihu Burritt's League of Universal Brotherhood, the international law societies and Interparliamentary Union, the Church Peace Union and International Association for Friendship Through the Churches, the Carnegie Endowment with its overseas branches, the American Friends Service Committee through relief and reconstruction work, the Cosmopolitan Clubs, International Fellowship of Reconciliation, War Resisters International, Women's International League for Peace and Freedom, the League of Nations Association in cooperation with national unions, Amnesty International, and the International Peace Research Association. Moreover, the movement has consistently interpreted itself in terms of universal ideals. For all of its world contacts

and values, however, the movement has for the most part responded to national constituencies and has dealt with issues of national
interest.

Contemporary peace reform, on the other hand, is addressing
itself to issues globally conceived. It is interpreting even national
issues in terms of interrelated world processes and systems.
According to the World Without War Council:

> We believe the United States should lead in creating the global
> political processes which can reduce world problems and resolve
> international conflicts. Without adequate political processes,
> the world is left with the insecurity and expense of expanding
> military systems and without the means to alleviate hunger,
> secure human rights, preserve the environment and prevent war.
> These global problems threaten the quality, if not the continuance
> of human life and will be solved politically and internationally,
> or not at all.[17]

That statement is the preamble of a 'Peace Platform' sponsored by
an internationalist coalition and addressed to electoral candidates in 1976. Similarly, a study of *The United States and Latin
America Today*, published by the American Friends Service Committee in 1976 puts hemispheric relations into a global context,
interprets development in terms of dependency, recommends
structural changes in international systems, and argues that 'major-
problems are global and ... not even the U.S. can attempt
solutions on its own'.[18] The same emphasis is found in the World
Order Models Project of the Institute for World Order, in most
peace education literature, and in new future studies programmes.
It is reflected in the reorientation of major church bodies which
envision themselves as sharing a mission in the world with
churches in other societies (as opposed to having a mission to
them). Problem-oriented organisations such as Bread for the World
are reaching specific publics with integrated concerns for global
ecology, hunger, and social change, and they are finding the national media supportive. The Institute for Policy Studies is adopting
a transnational approach to problems of economic inequality and
human rights. Along with the organised peace movement, these
groups reflect the search for 'newer ideals of peace'.

Jane Addams coined that phrase in a series of lectures at the
University of Wisconsin in 1906. She described the cooperative-
ness of slum immigrants, municipal reform, social legislation,

the protection of children, and public-consciousness among women as evidence of a new 'cosmopolitan interest in human affairs with the resultant social sympathy'.[19] Is it too much to hope that the 'cosmopolitian interest in human affairs' and the awareness of their interrelatedness which Jane Addams offered for American society is being extended to the world? Is it too bold to suppose that the ethos of internationalists and pacifists alike is being fused in new ideals of peace?

The contemporary peace-movement has a heritage of over 150 years of organised activity. It has diversified constituencies, an infrastructure for public debate and influence. It knows the tensions of coalition politics. Dividing sharply over participation in specific wars and obscuring important issues it could not reconcile, always struggling for meager resources and attention, it has measured foreign policy against varying ideals of peace. It appears to have identified unifying, transnational criteria of national interest that are rooted both in social impulses (the cosmopolitan sympathies of pacifist heritage) and in systemic analyses (through which internationalists can relate national sovereignty to global systems). Such a movement is more than dovish, in Devere Allen's phrase—more than flighty, naïve, and self-annointed. In the marketplace of American ideas, where the national interest will be defined, it has been the function of the organised peace movement to advance and assess alternative ideals in the public philosophy.

Notes

1. I have summarised the extended version of this story by Devere Allen, 'Only Doves,' *Christian Century*: 45 (17 May 1928), pp. 636–37.
2. Constitution of the American Peace Society, as revised at the Ninth Annual Meeting, reproduced as an appendix to the thorough analysis of early peace movement thought, David Lawson, 'Swords into Plowshares' (unpublished Ph. D. dissertation, University of Arizona, 1975), pp. 537–38.
3. William Ladd, *On the Duty of Females to Promote the Cause of Peace* (Boston, 1836), pp. 3–4. *
4. Quoted from the full text of the platform in Marie Louise Degen, *The History of the Women's Peace Party* (Baltimore, 1939, 41.). *
5. Roland Marchand, *The American Peace Movement and Social Reform, 1898–1918* (Princeton, N. J.: Princeton University Press, 1972), p. x.
6. This period has been definitely established in: Roland Marchand, *ibid.*: Sondra Herman, *Eleven Against War: Studies in American Internationalist Thought, 1898–1921* (Stanford: Hoover Institution Publication 1969); David

Patterson, 'The Travail of the American Peace Movement, 1887–1914' (unpublished Ph. D. dissertation, University of California, Berkeley, 1968); and Michael A. Lutzker, 'The 'Practical' Peace Advocates: An Interpretation of the American Peace Movement, 1898–1917' (unpublished Ph. D. dissertation, Rutgers University, 1969).

7. 'The State,' in Carl Resek, Ed., *War and the Intellectuals: Essays by Randolph Bourne*, 1915–19 (New York: Harper & Row 1964), p. 89.

8. *Peace and Bread in Time of War* (New York, 1945), p. 150.*

9. Bruce Catton *U.S. Grant and the American Military Tradition* (Boston: Little Brown, 1954), p. 132.

10. *The Human Harvest: A Study of the Decay of Races Through the Survival of the Unfit* (Boston, 1907), pp. 118, 121.*

11. *Imperial Democracy* (New York, 1899), pp. 42–43.*

12. Page to "Dear Ones," October 20, 1917, and elsewhere in the Kirby Page manuscripts, Claremont, Calif. Page subsequently becomes the most published and widely influential pacifist concerned with social and international issues.

13. 'What is Worth Fighting For?' in Charles Chatfield, ed., *The Ethics of War: Bertrand Russell and Ralph Barton Perry on World War I* (New York, 1972), p. 831.*

14. *War, Peace and Change* (New York, 1939), pp. 50, 97.*

15. *The International Mind: An Argument for the Judicial Settlement of International Disputes* (New York), p. 102.*

16. *The International Mind: An Address* (Boston, 1916), p. 17.*

17. *Building a World Community: A Peace Platform for* 1976 (Chicago: Peace Platform Committee, 1976).

18. *The United States and Latin America Today: A Critical Examination of U.S. Economic and Military Presence in Latin America* (Philadelphia: American Friends Service Committee, 1976).

19. Jane Addams *The Newer Ideals of Peace* (New York: Macmillan 1907), p. 9. *These works are available with new introductions in the reprint series, *The Garland Library of War and Peace*, eds., Blanche Wiesen Cook, Charles Chatfield, and Sandi Cooper (New York, 1972–75).

Law, Peace, and War in American International Legal Thought

James P. Piscatori

Benjamin Franklin, upon whom Americans rely as the great aphorist, believed that there is no such thing as a bad peace nor a good war.[1] Fortunately, American international legal thought on the subject has been both more diverse and more subtle. The American consciousness of the law of nations in general was early asserted, as evidenced by the revolutionary wartime regulations governing the capture of vessels 'according to the general usages of Europe'[2] and in Article VI of the Constitution making treaties the 'supreme law of the land'. But the importance and content of the higher law have varied with the interpreters who in the nineteenth century were mostly diplomats, judges and military officers. The breadth of interpretations increased in the present century as the government's interest in world politics expanded and as international law courses and degree programmes were developed in the universities, as private institutions like the Carnegie Endowment for International Peace encouraged research on the abolition of war, and with the American Society of International Law helping to establish a body of professionals.

An examination of the broad assumptions held by American international legal specialists would reveal that they reflect elements of the 'American' culture—for example, the preference for law over politics, the belief in progress through law, and the enthusiasm for unfettered economic intercourse. The values of liberalism have been firmly embedded, but there is nothing so neat as *American* international law, nor are American international lawyers so homogeneous that they constitute a distinct school. Perhaps the most distinctively American trait is the novelty, if not also the infelicity, of the language used by the American lawyers. They have replaced the Old World, Latin obscurities of legal study, the 'ipse-dixitism' of which Bentham complained,[3] with such New World obfuscations as 'configurative jurisprudence', 'phase analysis', 'authority structures' and 'judicial paradigms'. A diversity of views on specific legal problems, however, has been assured among American international legal writers by the imprecise contours of the law itself and by the heterogeneity of individual backgrounds. The latter can in part be attributed to the fact that several influential lawyers of the present century emigrated to the United States after substantial training in European law centres.[4]

Thought-Provoking Crises

The problem of war and peace has generated a variety of legal positions, and it should not be surprising that the problem has been most salient in times of crisis. In the nineteenth century, the wars with Mexico and with Spain provoked arguments, albeit few, as to the legality of the particular ventures, but it was only the Civil War which stimulated thought on the general problem. The internal nature and brutal intensity of the fighting made it appropriate that if any international law would be involved, it would be the laws governing the conduct of warfare, the *ius in bello*. The 'Instructions for the Government of Armies of the United States in the Field' of 1863 did not differ much from the customary law, but they are notable because they both endorsed the application of international law to civil wars and codified the traditional law. These instructions were the first clear statements of the laws of war, and they influenced subsequent thinkers in Europe as well as the United States. Their author, Francis Lieber, professor of international law and political science at Columbia University, defended the view that although wars are means to national ends, their conduct should not be unlimited, even in civil wars where the end is considered absolute: 'Men who take up arms against one another in public war do not cease on this account to be moral beings, responsible to one another, and to God'; and 'humanity induces the adoption of the rules of regular war towards rebels'.[5]

The crises of the twentieth century have provoked more international lawyers to tackle the general problem of war. World War I did more than any previous conflict to inspire abhorrence of inter-state violence, yet there were different approaches even among those investing faith in the principle of 'peace through law'. One school, emphasising both the obligation of states to exhaust pacific settlement procedures before resorting to force and the collective responsibility of states to oppose an aggressor, saw its thinking embodied, partly, in the Hague Conventions and, more fully, in the League of Nations Covenant. The American proponents were numerous, particularly since under President Wilson this collective security approach was official United States policy. One international lawyer and eventual judge of the Permanent Court of International Justice, Manley O. Hudson, was an especially articulate defender of the view that the Covenant signified a revolution in international relations thinking, which had regarded war as acceptable.[6]

The second school of thought, which was critical of the Wilsonian approach for its conservatism, was represented by the 'outlawry of war' movement, led by Salmon O. Levinson and Charles C. Morrison and endorsed by the philosopher John Dewey. The group was active between 1919 and 1929 in arguing that the League did not go far enough for it merely substituted one war, the war waged by the community, for another, the war waged by the aggressor. The movement was not one of international lawyers, but the financial lawyer Levinson and the minister Morrison looked forward to a development in international law where a treaty would be concluded in which states would abjure for all time the use of war and would pledge to submit disputes to an international court. In arguing that the League was not to be trusted because it was a 'political arrangement' whereas a 'wholly' juridical solution was required,[7] the movement's proponents assumed an extreme position not shared by the overwhelming majority of American international lawyers and, in so doing, displayed an overzealous commitment to the American ideal of law. However, the position may well have led many international lawyers to argue that war indeed had already been 'outlawed', provided, of course, that war is understood to be synonymous with aggression.

The response of most American international lawyers to World War II was support for the government's commitment to the

United Nations Charter, which outlined an international order similar to that outlined by the League Covenant. The days of bipolar confrontation that followed within a decade of the Second World War's conclusion prompted other legal reactions. It is simplistic to say that the debate pitted Realists against Idealists, but the positions did reflect a difference over the capacity of law to deal with threats to international stability by the great powers. One group, arguing that international law is only what the major states allow it to be, concluded that the United Nations Charter would be virtually suspended in the case of conflict between these states. Morton Kaplan and Nicholas De B. Katzenbach, for example, suggested that political restraints are more effective than legal norms in regulating inter-bloc tensions,[8] and Stanley Hoffmann has found the 'law of the political framework' a very modest law in part because of the vast increase in power created by the possession of nuclear weapons.[9] Edwin Borchard, though writing within a year of the conclusion of World War II, expressed best the general position that, whatever the relationship between law and war in general, law damages itself when it pretends to regulate what it clearly cannot: '. . . it so happens that the Great Powers will rarely see the same way on important matters. It is just as likely that the United Nations Organisation will make for war as for peace, since (Great Power) conflicts do not leave the relations among nations unaffected.'[10]

Other American international lawyers have argued that, regardless of how difficult it may be to apply the law equally, the great powers cannot escape the regulation of the Charter. Quincy Wright, for one, insisted that it does not bode well for the prospects of peace to maintain that international law cannot regulate conflict of the important states, and he applied the law of the Charter to the major instance of American-Soviet confrontation, the Cuban missile crisis. Examining the position of the United States, he concluded that Cuba and the Soviet Union had not violated international law by the emplacement of missiles on Cuban soil and, more importantly, that the United States by the imposition of the quarantine did violate the preeminent Charter norm, Article 2(4), forbidding the use of force by states. The example, he concluded, highlighted the need for limitations on the exercise of sovereignty, particularly when the unrestrained freedom of the great powers portends great damage.[11] Louis Henkin has echoed the basic point that the rivalry of the nuclear giants, though not clearly anticipated in 1945, only increases the need for the application of the Charter law.[12] In short, these writers have maintained that if the general prohibition on force is to have meaning, it must apply to the big as well as the small.

The Vietnamese conflict has recently stimulated intense controversy within the ranks of American international lawyers. The facts and relevant rules have been subjected to widely varying interpretations, yet the discussions on how the experience affects international law are more noteworthy. One position is that this war indicates that there is a need to prohibit directly third-party interventions. In effect, a revision in the *ius ad bellum*, the law governing resort to war, is demanded so that states can no longer exploit the ambiguity of existing international law on the subject. Percy Corbett has advanced the suggestion that the International Law Commission draft a convention prohibiting both external encouragement of and direct intervention in civil wars. The experiences of Vietnam convinced him that legal reforms dealing with regulations of such conflicts are not sufficient; nothing short of rendering intervention itself illegal is demanded, especially since states like the United States are prompted to intervene often out of 'misguided benevolence'.[13] Prohibition thus takes precedence over regulation.

A second response to the Vietnamese war is that, because outright prohibition is not likely, control of the conduct of such wars is an imperative. Telford Taylor, American chief counsel at the Nuremberg war crimes trials and author of the controversial *Nuremberg and Vietnam: An American Tragedy*, argues that whatever the legal status of the Vietnam War, the laws of warfare increase in importance because of the temptation to excesses in irregular, unconventional fighting. He acknowledges the difficulty of determining whether American actions constituted aggression, but stresses that the range of permissible acts in war must be limited. However impossible it had become to distinguish combatants and noncombatants, the laws of war must be followed, he concludes, because they serve both the self-interest and conscience of the belligerents.[14] An imperfect *ius in bello*, in short, is better than none.

A third position complements the second by suggesting that the laws of war must be modernised to meet the type of warfare Vietnam represented. The use of napalm, the massive bombardment of North Vietnam, the 'pacification' programme, and the difficulty in identifying combatants, are all problems with which the traditional law does not deal. Hamilton De Saussure and Robert Glasser, in *Law and Responsibility in Warfare: The Vietnam Experience*, which is the product of a conference sponsored by the American Society of International Law, have analysed one of these problems, aerial bombing, and have concluded that the Nixon-Kissinger employment of this military approach to induce North Vietnam to negotiate should have been illegal. The Geneva Conventions, they feel, should be changed to ban bombing for expressly 'political' reasons and to allow only bombing designed to 'achieve a distinct military advantage'.[15] Updating and revising the general laws binding on all combatants are thus demanded, but it is obvious that the revisions would leave open the matter of precisely defining what is political purpose and military advantage.

A fourth position, a modification of the third, argues that the laws of war must recognise differences among the belligerents. Richard Falk has been particularly vocal in arguing that because the conflict was civil in nature and because the United States was so militarily strong, American involvement in Vietnam was both illegal and unfair. The guerrillas, he declares, were at a disadvantage and so could hardly be expected to follow the traditional regulations. Terror was permissible for them but not for the Americans, and the disparity in status is justified, partly, by the numbers endangered: 'An important element of differentiation is that insurgent terror tends to be discriminating in its application and to involve relatively small numbers of victims.'[16] It is also justified as a necessity for guerrillas with no other recourse. This proposed change in the *ius in bello* for the insurgents not only would create a dual system of laws but also would enhance the concept of military necessity,[17] even though the intent of the conventions of the first half of the century was to limit the instances when belligerents might justify their acts on that basis.

The preceding brief summary indicates that it is difficult to characterise American international legal thinking at a specific time. A foreign observer, however, has recently generalised that at least American foreign policy attitudes and the prevailing international law have been at odds.[18] Throughout most of American history, it is argued, the American suspicion of European power politics and the messianism best represented by Wilson combined to produce a policy antagonistic to the traditional system of interstate law. More recently, realism has become the government's philosophy while international law has developed into a nascent community law. The American attitude towards international law, in other words, was at one time premature but is lately outdated. One difficulty with this argument is the simplification or condensation of American official thinking, and another, more important, difficulty is the assumption that international law could be so broadly categorised. The law is not only what statesmen say it is but also what jurists and publicists say it is—and the record is by no means uniform. When only international lawyers are considered, American views on the legality of war, apart from reactions to particular events, can be fitted into three categories, each of which contains substantial variations. The first approach deals with the problem by setting out various dichotomies such as law and war, war and peace, and permissible and impermissible conflict. The second approach tries to go beyond these dualisms by adding a third, intermediate state between war and peace. The third main approach views the problem in terms of a continuum of coercion.

Dualistic Approaches to the Legality of War

Most international legal thinkers, including Americans, have viewed the matter of conflict in dualistic terms. One school of thought concentrates on the two elements of law and war and finds them opposed. The assumption is that law is based on the ordered, authoritative resolution of disputes; in short, law is tied firmly to peace. Alexander Hamilton, who, admittedly, used strong language in order to advance the cause of federation, expressed succinctly this line of thought in the fifteenth Federalist Paper when he presented the choice: either 'the coercion of the magistracy' or 'the coercion of arms'.[19] A second position, which is a modern variant of the law-war dichotomy, says that if international law exists, it has little to say about warfare. Although Dean Acheson would not outrightly deny the validity of the *ius in bello*, the distance is small between the views of mutual exclusiveness held by Washington's Secretary of the Treasury and the view held by Truman's Secretary of State that law must beat a hasty retreat when overriding national interests are endangered, as he thought true of the Cuban missile crisis.[20] In the first position, war is seen as *antithetical* to law, and in the second, law is seen as *irrelevant* to war.

A third general approach follows the dichotomy of the European international law of the eighteenth and nineteenth centuries whereby there were two laws—the law of peace and the law of war. War, in this perspective, is a legal *state* which gives rise to rights and obligations, such as those dealing with military occupation and interruption of commerce, that differ from those that prevail in peacetime. The primary emphasis is on the laws governing the conduct of warfare; war is thus considered a state *within* the law, to be regulated and curtailed. It is not often understood that the proponents of this position have regarded the emphasis on a restrictive code of conduct as revolutionary, in much the same way that the post-League proponents of a restrictive *ius ad bellum* have called themselves legal radicals. For example, James Kent, Chancellor of New York and a state Supreme Court justice, described in his famous *Commentaries on American Law*, the first edition of which appeared in 1826, the unpleasant character of unrestrained conflict and concluded that 'these barbarous rights of war' have been circumscribed by the development of civilised laws of warfare.[21]

John Bassett Moore, professor at Harvard and a judge of the Permanent Court of International Justice, agreed with Kent that the elders of international law had led a 'moral revolt' in creating legal curbs on warfare. So convinced was he of the importance of the laws of war that he forcefully defended their vitality against both the deniers and the zealots of international law. To the former, he argued that the experience of World War I had proven the wisdom of distinguishing between combatants and non-combatants and between absolute and conditional contraband. To the latter, he suggested that since the phenomenon of war, whether it be international or civil, is likely to persist, it does no credit to international law for it to bypass what it can accomplish—restraint—in favour of what it probably cannot achieve—abolition.[22]

However strong the emphasis in this general approach on the laws of war, there is not so marked a contrast as is commonly assumed with the medieval conception of legitimate wars. Indeed, there are residues of the just war theory in the thinking of American international lawyers holding to the dichotomy between the laws of peace and the laws of war. One view is that war, generically considered, is not illegal, and it is implied by Kent who said that although public opinion might condemn a nation for going to war when uncertain of the legality of its action, there is a built-in uncertainty in the nature of public policy. The only legal obligation that is certain, he felt, is the need to exhaust pacific settlement procedures before the resort to war. War *per se* might not be unambiguously legal, but specific conflicts could be legal if waged to redress an injury and if peace is more odious than the war itself. The thought is implicit that the legality of individual wars depends upon the legitimacy of their ends, although it is not clear who determines what is legitimate. In the last analysis Kent indicated that a war is rendered illegal more definitely by the breach of a treaty than by its illegitimacy: 'To recommence a war by breach of the article of a treaty of peace is deemed much more odious than to provoke a war by some new demand and aggression; for the latter is simply injustice, but in the former case, the party is guilty both of perfidy and injustice.'[23] *Pacta sunt servanda* thus triumphed over the *ius ad bellum*.

H. W. Halleck, Secretary of State in California during the American-Mexican war and a legal adviser to the Navy, similarly dealt with the legality of particular wars. More explicit than Kent, Halleck both believed that an unjust war is illegal and specifically refuted the suggestion that the usage of all force is criminal.[24] Both international lawyers seem to have been grappling with the difficulty of reconciling the prevailing assumption that international law should not regulate the resort to war and the lingering influence of the just war approach. Kent resolved the matter by relegating substantive issues of justice to a position inferior to procedural norms. Halleck handled it by flirting with a tautology. In arguing that laws must be just and that the justice of a war is found in respecting the belligerent rights of the *ius in bello*,[25] he effectively said that war is a legal state *only* if waged within the law. The common element that emerges, however, is the view that because of the existence of some restrictions on the legality of individual wars, the general phenomenon can not be considered either legal or illegal.

Another view is that considerations of justice are not applicable to the legality of war. In this perspective, war is not only a state within the law, which is the general belief of the third type of dichotomy, but it is also a state *of* law; since 'war' itself is legal, every individual war must be legal. Henry Wheaton, who was rapporteur of the United States Supreme Court, a diplomat and author of a treatise on international law which was influential in the early nineteenth century, made the underlying assumption of this view manifest when he wrote that it is the right of every state to go to war. An international legal order predicated on sovereignty could hardly make a sovereign act illegal or even legal.[26] Other international lawyers have suggested that war is legal, in part at least, because it is often beneficial. For example, the author of the much-used manual on American international legal practise, Charles Cheney Hyde, found war to be sometimes 'honourable and reasonable'.[27] Theodore Dwight Woolsey, a late nineteenth century international lawyer, argued that war is an abnormality which also has certain advantages—e.g. the restoration of national honour and the reform of internal disequilibria.[28]

George B. Davis, a judge-advocate of the last century, presented the interesting argument that war is only temporarily legal: 'When its object is attained,... war itself becomes unlawful and must cease.'[29] This argument is interesting because although it is really a variant of the medieval approach which assigned justice to a war until it fulfilled its real purpose—peace—Davis was definite in rejecting considerations of moral propriety in international law and in asserting that war is simply a fact of life. Nevertheless, the time limitation approach, like the others, was intended to limit the fighting. Whether war is regarded as simply an entity the conduct of which is governed by law, or, combined with the first alternative, as legal in itself because it is a prerogative, useful or temporary, the common impulse is the purpose of the *ius in bello*—to curtail the ravages of conflict.

The fourth type of dichotomy, reverting back to the just war theory, places emphasis on the *ius ad bellum* and deals with the two concepts of permissible and impermissible conflict. In this perspective, most wars are considered *crimes*. The theory shaped by Augustine, Isidore and Aquinas concentrated on the ethical dimensions of warfare, but modern international lawyers have been more concerned with its legal dimensions. The legal-illegal dichotomy has varied slightly, however; one approach assigns legality to only a few types of war and another argues that 'war' itself is illegal. Telford Taylor, representing the first group, has spoken of a simple equation whereby aggression is a crime and self-defence is legal warfare, but there is no exact specification of what the terms mean. Hans Kelsen presented a variant which is the logical outcome of his 'pure law' theory. Seeing forcible acts as acts either of wrong-doing (delicts) or of right-doing (sanctions), he concluded that the only illegal usage of force in international law is that which is not intended to punish a delict. The reasoning is somewhat tortuous: force is a crime when not employed as a sanction; the antithesis of a sanction is a delict; force is a crime when a delict. Although he avoided the term 'war', it at least is clear that he included the phenomenon in the appellation 'coercive act'.[31] The resort to coercion-as-sanction is thus legal for Kelsen and the resort to coercion-as-delict illegal.

The second approach really follows the Kelsenian flair for reconstructing 'word order'. Rather than finding some wars illegal depending on their purpose, Quincy Wright preferred to consider all wars illegal. In effect, he established his own dichotomy of war and legal force; whereas Taylor says that aggression is a crime and self-defence legal, and Kelsen said that a forcible delict is a crime and sanction legal, Wright recast the substantive thought by removing what is legal from the very category of war. This approach, perhaps influenced by the outlawry movement of the 1920s, was possible because there could be only *one* type of war for Wright—aggression. It may be protested that war was outlawed by terminological preference, but Wright at a minimum deserves credit for clarifying what he meant by aggression. He suggested that it meant the use or threat of force across an internationally recognised border unless the state relying on armed means is acting under express authority of the United Nations or in self-defence.[32]

Charles C. Fenwick echoed Wright's conceptualisation, though he was perhaps more cautious in interpreting existing law, as indicated by his statements that the Kellogg-Briand Pact and League Covenant deprived war of 'much' of its legal character and that the Charter makes war illegal among members of the United Nations without specifying the effect on non-members.[33] But Fenwick's aspiration was clearly ambitious in 1942 when he called for the stripping of every vestige of legality associated with war.[34] Regardless of whether war is a crime *when* it is aggressive (i.e. only aggressive wars are crimes) or *because* it is aggressive (i.e. all 'wars' are aggressive and so are crimes), the common concern is to make war increasingly illegal. This type thus contrasts with the third kind of dichotomy which is concerned to consider war as legal or at least not illegal.

There are at least three rationales as to why war would be considered criminal, and all three have often been invoked by the same theorist. The first asserts that war is morally wrong; the attack is thus against war as an *institution*, an engrained practise which must be extirpated. The attack was most clearly made by the 'outlawry' advocates, but lighter shades of similar moral outrage permeate the works of Wright, Fenwick and the critics of American involvement in Vietnam such as Falk. A second rationale is that war is dysfunctional and so the assault is concentrated on war as a *method*, an instrument of national policy and prestige. This perspective is a reaction to the belief described earlier that war can be beneficial; indeed, Amos Peaslee rejected it as long ago as 1916 when he wrote that war cannot be considered 'beneficial as a sort of national virulent exercise'.[35] The most prevalent argument since World War II is that nuclear war as a means to foster states' interests would be utter folly. Finally, it has been proposed that war is a collective *malady*, a psychosis which requires a fundamental shift in public and private thinking to cure it. Kenneth Carlston made the point succinctly: 'Rationally and ethically, war is a cultural disease.'[36]

The fervour with which war is attacked makes understandable the elimination of another legal category—neutrality. The 'grand' theorists, such as Wright, maintain that there can be no neutrals in a legal order where the state is either an aggressor or a participant in collective security measures.[37] The unacceptability of neutral status flows from the interrelated beliefs in the indivisibility of peace and the illegality of war. It is a position that fits well into the American habit of bifurcating the world into those 'with us' and those 'against us', as evidenced by the attack of John Foster Dulles on the political ideology of neutralism as immoral in an era of bipolar confrontation. It is clear, however, that the anti-neutrality stand, like the premature obituary of other evils, is prompted more by logical rigour and pious aspiration than by attention to reality. Neutrality has to be an outmoded concept, the theory runs, because the principle of collective security requires a crusade of all against the aggressor. It is additionally believed that neutrality must be abandoned because it serves the avoidance of armed conflict for some, not its prevention for everyone. This latter point illustrates the 'as if' mentality:[38] states should behave as if neutrality is unacceptable so that potential aggressors will be deterred; in so doing, neutrality will in fact become a dead concept.

The obvious gap between theory and practice animates most American international lawyers to acknowledge the vitality of the neutrality principle. There has been, in effect, a reaffirmation of the nineteenth century view that it is an important part of international law. James Kent revealed the particularly American interest in neutrality when he recommended its study to his fellow citizens 'inasmuch as it is our true policy to cherish a spirit of peace, and to keep ourselves free from those political connections which would tend to draw us into the vortex of European contests.'[39] In this century, the defence was less self-righteous in tone and more pragmatic in content; John Bassett Moore, for example, defended the laws of neutrality in the wake of World War I because they serve state interests and largely work.[40] Even Quincy Wright had to acknowledge that the concept of neutrality has endured in international law.[41]

If neutrality remains a constant in international law, the laws governing the actual conduct of hostilities have also persisted. The restrictive *ius ad bellum* approach would naturally affect views of the *ius in bello*, and so it is not surprising that those writers believing the United Nations Charter has outlawed aggression have concluded that there must be a difference in application of the law. For Wright, reason demanded that if the law governing resort to war is to have any significance, the laws governing its conduct must discriminate between those who obey and disobey the former.[42] In proposing that aggressors be stripped of rights and burdened with duties, Wright came closer to Van Nispen, who denied all protection of the laws of war to aggressors, than to Lauterpacht, who argued for unequal treatment only with respect to property relations.[43] At least one American international lawyer, Manley Hudson, who was a firm supporter of the post-World War I institutions designed to promote peaceful change, feared an adverse development in applying the laws of warfare because of the aggressor-collective policeman dichotomy: 'When society sends out a policeman to clean up a gang of crooks, it is not over-meticulous as to the method which he uses.'[44]

However undeniable the logic that the essential correlate of the *ius ad bellum* is an inequality of status within the *ius in bello*, and however unrestrained the implementation of that logic might be, Holmes' dictum that the life of the law is experience is convincing. The obvious experience is the persistence of wars despite their prohibition and the inability of the United Nations to conduct police actions despite the Charter. The proponents, like Fenwick, of the war-is-a crime approach conclude, rather begrudgingly, that if the illegal should occur, it still gives rise to the same rules of conduct that dominated the 'old' international law.[45]

Adding a Third Category

It is the difficulty of reconciling reality with the law that led some American international lawyers to break away from the use of dichotomies. In particular, Philip Jessup, who at one time was the American judge of the International Court of Justice, argues in a 1954 article for recognition of a third state of law coexisting with war and peace. Because the implicit assumption is that war and peace are states of law, this view may be seen as an outgrowth of the third kind of dichotomy which sees war itself as a legal entity giving rise to belligerent rights and obligations regulated by the law. Jessup himself finds a preliminary version of his concept in that of 'imperfect' war;[46] this concept was indeed common in nineteenth-century jurisprudence and was defined by Henry Wheaton as a war limited in scope, area and participants.[47] Jessup's term for a condition of hostility that is less than a formally waged war and more than what is allowed in peacetime is 'intermediacy'. The word applies to situations where there is sustained, perhaps ideological, stress, where deep-rooted differences cannot be resolved by settling a particular issue, and where there is the absence of an intention to go to war to solve the differences.[48]

The conceptualisation is vague and the distinction from 'cold war' is especially unclear. Jessup, arguing for a break with that common term, suggests, nevertheless, that the disputes usually associated with the Soviet-American cold war such as Korea, Germany and Austria, are examples of intermediacy. In the end, it seems that Jessup is taking exception with the terminology and feels that the psychological effect of removing the word 'war' from this nebulous area would lessen the pressures for outright hostilities: 'If the mind is wedded to the idea that there is no alternative between war and peace and the actualities seem to deny that there is "peace", the argument for war seems to command the support of a certain logic if nothing else.'[49] The legal implication is that international law should be revised to recognise the reality of intermediate situations and to refrain from exacerbating these tensions by according them the label of 'war'. It is interesting to note that this analysis, clearly influenced by the bipolar confrontations of the early 1950s, is not evident in Jessup's earlier *A Modern Law of Nations*. Rather, in that 1948 work which has been reprinted many times, he adheres basically to a dichotomous approach whereby the only permissible use of force is self-defence. There is, however, the recognition that not every conflict situation can fit into two categories.[50]

Another American international lawyer, Wolfgang Friedmann, found the concept of intermediacy applicable to the American quarantine in the Cuban missile crisis. Friedmann argued that, though traditional international law incorporated such measures short of all-out war as reprisals, the 1962 quarantine could only be classified as a reprisal if it came in response to an illegal act; the difficulty of making a legal determination of the facts thus suggested to him the relevance of an intermediate legal condition between aggression and self-defence.[51] Elsewhere, Friedmann spoke of other in-between acts of hostility, such as indirect, ideological aggression and intervention in civil wars, but he clearly aggregated world affairs into three broad categories: 'military war', 'lesser forms of warfare' and peace.[52]

The Vietnamese conflict has given rise to a concentration on the 'intermediate' act of intervention. Contemporary American international lawyers, having witnessed their government's intervention in Cuba, the Dominican Republic, and Vietnam in the 1960s, have become increasingly concerned with the legal status of an act which is not covered in the United Nations Charter and which is ambiguously treated in customary law. The existence of ambiguity, of 'gray areas' as Jessup called them, is the very rationale for the trichotomous approach, and in the case of intervention it has given rise to at least three arguments. The suggestion that intervention should be outlawed, as proposed by Percy Corbett for one, is not pertinent here because, seeking to place intervention firmly in the category of illegal force, it is part of the dichotomous approach.

Louis Henkin, however, represents well the position that intervention is neither peace nor war. He has suggested that international law is not likely to have a solution to the problem because of several complicating factors: there are many types of intervention; it is not certain what constitutes a legitimate request for intervention nor even what is a *bona fide* civil war; and ideological rivalries exacerbate the problem of reaching agreement. In light of the difficulties, he concluded that international law should concentrate on prohibiting 'cases of direct, overt aggression that are generally capable of objective and persuasive proof.'[53] Intervention, in other words, is a political matter which is not susceptible to successful legal regulation. Perhaps one reason why Henkin does not urge a legal solution is his belief that intervention in an internal war is not as serious an aggression as that directed against a state's territorial integrity and independence; it is a view sharply rejected by Corbett who believes that intervention and internal wars constitute the gravest threats to contemporary world order.[54]

A second approach acknowledges the reality of interventions but seeks to set some limits. John Norton Moore, for example, has suggested that it is legal for a third state to assist a recognised government besieged by forces of another state or by insurgents assisted from outside. It is, however, illegal for a third state to help a group involved in 'any type of authority-oriented internal conflict' or to use force in the territory of another state to change or support 'authority structures'—unless, of course, they are under some form of externally-fed attack.[55] Intervention *per se* is thus not illegal; the legality is tied to the actors under attack, attacking and assisting. According to Moore, United States actions in Vietnam were permissible since they constituted support for the widely-recognised government of South Vietnam which was under attack by an insurgent group assisted by North Vietnam.[56] The legal status of this 'intermediate' action was, in short, dependent on the circumstances.

The third position questions the wisdom of tying legality to circumstances the definiteness of which cannot easily be ascertained. It may be asked, for example: when are governments widely recognised? how is external support of insurgents to be determined? what kind of support is sufficient to warrant a response? Moore's concept of legal intervention is really counter-intervention, the argument would run, and legality-twice-removed is an obscure legality. Thomas Farer adds a cultural dimension to this position when he criticises the second approach for a Western, anti-reformist bias, particularly because of Moore's insistence that intervention be on behalf of legitimate governments with legitimacy largely endowed through the electoral process.[57] Counter-intervention, in this sense, is counter-revolution. Farer argues, by way of contrast, that revolutionary upheavals are often better means to effect social justice, but he does not carry out the logic of his thought by according legality to interventions designed to advance the overthrow of corrupt regimes.

The positions, in the end, are as nebulous and indefinite as the reality upon which they pronounce. Like Jessup in 1954, these international lawyers of the 1960s and 1970s have mainly sought a new psychological climate in which to place hostilities that are at once removed from peace and are not yet war in the traditional, interstate sense. For Jessup, the hope is to recognise cold war-type tensions as legal so as to minimise pressures for bellicose solutions that are implied in the war-peace mentality. For Henkin, the hope is to remove, provisionally at least, interventions from the Article 2(4) prohibition on military force so that political forces can have a chance to reach agreement; for Moore, to specify the conditions of legal intervention so as to educate statesmen and their publics that force is to be sparingly used; for Farer, to urge consideration of the reasons for internal strife before intervention so as to prevent the support of oppression in the name of defence against aggression and so as to persuade the oppressed that Western states are not automatically opposed to them. The common impulse, then, is to prevent the 'gray' acts from deteriorating into all-out warfare.

Law and the Continuum of Coercion

A final approach sees instead of two or three categories an entire spectrum. The view, simply put, is that a great number of forceful acts, ranging from the little harmful to nuclear warfare, exist and that the law should reflect this complexity. There is a continuum of *coercion*, in other words. Whereas other emphases have been on war as a legal state or crime and on intermediacy as quasi-legal, this approach emphasises coercion as a series of facts generating legal *consequences*.[58] The primary exponents are Myres McDougal and his co-workers in the policy science school of international law. The basic assumption of the group is that, since law is intimately related to the decision-making process, the responses of decision-makers to acts of coercion are as varied as the acts themselves and hence defy convenient legal cataloguing.

It follows that the rôle assigned to international law in conflict management is modest. Abolition of warfare is certainly beyond its purview, McDougalians argue, but law can have some success in dealing with regulation. The goal is to create 'minimum world public order', though it is never clearly defined. It is clear that McDougal hopes for the increasing recognition by statesmen that force must be curbed for their own most basic interest, self-preservation. The most productive work that can be done by the international lawyer is to observe the complex intermixture of acts, responses and processes from which the law dealing with coercion emerges.[59]

One of the vigilant scholars has been Richard Falk, who follows the continuum model in his typology of conflicts. His Type I refers to conflicts in which force is directed across established frontiers by organised groups; Type II refers to large-scale intervention in an internal conflict; Type III refers to internal strife apart from external involvement; and Type IV refers to conflicts collectively authorised.[60] If vigilant, Falk has also become impatient and so has urged the development of 'global-populist' norms whereby conflict would be controlled by the international community. Moving away from the strict McDougalian line, Falk has argued: 'Legality depends more upon the *identity* of the authorising decision-maker than upon the *facts of coercion*.'[61] In developing the line of thought that legal conflicts are those which are properly authorised, Falk comes close to Quincy Wright who argued that legal conflicts are those which are collectively author-ised; it is not surprising that, though arguing along different specific lines, the two American lawyers concurred in their con-demnation of American actions in Vietnam.[62]

The continuum approach, of course, is neither the discovery nor the domain of the New Haven School. McDougal, in his 1955 article on the subject, quite properly acknowledges the pioneering work of others in examining the forms of war in law and history. In addition, the concept of the law of 'armed conflicts', implying a number of conditions of force, was included in the Geneva Convention of 1949 and so preceded McDougal's work. All the international lawyers considered have, in some form, acknowledged the reality of diversity of force; indeed, the traditional law itself was replete with references to reprisals, blockades and embargoes. The contribution of McDougal is to have taken Wright's distinction between war in a material and legal sense[63] and to have broadened it into the conception of a series of policy decisions in response to a multiplicity of coercive facts. McDougal, in other words, has broken the legal moulds in which every act was placed. In freeing international law of its stereotyping role, McDougal, ironically, has also largely isolated the law from the value standards which guide as well as categorise.

Conclusion

Whether or not legalism is a 'red skein' running through American diplomatic history,[64] it is clear at least that American legal knitters have been manifold. It is hard to determine the extent to which their thinking on war and peace reflects the American character, probably because that character is so heterogeneous and so amorphous. The most that can be said is that their writing illustrates well the element of diversity prevalent in American life, and in so doing reflects part of the American character. Most American legal writers have perceived the relationship of law, war and peace in dualistic terms, but there have been several types of dichotomy. One type finds war opposed or irrelevant to law, another conceives of both war and peace as legal states, and yet another accords legality to certain conflict situations and illegality to others. The problems of thinking in either—or terms led other lawyers to speak of a third state which is neither outright war nor peace in the accepted sense. The legality of the inter-mediate condition, whether it be cold-war-type tension or intervention, has not been made certain, yet the point is clear that the third state deserves special attention in both politics and law. Still other lawyers have been influenced by theories of decision-making and have preferred to abandon discrete categories in favour of a greater range of acts which are both influences on and outcomes of the policy process. The reader will be forgiven if he wonders, in the manner of Mr. Dooley's Admiral Dewey, if international lawyers' ideas on war, in all their variety, are any more helpful than ideas on 'how to r-run a quiltin' party'.[65]

If the positions have been maddening in their differences, they are also reassuring. Public discourse is inevitably advanced by the availability of a variety of well-articulated, refined opinions. Although most Americans are hardly likely to be excited by the respective merits of dichotomy, trichotomy and continuum as approaches to war and peace, there is a chance that some citizens will be influenced by the application of these approaches to the evaluation of specific wars. No one can reasonably anticipate the public's easy familiarity with the work of theorists, but the assumptions they make clear and the goals they advance often enter into and shape popular reactions when peace and war become life and death issues; the case of Vietnam is, of course, instructive. It is perhaps particularly American that the public cares what the international lawyers say more than the lawyers reflect what the public values.

The diversity of thought is also reassuring in terms of the general development of the international law of conflict. Since the writings of 'publicists' are a subsidiary source of the law, according to Article 38 of the Statute of the Court of International Justice, they are clearly meant to stimulate and influence thought, not to make and certify legal decisions. There is flexibility in this approach, and the lack of uniformity of opinions among Americans on what law should do about war and peace both confirms the wisdom of the subsidiary status of legal thought and enhances the pick-and-choose method of legal codification.

Notes

1. Franklin expressed the view in two letters, one to David Hartley and the other to Josiah Quincy in which he wrote: 'May we never see another war! For in my opinion there never was a good war or a bad peace.' See: Carl van Doren, *Benjamin Franklin*, Garden City, N.Y.: Garden City Publishing Co., Inc., 1941, pp. 621, 698, quote at p. 698.
2. Ordinance of 4 December 1781, as quoted in James Kent, *Commentaries on American Law*, 11th edn., Boston: Little, Brown and Company, 1867, p. 1.
3. See: George W. Keeton and Georg Schwarzenberger (Eds.), *Jeremy Bentham and the Law*, London: Stevens & Sons, 1948, pp. 156–57.

4. It is assumed in this paper that an international lawyer is American if he has spent a significant portion of his professional life in the United States.

5. The 'Instructions' are reproduced in George B. Davis, *Outlines of International Law*, New York: Harper & Brothers Publishers, 1899, pp. 397–428, quotes at pp. 401 and 426, respectively.

6. Manley O. Hudson, *By Pacific Means: The Implementation of Article Two of the Pact of Paris*, New Haven: Yale University Press, 1935, pp. 24–25.

7. Charles C. Morrison, *The Outlawry of War: A Constructive Policy for World Peace*, Willett, Clark & Colby, 1927, pp. 58–75, *et passim*; quotes at p. 63. There is an excellent introduction by Charles DeBenedetti in the 1972 reprint of Morrison's work and of *Outlawry of War* by Salmon O. Levinson, reprinted together by Garland Publishers, New York.

8. See, generally: Morton A. Kaplan and Nicholas DeB. Katzenbach, *The Political Foundations of International Law*, New York: John Wiley & Sons, Inc., 1961.

9. Stanley Hoffmann, 'International Systems and International Law', in Klaus Knorr and Sidney Verba, eds., *The International System: Theoretical Essays*, Princeton: Princeton University Press, 1967, pp. 212, 223–233.

10. Edwin Borchard, 'The Effect of War on Law', *The American Journal of International Law*, 40, No. 3, July 1946, p. 621.

11. Quincy Wright, 'The Cuban Quarantine', *The American Journal of International Law*, 57, No. 3, July 1963, pp. 546–65.

12. Louis Henkin, *How Nations Behave: Law and Foreign Policy*, New York: Praeger Publishers, 1970, pp. 130–134.

13. Percy Corbett, *The Growth of World Law*, Princeton: Princeton University Press, 1971, pp. 153–69, quote at p. 164.

14. Telford Taylor, *Nuremberg and Vietnam: An American Tragedy*, New York: Bantam Books, 1971, pp. 40–41, 98–99, 152.

15. Peter D. Trooboff, ed., *Law and Responsibility in Warfare: The Vietnam Experience*, Chapel Hill: The University of North Carolina Press, 1975, pp. 119–139, especially pp. 138–39, quotes at p. 139.

16. Richard A. Falk, *The Six Legal Dimensions of the Vietnam War*, Princeton University Center of International Studies, October 1968 (Research Monograph No. 34), pp. 3–4, 30–32, quote at p. 31. Also see: Trooboff, *op. cit.*, pp. 37–53.

17. See: Taylor, *op. cit.*, p. 137.

18. Charles Zorgbibe, 'Droit international et réalisme politique dans la politique étrangère américaine', *Politique Étrangère*, 41, N° 1, 1976, pp. 27–41.

19. *The Federalist Papers*, Washington Square Press, Inc., 1968, p. 42. Norberto Bobbio speaks of this antithesis in 'Esquisse d'vne théorie sur les rapports entre guerre et droit', in *La querre et ses théories*, Paris: Presses Universitaires de France, 1970. (Annales de Philosophie Politique, 9), pp. 11–12.

20. 'Remarks by the Honorable Dean Acheson' in discussion of 'Cuban Quarantine: Implications for the Future', *Proceedings of the American Society of International Law*, April 25–27, 1963, pp. 13–15.

21. Kent, *op. cit.*, p. 95.

22. John Bassett Moore, *International Law and Some Current Illusions*, New York: The MacMillan Company, 1924, pp. 1–70, 99, quote at p. 13.

23. Kent, *op. cit.*, pp. 56–57, quote at p. 177.
24. H. W. Halleck, *International Law; or, Rules Regulating the Intercourse of States in Peace and War*, New York: D. Van Nostrand, 1861, pp. 319–322.
25. *Ibid.*, p. 347.
26. Henry Wheaton, *Elements of International Law*, 6th edn., Boston: Little, Brown, and Company, 1855, p. 361.
27. Charles Cheney Hyde, *International Law Chiefly as Interpreted and Applied By the United States*, Boston: Little, Brown and Company, 1922, p. 187.
28. Theodore Dwight Woolsey, *Introduction to the Study of International Law*, 6th edn., New York: Charles Scribner's Sons, 1898, pp. 177, 399.
29. Davis, *op. cit.*, pp. 199–202, quote at p. 199.
30. Taylor, *op. cit.*, pp. 73–74.
31. Hans Kelsen, *Law and Peace in International Relations*, Cambridge, Mass.: Harvard University Press, 1942, pp. 27–55.
32. Quincy Wright, 'The Prevention of Aggression', *The American Journal of International Law*, 50, No. 3, July 1956, p. 526.
33. Charles G. Fenwick, *International Law*, 3rd edn., New York: Appleton-Century-Crofts, Inc., 1948, pp. 543, 551.
34. Charles G. Fenwick, 'The Fundamental Principles of International Law', *The American Journal of International Law*, 36, No. 3, July 1942, pp. 446–47.
35. Amos J. Peaslee, 'The Sanction of International Law', *The American Journal of International Law*, X, No. 2, April 1916, p. 329.
36. Kenneth S. Carlston, 'A Framework for the Legal Analysis of War-Peace Issues', *The American Journal of International Law*, 60, No. 4, October 1966, p. 733.
37. Quincy Wright, *The United States and Neutrality*, Chicago: The University of Chicago Press, 1935 (Public Policy Pamphlet No. 17), p. 19; Wright, *Contemporary International Law: A Balance Sheet*, New York: Doubleday and Company, Inc., 1955, p. 18.
38. Inis L. Claude, Jr., 'The Present and Future of World Order: A Review, *The Journal of Conflict Resolution*, XIII, No. 4, December 1969, p. 532.
39. Kent, *op. cit.*, p. 119.
40. John Bassett Moore, *op. cit.*, pp. 5, 40–42
41. Wright, *Contemporary International Law, op. cit.*, p. 19.
42. Quincy Wright, 'The Outlawry of War and the Law of War', *The American Journal of International Law*, 47, No. 3, July 1953, pp. 370–71.
43. *Report of the Conference on Contemporary Problems of the Law of Armed Conflicts*, New York: Carnegie Endowment for International Peace, 1971, p. 46.
44. Manley O. Hudson, 'The Stacking of the Cards', in Norris F. Hall, Zechariah Chafee, Jr., and Manley O. Hudson, *The Next War*, Cambridge Mass: The Harvard Alumni Bulletin Press, 1925, pp. 93–95, 106, quote at p. 93.
45. Fenwick, *International Law, op. cit.*, p. 543. Fenwick recognised the impossibility of applying the 'new' law after the development of nuclear weapons, in Fenwick, 'International Law: The Old and the New', *The American Journal of International Law*, 60, No. 3, July 1966, pp. 479–480, 483.
46. Philip C. Jessup, 'Should International Law Recognize an Intermediate Status Between Peace and War?', *The American Journal of International Law*, 48, No. 1, January 1954, p. 99.

47. Wheaton, *op. cit.*, p. 365.

48. Jessup, *op. cit.*, pp. 100–101.

49. *Ibid.*, p. 102.

50. Philip C. Jessup, *A Modern Law of Nations*, New York: The MacMillan Company, 1948, pp. 157–87.

51. Wolfgang Friedmann, 'United States Policy and the Crisis of International Law', *The American Journal of International Law*, 59, No. 4, October 1965, pp. 864–65.

52. Wolfgang Friedmann, *The Changing Structure of International Law*, New York: Columbia University Press, 1964, pp. 273–74.

53. Henkin, *op. cit.*, pp. 141–51, quote at p. 149.

54. Compare: Henkin, *op. cit.*, p. 150 and Corbett, *op. cit.*, 154–55.

55. John Norton Moore, ed., *Law and Civil War in the Modern World*, Baltimore: The Johns Hopkins Press, 1974, p. 26.

56. See, generally John Norton Moore, 'The Lawfulness of Military Assistance to the Republic of Viet-Nam', *The American Journal of International Law*, 61, No. 1, January 1967, pp. 1–34.

57. John Norton Moore, *Law and Civil War*, *op. cit.*, pp. 554–56.

58. Myres S. McDougal, 'Peace and War: Factual Continuum with Multiple Legal Consequences', *The American Journal of International Law*, 49, No. 1, January 1955, pp. 63, 66–67.

59. Myres S. McDougal and Florentino P. Feliciano, *Law and Minimum World Public Order; The Legal Regulation of International Coercion*, New Haven: Yale University Press, 1961, pp. 1–96.

60. Richard Falk, *Legal Order in a Violent World*, Princeton: Princeton University Press, 1968, pp. 227–28, 273.

61. *Ibid.*, p. 308. Emphasis in original.

62. See: Quincy Wright, 'Legal Aspects of the Vietnam Situation', *The American Journal of International Law*, 60, No. 4, October 1966, pp. 750–69.

63. See: Quincy Wright, 'Changes in the Conception of War', *The American Journal of International Law*, 18, No. 4, October 1924, pp. 756. Also: Wright, 'History of the Concept of War', *Indian Year Book of International Affairs*, 1964, p. 116.

64. George F. Kennan, *American Diplomacy*, 1900–1950, New York: Mentor Book, 1951, p. 82.

65. *Mr. Dooley in Peace and War*, Boston: Small, Maynard and Company, 1919, p. 21.

The Ethical Dimension in American Thinking about War and Peace

Kenneth W. Thompson

Americans have been prone both to exaggerate the scope and overstate the limitations of ethical thinking on war and peace. Paradoxically, these two tendencies have been expressed by the self-same leader or scholar. Thus President Theodore Roosevelt in his early associations with Andrew Carnegie encouraged the most utopian dreams of the powerful industrialist. (It was Carnegie who instructed the Trustees of the Carnegie Endowment for International Peace to direct their attention first to the elimination of war and when this objective had been realised to turn then to other urgent problems.) Yet it was also President Roosevelt who spoke of 'speaking softly and carrying a big stick' and heaped scorn on those, including Carnegie, who when planning for the Second Hague Conference proposed that the United States reduce substantially its national defence capacity. General Douglas MacArthur was an outspoken champion of world government; yet he favoured a military policy in Korea which took United Nations troops to the borders of China and beyond. Utopianism, pacifism, and cynical realism more than once have been co-mingled in the thinking of an individual leader as with the respected Senator from Ohio, the senior Robert Taft, who in the 1940s, opposed American participation in NATO and questioned U.S. involvement in the United Nations while simultaneously favouring an international régime based on the rule of law. Secretary of State, John Foster Dulles, as Chairman of the Commission on International Relations of the National Council of Churches supported universality of membership for the United Nations including the admission of Communist China; yet as Secretary of State he was the author of a foreign policy dedicated to rolling back the Soviet sphere of influence in Eastern Europe if need be through 'massive retaliation,' 'liberation' and 'brinksmanship.'

What these examples have in common is a tendency to espouse different views according to time and circumstance. Nor have academics been immune to this tendency. Professor Robert Tucker of The Johns Hopkins University, a student of Hans Kelsen, founder of the pure theory of law, criticised the amoralism of the political realists in the 1950s but by the 1970s was proposing a preemptive strike against the oil rich Gulf states in the Arab-Israeli conflict. Hans J. Morgenthau, who was the leading proponent of negotiations and accommodation with the Russians in the 1950s, became one of Secretary Kissinger's severest critics in the 1970s for his foreign policy of *détente*. David Easton, of the faculty of the University of Chicago, announced in the 1950s that all the fundamental answers to the understanding and practice of politics were to be found in the behavioural sciences but later changed his mind and wrote of the need for new insights and approaches in what he christened the post-behavioural era. Arthur Schlesinger, Jr., wrote throughout the Roosevelt-Truman, Eisenhower, and Kennedy-Johnson years of the need for strong executive leadership; yet the Nixon Presidency provoked him to condemn in the most devastating terms 'The Imperial Presidency.' International lawyers who in the interwar period linked the future of mankind to the growth of a system of universal international law were far more likely in the 1950s, 1960s and 1970s to approach principles of law as they applied to regional and functional problems such as the European Community and the law of the seas.

Cynics, Utopians and Ideologists: Three Viewpoints on the Ethical Problem in War and Peace

It should be clear from the examples above that statesmen and scholars have been more successful in proclaiming what is right and wrong in international relations and politics than in sustaining their views in some coherent fashion over any significant period of time. We seek to do what is right and to follow ethical precepts, but the question that haunts us is 'What is right?' Most of us are all too conscious of the inescapable character of ethical dilemmas in our personal lives. The difficulty of perceiving what is right, however baffling this may be, is surpassed in complexity and uncertainty by the virtual impossibility of judging the consequences of our actions. The history of men and nations makes it abundantly clear that good and decent men make choices that bring on appalling consequences for themselves and the world. Chamberlain at Munich following the dictates of a responsible Birmingham business man sought to strike a bargain with Hitler to preserve the peace of Europe. Historians looking back point to his policy as a primary cause of World War II with its unspeakable brutalities and carnage. Churchill, by contrast, with a rather vainglorious concept of the British Empire and a quite limited perspective of the rights of dependent peoples, successfully organised and united the Grand Alliance to defend and preserve western civilisation. Franklin D. Roosevelt continues to receive harsh words and disparagement as a leader devoid of all moral and political convictions from such revisionist historians as Gabriel Kolko. Yet not only his wartime leadership but also his New Deal economic policies helped avert political and economic catastrophe[1].

Throughout American history, good men have often initiated policies that produced or hastened disaster. Herbert Hoover, a decent and honourable leader, may not have caused the great depression but his policies did little to prevent a deteriorating situation from growing worse. By contrast men whose intentions were suspect or morally ambiguous have often taken actions which brought about positive results. Lyndon B. Johnson as a Texan was not the first choice of blacks or other minorities, but more civil rights legislation was concluded in his years as President than in those of any other chief executive before or since.

Faced with the problem of the ambiguity of good and evil, American writers on the ethical dimension of international relations group themselves into at least three distinct categories: the *cynics*, the *utopians*, and the *ideologists*. Ethics, say the cynics, has little if anything to do with war and peace. Most decisions in foreign policy are made either with no reference to ethical principles or are determined by the harsh necessities of international politics where force and fraud prevail. Beginning in the late 1940s, a spate of books and articles by foreign policy practitioners have appeared in the United States which reiterate a common theme.

The authors of these studies who have earned public respect and trust report that for most of the decisions they helped to make, they cannot recall anyone raising the issue of morality. Instead the overwhelming proportion of such choices involved practical questions such as whether or not to grant diplomatic recognition to a new or changing government, to grant or not grant a visa, or to undertake or not undertake programmes of economic assistance or cultural exchange. The data they were called upon to evaluate involved matters of fact such as whether or not foreign governments exercised control within given territorial boundaries, whether or not American citizens travelling abroad could be protected by their government, and whether or not treaties or agreements acceptable to the participating governments could be successfully negotiated. It may be stretching a point to describe the authors of this approach as cynics, yet the implications of some of their viewpoints have been interpreted in this way.

However, more clear-cut expressions of moral cynicism occur in those writings which view international relations almost entirely as a matter of adversary relations. Nation states are laws unto themselves. They are locked in mortal struggle. Their rivalry can best be described as protracted conflict. Given the incompatibility of their goals and interests, their differences can be resolved only by war, whether it be a hot or cold war. Their relations proceed without benefit of moral consensus, contrasting with the shared values of eighteenth and nineteenth century monarchs and rulers who constituted a self-conscious aristocratic élite. The example most often cited as characteristic of the earlier period is Frederick the Great who all his life spoke better French than German. The comparison is often made between the relative civility of international relationships among such rulers and the fierce polemics of Soviet and American leaders in the Cold War. Viewing the latter, cynics ask where is the ethical dimension in present day international relationships.

Utopian writers who study contemporary statecraft agree with the cynics on at least one point. As presently constituted the international system promotes force and violence, not peace and justice. The need, therefore, is to transform the system. Utopians divide among themselves on at least two basic issues. Some believe in the improvement if not the perfectability of institutions, provoking the historian Carl Becker to ask *How New Will the Better World Be?*, while others believe in the perfectability of man. Illustrative of the first viewpoint is the utopianism of some who have espoused world government. An example of the latter is the thought underlying certain social-psychological or economic approaches which consider man as good and society as evil. Change society or the social circumstances under which men live and their natures in turn will be transformed.

Those who espouse utopianism may be separated into soft and hard utopians. The 'soft' utopians assert that every political ideology at root is basically the same. Each serves a part of mankind, and mankind's needs and interests are everywhere the same. Sooner or later, nation states will learn this and give their free and voluntary consent to a common régime for mankind. The pathway, as the soft utopians see it, to such a regime is through national choice largely free of the taint of domination or coercion.

'Hard' utopians, by comparison, insist that one political system is unmistakably superior, that men and nations outside it may from ignorance or false precepts resist, but the righteous and the committed, having been summoned by history, must instruct and if necessary coerce those who are backward and wrong-headed. To this end, the chosen few have a sacred mission, whether they are in the vanguard of the proletariat, the party of liberty, or the more self-righteous of Third World nations. And tragically, history records that having set out to pursue their mission by preaching and teaching they may in the end be tempted to conflict and coercion and sometimes holy wars, living by fire and the sword because their cause is pure.

Finally, ideologists join with the cynics in affirming that genuine moral purpose in foreign policy is an illusion. They part company with the cynics, however, in insisting that broad moral statements serve a valued purpose. Nations and their leaders act from hard and cynical practical interests but their success depends on covering their interests with a tissue of ideological and moral justification. Here again the ideologists group themselves in two separate aggregations. For one group, ideologies are no more than a means to an end. However selfish and cynical in their goals, national leaders use ideological means to give their acts an ethical justification. They make the worse appear the better cause. For another group of ideologists, including some communist and religious spokesmen, ideology is an end in itself—and it is the sole end and purpose that groups and nations follow in shaping their policies toward other nations. According to this view, China or the Soviet Union act not as traditional nation states but as the instruments and purveyors of a single dominant ideology. They are the select vehicles of history for carrying forward a high political and moral creed. Their decisions are the product not of selfish calculations based on national interests but of the ongoing historical process and the advance of the ideology they speak for and represent.

Monist and Pluralist Approaches to the Ethics of War and Peace

There is a more fundamental distinction to be made, however, in characterising different American approaches to the ethical dimension of war and peace. It is by and large true that the main body of statesmen and thinkers who have concerned themselves with morality and international affairs have fallen within one or the other of two prevailing schools of thought. If we employ terms that have been used in another context by political theorists and theologians, one group may be designated monists and the other pluralists. Monists have found the answer to the question of right and wrong in international relationships by focusing attention on a single moral value; pluralists have chosen to relate one value or set of values to other values in the decision-making process.

In the interwar period, the dominant approach in American universities and colleges was that of international law and organisation. Following the repudiation of the League of Nations by the Senate of the United States, a widespread sense of guilt swept over the intellectual community. Scholars took the lead in promoting renewed interest and commitment to American responsibility in world affairs. Practically every chair in international relations was occupied by professors of international law. The mandate of this professoriat, often explicitly stated, was not only the study of the subject but also the advancement of the principle and practice of international law. A remarkable group of scholars including such men as George Grafton Wilson, Charles C. Hyde, James Berdahl, and James Shotwell accepted the calling of being the spokesmen for and missionaries of international law. It is instructive in this connection to re-read the publications of the conferences of Teachers of International Law and Related Subjects sponsored by the Carnegie Endowment for International Peace. The main thrust of the conferences was plainly the inculcating of widespread scholarly support for international law. A tiny handful of marginal thinkers apparently felt compelled to introduce dissenting opinions to this dominant viewpoint, but they were for the most part voices crying in the wilderness. Noteworthy in this connection were Nicholas J. Spykman, who championed the sociological approach to international law in arguing that law must be studied in relation to wider social and political forces, and Hans J. Morgenthau, whose writings at the time dealt primarily with the limitations of international law. This little group made common cause with such British writers as Professors Keeton and Schwarzenburger of London University and European jurists such as Charles de Visscher. It is difficult to escape the conclusion, however, that the majority of influential international lawyers in the 1930s were monists in their approach to international values.

Among statesmen, a similar concentration on single values was apparent. The pre-Presidential writings of Woodrow Wilson, to which historians such as Arthur Link and Arthur Walworth have called attention, demonstrate that the great reformist President was acutely aware of the vagaries of American politics. He saw the inevitable struggle between the Congress and the President in the shaping of public policy. Conspicuous by its absence was any significant discussion of foreign policy, and yet this was the sphere in which Wilson as President can most convincingly be judged a monist. Not only did Wilson defend the League of Nations as a panacea in the resolution of world problems, but he discovered in the doctrine of national self-determination the single important value for resolving conflicts among nations. (John Maynard Keynes, Walter Lippmann, Sir Harold Nicolson and others in writings on the Paris Peace Conference have pointed up Wilson's supreme indifference to the complexities of settling the hard questions of territorial boundaries in Europe.) He was seemingly oblivious to the high price of nationalism in the economic consequences of the breakup of the Austro-Hungarian Empire in the heart of Europe. It remained for another Wilsonian, Cordell Hull, the Congressman from Tennessee who was to become Secretary of State under Franklin D. Roosevelt, to substitute for national self-determination the single value of freedom of international trade. Trade rather than nationalism was to bring international strife to an end.

In opposition to the monist approach, another group of thinkers and political leaders have adopted a pluralist perspective on values. In this they have drawn on the ancient tradition of moral reasoning. Hannah Arendt, one of the few American political philosophers in the mid-twentieth century whose writings promise to have enduring value, summoned political scientists to re-examine the Platonic dialogues. Socrates, Dr. Arendt pointed out in her lectures and in a little-known article in *Social Research*, approached the great issues of values through conversations between individuals of divergent political views.[2] To such individuals, Socrates posed timeless questions regarding justice, virtue and the good state. Their conversations characteristically took the form of what may seem little more than meandering reflections on the many facets of the question of right and wrong. Their reflections and debates left most of the basic issues unresolved, but having uncovered the contradictions and complexities of moral reasoning about the great issues of the nature of man and the state and having pointed out to the participants that they had come full circle, Socrates said, 'Let us start over again and think about our problems in a new light.' Dr. Arendt insisted that out of this seemingly wandering and inconclusive discourse, new levels of understanding emerged. The moral problem as Socrates viewed it was not to be solved once and for all but required continuous re-examination.

In another realm of political discourse, Paul Freund, the renowned Professor of Constitutional Law at Harvard University, has been a spokesman for the pluralist approach. Values in law and politics, Freund has stated, cluster and compete with one another. The choice of right or wrong is seldom one involving action based upon a single good. Instead choice in law and politics commonly involves discriminate judgement between competing goods. Rights compete with rights, and justice for one man or group can mean injustice for another; moral reasoning, therefore involves an unending process of balancing competing rights and interests. In politics and law men are required to live without benefit of absolute truth. Instead, for every truth there is a balancing truth, and only demagogues or fanatics are freed of such constraints. Reporters in covering court-room trials affirm the rights of a free press and the public's right to know, but American constitutional law also provides for a fair trial for defendants. The peculiarities of the American system of trial by a jury, presumed to be impartial and objective throughout the trial and unswayed by public passions, set limits to premature public disclosure. Such limits clash with the freedom of the press.

The problem of competing values runs the gamut of war and peace issues. There is widespread popular appeal in the Wilsonian doctrine of 'open covenants openly arrived at'. For the monists have always addressed themselves to the evils of secret diplomacy, and Congressmen have railed against the lack of full and open disclosure of negotiations by the executive branch of government with leaders of other states. (Diplomatic columnists have speculated that Secretary of State Henry Kissinger spent a substantial part of his time out of the country partly to escape continuous questioning and scrutiny by the numerous committees of Congress on delicate and sensitive negotiations with foreign powers.) Walter Lippmann frequently reminded his readers that individuals not assemblies are alone capable of diplomatic negotiations. The limited truth of the Wilsonian formula of 'open covenants' is evident in its subsequent modification to read 'open covenants secretly negotiated.'

Examples of Monism in Contemporary Ethical Approaches

The clash between the monist and pluralist outlooks may take on more specific and concrete meaning if we examine a few of the popularly held philosophies of war and peace and go on to consider the ways in which they have been tested and applied to important issues. We begin then by outlining three philosophies of war and peace which emphasise a single factor.

Pacifism stands out among the leading war and peace theories as perhaps the most attractive to liberal and humane people. It selects from the range of possible objectives nations may pursue in foreign policy one fundamental aim—the quest for peace. The distinction is sometimes made between absolute and pragmatic pacifists, the latter being more inclined to take part in social and humanitarian endeavours in devastated areas or inside oppressed societies. The merit of pacifism lies in its providing a noble example of human behaviour for others to emulate. Its weakness lies, in the words of Reinhold Niebuhr, in trying to make 'a success story of the Cross'. Norman Thomas, the Socialist Party candidate for President in successive Presidential elections, may be the best known American political leader to embrace pacifism although various local and regional leaders have been outspoken advocates of the doctrine, and the American Friends Service Committee and the Fellowship for Reconciliation have made considerable headway in institutionalising it. Scholars such as Kenneth Boulding, Clark Kerr, and Gilbert White and publicists such as the doughty A. J. Muste have gained the respect of pacifists and non-pacifists alike. No one in the United States has achieved the towering political heights of Gandhi in India, and it is fair to ask whether this great leader's political strategy could have succeeded if Germany or the Soviet Union and not Britain had been the ruling colonial power.

Militarism occupies a place at the opposite end of the spectrum from *pacifism* and it is not difficult to show that it too has concentrated on a single factor. For a country which in modern times has had an aversion to standing armies, the United States has done an abrupt about-face. Military expenditures averaging considerably above $100,000,000,000 are second only to those of Health, Education and Welfare. The trend toward militarism had gone so far by the 1950s, that President Dwight D. Eisenhower saw fit in his farewell address to warn against the mounting power of the military-industrial complex. Administration spokesmen who went before Congressional Committees found that economic assistance programmes were more likely to be accepted when they were linked with military assistance. Pentagon officials have on many occasions opposed concessions that diplomats were contemplating because in the armed forces lexicon political advantages took distinctly second place to military superiority. The retired Admiral and Chief of Naval Operations, Elmo Zumwalt, fought a campaign for the Senate on the principal issue of a decline in military preparedness, and opposed diplomatic concessions proposed by Secretary of State Henry Kissinger as essential to Soviet-American accommodation.

Peace through economic development and human rights is a third and for many a more convincing expression of single factor analysis. It is rooted in the belief that war comes about primarily as a result of economic disparities among peoples or gross violations of human rights. While the coupling of the two forms of monism in peace theories may appear arbitrary and even contradictory, it has often been true in the United States that the same individuals and organisations have been supporters of the two approaches. Thus Father Theodore Hesburgh, President of Notre Dame University, has written and spoken with force and eloquence on the need for increased technical assistance to the developing countries while at the same time spearheading the drive for human rights around the world. The Overseas Development Council in Washington, D.C. has chosen as twin focal points for its efforts economic development and human rights. Not only are these goals congenial to the liberal spirit of many Americans, but they happen to coincide with the principal goals of the republic. And much as Woodrow Wilson was persuaded that the goals of America were the goals of all mankind, present day champions trumpet not peace or international understanding as a goal but the establishment of human rights. In the words of Senator David Patrick Moynihan of New York:

> The case for making human rights concerns fundamental to our foreign policy is twofold. First, these are the issues we care most about, or ought to care most about . . . But second, there is a profound strategic point. To press human rights is to press the natural advantage of the United States. For we, and a few like us, maintain free societies, while most of the nations of the world do not.[3]

Senator Moynihan goes on to support his cause by citing results from a Freedom House survey quantified to his delight to show there are 41 free nations in the world of which two are in South America, two in Africa, two in Asia. (On the numbers he comments parenthetically 'the virtue of human rights as an issue is that it is . . . quantifiable: morality can mean anything and hence usually means nothing.') And the Senator concluded that:

> . . . if we are to adopt the human rights standard, it must be a single standard. No distinction between military aid and economic aid. No distinction between aid that helps the poor as against other kinds. None of these distinctions bear scrutiny.[4]

In other words American foreign policy ought to rest on a single factor.

Contemporary Problems and Monism

After outlining three monistic philosophies of war and peace, we are now in a position to consider the ways in which they have been tested and applied to important issues.

Peace in Vietnam was the battlecry of the critics of American policy in Vietnam, especially of those who were in the vanguard of the youth movement. A full assessment of what some have come to call the Vietnam débâcle remains the task of future historians. The main question of the initiation of the defence of Vietnam proliferates into related questions such as the connection between that country and the opening up of relations with China. There is bitter irony in the fact that the public debate between defenders and critics of our Vietnamese policy was joined between two contending absolutist viewpoints, the one grounded in the belief that peace ought to be our sole objective in Vietnam and the other that all aggression must be halted. The necessity of resistance to aggression was the lesson taught us by the belated and costly response of the Allies to Hitler's imperialism. For a whole generation of policy-makers no other principle of foreign policy was needed. It was the litmus paper to be applied to policy recommendations on any problem that arose involving a threat to peace in any area of the world whatever the political concerns.

Inevitably, a Thermidorian reaction set in. If resisting aggression everywhere in the world was the thesis, peace at any price was the antithesis. A host of questions and inter-related issues bore in on the policy-makers once the commitment to intervene in Vietnam had been made beginning with an assessment of the interests, objectives, and capacities of the major participants in the struggle and branching out into strategic issues involving Chinese and Soviet interests and capacities in the region. One need not construct an overall defence of the Kennedy-Johnson or the Nixon-Ford foreign policy and its various successes and failures to say that any administration and any group of public officials pursuing the national interest would have been obliged to take many factors into account, including the much criticised slogan 'peace with honour'. It was easier to decide that we should never have intervened than to know how to disengage once we were involved. The Vietnam issue was less a question of a handful of misguided leaders than the clarification of the requirements of national security.

To all this, the leaders of the peace movement remained largely indifferent. It was a sign of the nature and character of the movement that it disintegrated, once peace was achieved, although the need for peace in Berlin, the Middle East, and South Africa continued. Ending the bloodshed in Vietnam—a worthy moral and political purpose—was an end in itself. It brought about a public response powerful enough to terminate the political life and ambitions of President Johnson. But based on a single consideration, peace in that South-east Asian country was not sufficient to provide the basis for an ongoing foreign policy.

Militarism in Korea throws light on the hazards of another kind of single factor analysis. The United States following World War II had dismantled its military establishment to its lowest point since the inter-war period. Our commitments to South Korea and those of other members of the United Nations required that the invasion from the north be turned back. What began as a limited military buildup soon led to actions that raised the defence budget to a level approaching $30,000,000,000. The initial commitment to contain expansion from the north had as its corollary the assurance that China would not intervene and that the United States not be drawn into a land war on the mainland of China. The enemy was North Korea and every precaution was to be taken that China not be provoked to enter the conflict.

Once the struggle was joined, however, and battlefield considerations and requirements became dominant, the military and in particular the brilliant field commander, General Douglas MacArthur, assumed full authority. Korea was far away and the exigencies of battle were such that MacArthur was granted, or interpreted his orders as giving him, *carte blanche*. A war begun in part as a struggle to restore political equilibrium in the régime became almost exclusively a military struggle. Only when it was too late and China entered the war was the power of the Commander-in-Chief, President Truman, restored. Whatever the elements in the thinking of civilian and military authorities which brought the situation about, a military and not a political approach was maintained up to the point of the removal of MacArthur. Military objectives had prevailed to that point as the principal basis of foreign policy.

Technical Assistance and the Majority Poor. If a growing militarism has been one characteristic of American foreign policy since World War II, another has been the attempt by Americans to use their vast material resources to help others less fortunate to cope with their most vexing problems. Some observers have characterised technical assistance programmes as a secularisation of the missionary movement. Others point to enlightened self-interest as a primary motivation. Over a thirty-year period the technical assistance effort has continued with some programmes being more successful than others. In the past two or three years, a strenuous effort has been made to channel a far higher proportion of aid to the majority poor in the developing countries. Both in bilateral programmes and multilateral efforts such as those of the World Bank the emphasis has shifted from country programmes or attempts to build more viable structures and institutions for economic and educational growth to new designs for helping the poor. Recipient countries have been put on notice that any assistance given them must be directed to the needs of the more numerous poor rather than be drained off by the wealthy few at the top.

What began, however, as a worthwhile reorientation of foreign aid has brought growing criticism on several fronts. Leaders of some of the developing countries point the finger at American spokesmen whom they find guilty of moral hypocrisy. Not only have Americans failed to solve the problem of the poor at home (the lower 10% have 1.5% of the wealth while the top 10% have 26%), but when foreign governments such as India under Mrs. Gandhi, Chile under Allende, Jamaica, Tanzania, and Cuba set out on a drastic new course intended to help the poor, they are the first countries we repudiate and ignore. Friends in the developing countries are also frank to say that the United States has had two hundred years in which to solve its problems while they have been struggling with theirs for no more than ten to twenty-five years. Their most serious criticism though is that help to the poor requires policies, programmes, and the necessary infrastructure; and these will not emerge fully grown as from the head of Zeus. For a decade or two Americans have helped the developing countries build new institutions, for example, in higher education; and now that they are beginning to show signs of meeting the nation's most urgent needs, we announce that we have no interest in higher education but only in helping the majority poor in as yet undefined programmes of basic education.

Human Rights and Détente. The most controversial case of choosing to deal with one moral question in isolation from all the rest concerns the plight of the Jews in Russia. A growing awareness of the persecution by the Soviet government of this minority group has coincided with the foreign policy of *détente* initiated for the United States by President Nixon and Secretary Kissinger. Few responsible people debate the need for the relaxation of tensions in Soviet-American relations, although specific agreements have understandably come under question as to whether or not American negotiators have conceded too much. The Jackson Amendment, however, was designed to link the granting of favourable trade arrangements with relaxation of emigration rights of Soviet Jews. In part the debate has centred on a question of facts: Senator Jackson has argued that public pressure on the Soviets will increase the number of Jews given permission to leave while John Kenneth Galbraith and others have maintained that influential private contacts are more helpful and that emigration has fallen off sharply since the Jackson Amendment. The heart of the debate, however, has to do with priorities in foreign policy and whether the human rights of one small minority group should determine the fate of a major foreign policy initiative such as *détente*. Holding to the single factor of human rights puts all other issues including *détente* into a secondary position.

Moral Reasoning in American Thought on War and Peace

The somewhat bleak picture that emerges from a review of philosophies and policies that base ethical thinking on a single moral principle or goal is fortunately only half the story. Particularly since World War II, a significant group of thinkers has appeared on the American scene whose writings fall broadly within the tradition of moral reasoning. It is impossible in any brief survey to mention them all. Each has attracted his share of followers and critics. All have tended in their work, whatever their limitations, to direct attention to the multiple factors which affect moral reasoning. At the same time they have attempted to rank in order such factors, not being content with the general statement that 'morality is an aspect of foreign policy'.[5]

1. *Reinhold Niebuhr*

The first of these thinkers is the theologian, Reinhold Niebuhr, who in a vast outpouring of thought and writing beginning in 1929 with *Leaves from the Notebook of a Tamed Cynic* brooded about and sought to clarify the relation between ethics or religion and society.[6]

George F. Kennan has called Niebuhr 'the father of us all', implying an intellectual tradition going back to him which Kennan and others have continued. If Niebuhr is the father of a tradition, his children have chosen to interpret him in many diverse ways. Religious people who take pride in Niebuhr's commitment to what he called 'Christian realism' may prefer to forget his words, 'Religion is a good thing for honest people but a bad thing for dishonest people ... and the church has not been impressive because many of its leaders rationalise.'[7] Secular leaders were attracted to Niebuhr by the score perhaps because of what he called his 'dialogue with doubt', and a group was formed at Harvard called 'atheists for Niebuhr'. These groups must have been embarrassed by his words, 'No matter how far back I go ... I cannot get back to an atheistic mentality. As little can I reach a day when I was conscious of myself but not of God as I can reach a day when I was conscious of myself but not of other human beings.'[8]

This unique combination of a critical and a religious perspective made Niebuhr both the forerunner of other critically-minded thinkers and an irreplaceable figure on the American intellectual scene. Arthur Schlesinger, Jr., summed up the views of a panel attended by 500 scholars at the 1974 meeting of the American Political Science Association on Niebuhr's contribution by saying: 'No one has taken his place or the role he performed from the 1930s to the 1960s.'

Niebuhr sought to link his study of history and politics with a theory of human nature. His criticism of contemporary political science centred on its insistence that political theory was rooted in political institutions and statistically verifiable behaviour rather than in any historic view of the human condition, for he felt that any understanding of political phenomena is inseparable from the search for the intrinsic qualities of man. His celebrated Gifford Lectures began: 'Man has always been his most vexing problem.

How shall he think of himself?' Then Niebuhr went on in a mode of dialectical thought that was to characterise all his writings on the ethical dimension of politics, saying that any affirmation about man involves conflicts and contradictions. If the observer stresses man's unique and rational qualities, then man's greed, lust for power, and brute nature betray him. If the writer holds that men everywhere are the product of nature and unable to rise above circumstances, this tells us nothing of man the creature who dreams of God and of making himself God, nor of man, the creature whose sympathy knows no bounds. If the student of history declares that man is essentially good and attributes all evil to concrete historical and social causes, he merely begs the question, for these causes are revealed, on scrutiny, to be the consequences of the evil inherent in man. If he concludes that man is bereft of all virtue, his very capacity for reaching such a judgement refutes his conclusion. All these perplexing conflicts in human self-knowledge point up the difficulty of doing justice at one and the same time to the uniqueness of man and to his affinities with nature. The heart of Niebuhr's criticism is that modern views of man which stress exclusively either his dignity or his misery are fatuous and irrelevant, as they fail to consider the good and evil, the dualism in man's nature.

The deeper paradox arises from the fact that man is suspended perilously between freedom and finiteness, spirit and nature, the human and the divine. His ambiguous and contradictory position at the juncture of freedom and finiteness produces in him a condition of anxiety which is fundamental to understanding political behaviour. Man is anxious about the imperialism of others yet secretly fearful of his own vulnerability and limitations. Because of the finiteness of his reason, he can never wholly judge his own possibilities. So he endlessly seeks security in the pretence that he has overcome his finiteness and human limitations. Only through extending his power and influence is he safeguarded against the domination of others.

The most important observable expression of human anxiety politically is seen in the will to power. Man shares with animals their natural appetites and desires along with an impulse for survival. Yet being both human and divine, deriving his powers both from nature and spirit, his requirements are qualitatively heightened; they are raised irretrievably to the level of spirit where they became limitless and insatiable. To overcome social anxiety, man seeks power and control over his fellows, endeavouring to subdue them lest they came to dominate him. The struggle for political power is merely an example of the rivalry which goes on at every level of human life. It manifests itself in relations of husbands and wives; parents and children; spouses and in-laws; ethnic groups; children and remarried parents; cities, states and the nation, and the executive and legislative branches of government.

In the field of collective behaviour the force of egoistic passion is so strong that the only harmonies possible are those which manage to neutralise a rival force through balances of power, through mutual defences against its inordinate expression, and through techniques for harnessing its energy to social ends. Social unity is built on the virtuous as well as the selfish side of man's nature; the twin elements of collective strength for a nation become self-sacrificial loyalty and the frustrated aggression of the masses. From this it follows that politics, whether in organised political groups or in large organisations, is the more contentious and ruthless because of the unselfish loyalty and commitments of members of groups, which become laws unto themselves, unrestrained by their obedient and worshipful members. Niebuhr's conclusion is that within international society even a nation composed of men of the greatest goodwill is less than loving toward other nations. He observes: 'society ... merely cumulates the egoism of individuals and transmutes their individual altruism into collective egoism so that the egoism of the group has a double force. For this reason no group acts from purely unselfish or even mutual interest, and politics is therefore bound to be a contest of power.'

Translating this to the level of world politics, nations pursue the quest for power, influence, and prestige in a struggle which is heightened by the intensity of collective loyalties and compounded by the present day alienations and frustrations experienced by individuals in mass societies. All nations claim they seek security and follow their national interest; Niebuhr is willing to concede that nations on the whole are not particularly generous and a wise self-interest is usually the limit of their moral attainment. The demands of self-interest and national self-protection lead to acts which appear to override all accepted moral impulses. The decision in the early 1950s to build the hydrogen bomb gave offence to many sensitive people but Niebuhr replied: 'No nation will fail to take even the most hazardous adventure into the future, if the alternative of not taking the step means the risk of being subjugated.' Yet while saying this he was terrified and appalled by the prospect of nuclear proliferation.

Niebuhr was perusaded that men and states cannot follow their self-interest without claiming to do so in obedience to some general scheme of values. This belief led him to ask, first, whether a consistent and unquestioning emphasis upon the national interest is not as self-defeating in a nation as self-interest is in a person's life. Stated differently, does not a nation exclusively concerned with its own interests define those interests so narrowly that the very interests and securities, which depend on common devotion to principles of justice and established mutualities in the community of nations, are sacrificed? In American foreign policy, we claim more for the benevolence of our policies than they deserve, heightening thereby the resentments of people already envious of our wealth and power. At one time, therefore, national interest is imperiled by the hazard of moral cynicism and at another time by moral pretension, hypocrisy, and ideological justification. In his earlier writings, Niebuhr strongly denounced moral cynicism but later he became more concerned with hypocrisy and ideological justification, concluding that cynicism and pretension were two parts of a single problem. That problem involves our continuing ambivalence toward the moral issue and its principal dimensions, as we claim at one moment that nations have no obligations beyond their interest and at the next that they are engaged in a high moral crusade without regard for selfish interests.

Edmund Burke provided Niebuhr with a concept that became central to the last stages of the great theologian's thinking. Theorists, and more particularly 'scientists' of society, have often given themselves over to the belief that the historical realm is analogous to the realm of nature and that the adoption of proper scientific or theoretical techniques will assure men mastery over their historical fate. Most scientific studies for this reason have been largely irrelevant to the practice of statecraft where the watchword must be 'sufficient unto the day is the evil thereof'. For Burke the problem of relating theory and practice in politics is bound up with the concept of prudence. Prudence, not justice, is first in the rank of political virtues; it is the director and regulator. Metaphysics cannot live without definition, but prudence is cautious in its definitions for it has learned to live with ever-changing reality. As Niebuhr moved toward an increasingly more pragmatic view of world politics, he sensed the limits of rational as well as traditional normative thinking. In the largely irrational realm of politics, the struggle is usually so intense that the only possible peace becomes an armistice and the only order a provisional balance among forces. Even the proximate moral norms of politics are seldom realised in practice; statesmen must settle for uncertain compromises. It is as necessary to moderate the moral pretensions of every contestant in the power struggle as it is to make moral distinctions regarding the national interest. In the 1920s Niebuhr was a social reformer and optimist; in the Marxist 1930s he was a radical; but in his later years he became a Christian realist. When critics warned he was in danger of being little more than a pragmatist, he replied that his pragmatism was limited and instrumental, even while acknowledging that through it he risked standing 'on the abyss of cynicism'. What saved him from this position, he hoped, was his openness to criticism by friend, foe, and God. It was also the ability through religion and, in the American Constitutional system, through the higher law, to stand outside the world of events 'in order to get a fulcrum on it'. He paraphrased St. Paul in *The Irony of American History*: 'Nothing worth doing is completed in our lifetime; therefore we must be saved by hope ... Nothing we do, however virtuous, can be accomplished alone; therefore we are saved by love. No virtuous act is quite as virtuous from the standpoint of our friend or foe as from our standpoint. Therefore, we must be saved by the final form of love which is forgiveness.'[9]

2. *Hans J. Morgenthau*

Another writer who attributes much of the development of his thinking to Niebuhr is Hans J. Morgenthau whose classic text, *Politics Among Nations*, has educated several generations of students and practitioners in the realities of world politics. The fact that he wrote with such candour, about the harsher aspects of politics, cloaked an underlying compassion. Walter Lippmann turned to him at the end of a conference of theorists in Washington and said: 'You are not the hard-headed realist you are painted but the most moral man I know.' Morgenthau's writings, as Niebuhr's, are voluminous and include contributions both in political theory and foreign policy.[10]

Morgenthau more than any American scholar sought to turn American thinking on war and peace from its preoccupation with laws and structures to its core in international politics. For him as for Niebuhr politics at bedrock is a struggle for power. In the present world system, power and interests are linked with the security of the nation state, but nowhere is it preordained that nation states remain as the permanent political units of international society. The paradox of the present era is that nation states have become obsolete in providing for the most urgent needs of man, but no other unit has emerged effectively to take their place. The nation state will not disappear whatever its weaknesses until something better is available to take its place.

In this vein of thought, Morgenthau has remained sceptical of every other device or instrumentality proposed for doing away with the struggle for power. 'Power politics' when he set forth on his career in the United States were dirty and forbidden words. Politics was something world government or public administration were designed to eradicate. Politics epitomised all that was evil and had to be uprooted if men were to live in a civilised world. To these judgements Morgenthau responded in the most uncompromising terms by saying:

> Whatever the ultimate aims of international politics, power is always the immediate aim. Statesmen and people may ultimately seek freedom, security, prosperity or power itself. They may define their goals in terms of a religious, philosophic, economic or social ideal ... But whenever they strive to realise their goal by means of international politics, they do so by striving for power.[11]

To those who joined issue with him maintaining that power politics had not always existed and need not exist in the future, he answered:

> ... the struggle for power is universal in time and place and is an undeniable fact of experience ... Even though anthropologists have shown that certain primitive people seem to be free from the desire for power, nobody has yet shown how their

state of mind and the conditions under which they live can be recreated on a worldwide scale.... It would be useless and even self-destructive to free one or the other of the peoples of the earth from the desire for power while leaving it extant in others. If the desire for power cannot be abolished everywhere in the world, those who might be cured would simply fall victim to the power of others.[12]

Having rejected the optimistic views of those who predicted the end of power politics, Morgenthau devoted much of his writings to a discussion of the limitations of national power. He looked to international law, international organisation, world community, international cooperation and national purpose as effecting such limitations. He has had considerable to say about moral consensus within and among nations, and where it has been lacking he has expressed strong doubts about world government or political accommodation.

Furthermore, few writers have had as much to say about the clash of values and the interplay between values and interests. Where moral consensus is lacking among states, the best to be hoped for is a provisional accommodation of their interests and failing this, a redefinition of their interests. Treaties and agreements, Morgenthau says, must register an existing situation of facts; they cannot be imposed when the respective national interests of allies or foes are in conflict with one another. Soviet-American relations pointedly illustrate the conspicuous absence of such consensus, a fact that at least in part is the cause of Morgenthau's scepticism about *détente*.

More than Niebuhr, Morgenthau is inclined to say that politics most often involves a choice of lesser evils. There are fateful choices which involve not so much the balancing of rights against rights but judgements on which course of action is least likely to bring harmful results. Morgenthau's essentially tragic view of the course of action open to statesmen is based on his belief that two factors have brought about the deterioration of moral limitations on power: the substitution of democratic for aristocratic responsibility in foreign affairs and of nationalistic standards of action for universal ones. On the former, he writes:

Moral rules have their seat in the conscience of individual men ...
Where responsibility for government is widely distributed among

a great number of individuals with different conceptions as to
what is morally required in international affairs, or with no conception at all, international morality as an effective system of restraints upon international policy becomes impossible.[13]

In support of his views, he cites Dean Roscoe Pound who wrote:
'It might be maintained plausibly, that a moral ... order among
states, was nearer attainment in the middle of the eighteenth
century than it is today.'[14] On the latter change, that is the substitution of nationalistic for universalistic norms, Morgenthau,
having tested the manner in which the universal ethical command,
'Thou shalt not kill', is transformed by the national ethic, 'Thou
shalt kill under certain conditions the enemies of thy country,'
concludes:

> ... carrying their idols before them, the nationalistic masses
> of our time meet in the international arena, each group convinced
> that it executes the mandate of history, that it does for humanity
> what it seems to do for itself, and that it fulfils a sacred mission
> ordained by providence, however defined.
>   Little do they know that they meet under an empty sky from
> which the gods have departed.[15]

It is the tragic element in life and politics which more than any
other preoccupies Morgenthau: men seek power as the means to
worthy ends, but mankind and their ends are corrupted by the
pursuit of power; ideological foreign policy is a contradiction
to successful diplomacy, but foreign policy not rooted in national
purpose is aimless; and the national state is obsolete, but no
effective world community has yet come into being. Life is lived
at the point of such apparent contradictions and antinomies and
to obscure this is sophistry.

3. *Walter Lippmann*

Walter Lippmann began his intellectual journey in seeking to
understand the ethical dimension when he wrote in the first
issue of *The New Republic*: 'Every sane person knows it is a greater
thing to build a city than to bombard it, to plough a field than to
trample it, to serve mankind than to conquer it'. With Woodrow
Wilson, he was persuaded that those who were prepared to use
political reason would see the futility of war. He began, as a socia-

list and a foe of the European balance of power. As Secretary of the Inquiry engaged in preparing for the peace settlement after World War I, he collaborated in the formulation of the Fourteen Points.

By 17 February 1917 Lippmann and his colleagues at *The New Republic* sought to warn President Wilson that legalism and moralism were not enough and that an overall political strategy for war and peace had become essential. He acknowledged that both the blockade by the British and submarine warfare by the Germans were terrible weapons as war was terrible. In choosing between them, however, the United States would not be choosing between illegality and legality or even between cruelty and mercy. What mattered was that the United States in its own interest could not permit a German triumph and for this reason we accepted the closure of the seas to Germany and the opening of them to the Allies. He wrote:

> We are an inveterately legalistic people and have veiled our real intentions behind a mass of technicalities ... We have wanted to assist the Allies and hamper Germany, but we have wanted also to keep out of war. Our government therefore has been driven to stretch technicalities to the breaking point. We have clothed the most unneutral purposes in the language of neutrality.[16]

After the War, Lippmann continued his attack on moralistic pronouncements. We were told, he observed, that the United States would work for justice and peace. Such words are hollow vessels into which almost anybody can pour anything he chooses. Moral and political choices involved deciding what was vital in Europe to a stable peace and our interests. We needed policies that offered Europe something concrete. Instead, he continued:

> ... when it came to the test Wilson was to treat American policies like so many other ideals, something distant and of no material consequence. Calling ourselves disinterested, we behaved as if we were uninterested, and furnished the world with the extraordinary spectacle of a nation willing to send two million soldiers overseas, yet unwilling to project its mind and conscience overseas. ... When Mr. Wilson began, Europe believed that the Wilson program was an American program, a thing as vital to us as Alsace-Lorraine was to France. But in the course of

time the European statesmen discovered that Mr. Wilson's program was really nothing more than his gratuitous advice in a situation he did not thoroughly understand.[17]

The tragedy was that history was to repeat itself. We marched into Germany in World War II and once more winning the war became an end in itself. As we had no policy for the peace after World War I, we had this time the goal of ending alliances and the balance of power which we rather proudly announced had been the cause of all previous wars. The Russians and the British had political and territorial goals clearly in their minds though Stalin said that he, by comparison with Hitler, knew when to stop. We failed to remember that an international organisation— the major goal we worked for and advanced—cannot write the peace or establish a territorial *status quo* which it must defend. It is rather the nations, partners in war and peace, who must bring this about.

Lippmann's main proposition on the ethics of war and peace was based on his belief that ideals and goals can never be approached apart from political and territorial questions. For in ethics there is always a political dimension. To forget this is to place ethics on a remote and ceremonial pedestal of utopian thought.

4. *George F. Kennan*

George Kennan's contribution has been to carry farther Lippmann's thesis, elaborating, sharpening, and refining it. The areas of fundamental agreement of these men make even more poignant for Kennan Lippmann's criticism of his formulation of the containment doctrine in the Cold War. In *American Diplomacy*, Kennan wrote: 'I see the most serious fault . . . to lie in something that I might call the legalistic-moralistic approach to international problems. This approach runs like a red skein through our foreign policy of the last fifty years.' What was this approach? In Kennan's criticism it was the belief

> . . . that it should be possible to suppress the chaotic and dangerous aspirations of governments in the international field by . . . legal rules and restraints . . . instead of taking the awkward conflicts of national interest and dealing with them on their

merits with a view to finding the solutions least unsettling to the
stability of international life, it would be better to find some formal
criteria of a juridical nature by which the permissible behaviour
of states could be defined. Behind all this, of course, lies the
American assumption that the things for which other peoples in
this world are likely to contend are for the most part neither
creditable nor important and might justly be expected to take
second place behind the desirability of an orderly world, un-
troubled by international violence.[18]

What were the reasons for the all-pervasive character of the
legalistic-moralistic approach? In seeking an explanation, Kennan
mentions the dominant role of the legal profession in American
statecraft as well as a stubborn insistence that all states are like
our own, satisfied and content with their international borders
and status. Legalism by itself would be a serious impediment
to America's understanding of the world. Its association with
moralism compounds the difficulty. For moralism involves the
carrying over into the affairs of state the concepts of right and
wrong, the assumption, to quote Kennan's much-debated phrase,
that 'state behaviour is a fit subject for moral judgment'.

What Kennan would accept as a final interpretation of this
phrase is difficult to know despite several attempts to clarify it.
What he opposes is clear: The tendency of those who claim there
is a law on some contemporary problem and are indignant against
the law-breaker and feel a moral superiority to him; the spilling
over of their indignation into the conduct of a military struggle;
their impatience until they reduce the law-breaker to complete
submissiveness and achieve what became the Allies' objective
in World War II—unconditional surrender. Ironically, this
approach, rooted in a desire to do away with war and violence,
intensifies violence and makes it more destructive of political
stability than did the older motives of national interest. A war
that is fought in the name of high moral principle seldom ends
before total domination is realised. Kennan is a moral absolutist
on only one count—his denunciation of atomic weapons and war
which he said goes farther than anything the Christian ethic can
properly accept.

What would Kennan put in the place of the dangerous and
damaging approach of wars fought to end wars or for some other
moral principle? Despite his scepticism about international law

he would not wish to see it lose respect as 'a gentle civiliser of events.' What he urges instead is:

> ... a new attitude among us toward many things outside our borders that are irritating and unpleasant today—an attitude more like that of the doctor toward the physical phenomena in the human body that are neither pleasing nor fortunate—an attitude of detachment and soberness and readiness to reserve judgment ... the modesty to admit that our own national interest is all that we are really capable of knowing and understanding—and the courage to recognise that if our own purposes and undertakings here at home are decent ones, unsullied by arrogance or hostility toward other people or delusions of superiority, then the pursuit of our national interest can never fail to be conducive to a better world.[19]

A Concluding Note

It should be obvious that the four thinkers considered above are exemplars of pluralism in moral reasoning. Whatever the deficiencies of their thought, they can hardly be judged for paying heed only to a single factor such as peace or military defence. Each in turn has spoken out against exclusive concern for economic development or human rights. All contend that we must first 'know ourselves' before we can 'know others'. On the subject of Korea, they recognised the need for turning back North Korea's invasion and for maintaining a more stable equilibrium of forces in the region. But their criticism was loud and unqualified of the pursuit of the enemy heedless of the threat of drawing China into the struggle and changing the character of a limited war. On the Vietnamese war they each questioned from the beginning whether our national interest was involved and whether we grasped the true nature of the conflict, particularly its historical and political roots. On technical assistance and the majority poor, they doubted, as would Lippmann and Niebuhr if they had lived, the rather utopian view that America by itself could change the economic and demographic map of the world. On *détente*, it is likely that all four would favour such a policy while yet questioning whether Nixon and Kissinger had oversold it. Three of the four almost certainly would join the critics of *détente* in maintaining that concern for human rights in Russia should be weighed in the balance but in the context of the more fundamental need for the reduction of tensions between the United States and the Soviet Union.

However, a score sheet of issues and policies on which the four thinkers were more prescient than policy makers or the general public is not a justification of the main thesis of this discussion. The real issue to be pondered is whether their general approach of moral reasoning is more soundly based and central to the ethical dimension than are the monistic approaches which have tended to prevail in American thinking. It is their first and their principal merit that they offer us an alternative perspective which has not been tested by policy-makers and found wanting, but with a few notable exceptions, such as Kennan's containment policy, has been largely ignored or passed over, or when adopted has been distorted or misapplied as with containment in Asia. This alternative perspective represents a more hopeful approach and way of thinking about war and peace and morality than does any prevailing viewpoint.

Notes

1. Reinhold Niebuhr in his last years often said that Roosevelt had saved the republic; but Niebuhr also confessed he had twice voted against FDR because he, in Roosevelt's first years, considered him superficial. The contrast between Niebuhr who had the courage to change his mind and Kolko who did not is instructive.
2. Hannah Arendt, 'Thinking and Moral Considerations', *Social Research*, vol. 38, Autumn 1971, pp. 417–46.
3. *New York Times*, January 4, 1977, p. 27.
4. *Ibid.*
5. Cyrus Vance in an interview at the televised press conference at which his appointment as Secretary of State was announced.
6. Some of his most important books are *The Nature and Destiny of Man: Vol.* 1, *Human Nature, Vol. II, Human Destiny; The Children of Light and Darkness; Faith and History; Moral Man and Immoral Society; The Irony of American History; The Self and the Dramas of History; Christianity and Power Politics; Christian Realism and Political Problems; Pious and Secular America; Love and Justice;* and *The Structure of Nations and Empires.*
7. Reinhold Niebuhr, sermon at Union Seminary, New York, on 10 May 1960.
8. Quoted by June Bingham, *Courage to Change* (New York: Charles Scribner's Sons, 1961), p. 12.
9. Reinhold Niebuhr, *The Irony of American History* (London: Nisbet and Co., 1952), p. 54.
10. Among his books are *Scientific Man vs. Power Politics; In Defence of the National Interest; Principles and Problems of International Politics; The Purpose of American*

Politics; Dilemmas of Politics; A New Foreign Policy for the United States; and *Politics of the 20th Century.*

11. Hans J. Morgenthau, *Politics Among Nations*, second edition (New York: Knopf, 1954), p. 25.
12. *Ibid.*, p. 30.
13. *Ibid.*, p. 189.
14. Roscoe Pound, "Philosophical Theory and International Law", *Bibliotheca Visseriana*, 1923, Vol. I, p. 74.
15. Morgenthau, *op. cit.*, p. 196.
16. Quoted in Arthur Schlesinger, Jr., *Early Writings, Walter Lippmann* (New York: Liveright, 1970) p. 71.
17. *Ibid.*, pp. 88–89.
18. George F. Kennan, *American Diplomacy*, 1900–1950 (Chicago: University of Chicago Press, 1951), p. 93.
19. George F. Kennan, address at Princeton Theological Seminary printed in May, 1959 issue of *The Atlantic*, p. 100.

In Peace and War:
The Institutional Balance Reappraised

Catherine McArdle Kelleher

I. Introduction

To discuss the American organisation of warmaking and peace-making in the 1970s is to run the risk of a thrice-told tale of dire prediction. After Vietnam, the excesses of an all-powerful Executive capable of sustaining major hostilities on his own stand almost anywhere indicted. The hopes for a stronger, more activist Congress fulfilling the vision of the Founding Fathers seem forlorn, after so many decades of Congressional passivity and delegation of responsibility. And the search for viable, legitimate power-sharing formulae has already taken on a dated quality, as the United States enters its familiar post-conflict phase of forgetfulness.

Yet there is considerable value in re-examining the familiar, emotion-laden issues. The prescriptive significance for those Americans and others who are committed to 'No More Vietnams' is clear. The continuous nature of debate and criticism on these questions since 1789 allows a meaningful summary of trends and changes over America's growth as an international actor.

Most importantly, such a discussion can at least briefly bring a special perspective to what appear to be central questions facing the United States, indeed all advanced democracies now and for the foreseeable future: How adequate are the institutional mechanisms of the nation state to the issues and challenges of primary significance for national security in a nuclear age? To what extent can

they or should they cope with increasing international interdependence, both in the causes and in the impacts of even the
smallest conflict flashpoints? Are there indeed any meaningful
constraints which can be placed on the overweening powers
which centralisation and bureaucratisation have placed in the
hands of a few within the Executive?

This examination will proceed in three parts. The first will be
a general overview of the peculiarly American context in which
questions of who shall make war have arisen. We will then turn
to a brief analysis of the specific issues in the dispute over the
President's dominance of the peace and war powers. Finally, we
will assess the efficacy and the viability of the alternatives proposed,
now and in the past, for power-sharing and constraint.

II. The Context: Historical and Psychological

Over the past two hundred years, the questions about who is to
make war and wage peace have been the focus of bitter controversy
and continuing dispute within the American system.[1] Discussion
has been cyclical, with the proximity to conflict being the primary
determinant of the intensity, scope, and direction of debate. The
major protagonists have been the participants who share power
in the constitutional twilight zone of foreign policymaking:
the President as Commander-in-Chief and Chief Executive, and
the Congress with its secured prerogatives of declaring war, raising
armies, and overseeing general external relations. A feature of all
the cycles has been the shared conviction not only that the resolution of these disputes was central to the fate of the Republic, but
there has also been the common belief that a set of enduring answers
to the problems of power-sharing and limitation can be found and
expressed in legislation and constitutional understanding.

These discussions, however, have taken place within a framework of markedly consistent operational procedure: the increasing
centralisation in the Executive and in the Presidency itself of all
powers of war- and peacemaking. Since at least the first years of
World War II, the President has had the effective power to initiate
and conclude armed hostilities and to regulate all phases of national
life (economic and social, as well as political) which affect the military effort, without prior Congressional approval. The postwar
period has seen a whittling away of the need even for substantive

Congressional consultation or acceptance—as Kennedy's nuclear brinkmanship in the Cuban quarantine of 1962 shows as dramatically as Nixon's actions in Cambodia. There have been a series of Congressional predelegations of power and responsibility, most notably the resolutions on Formosa, the Middle East, Berlin, and the Gulf of Tonkin. The *coup de grâce* has been postwar bipartisanship—the Congressional and public commitment to 'let politics stop at the water's edge' and the related belief that the nature of 'the threat' requires basic submission to Executive decisions.

In part, these are not particular or irrational dilemmas. The United States is hardly unique in its Executive dominance in foreign policymaking or even in the resulting priority accorded domestic political considerations, especially Presidential politics. The emergence of the United States as one of the first democratic global powers, if not the very circumstances of its creation in 1776–83, made heightened appreciation of threats in the 'non-democratic' international system virtually inevitable. Moreover, it has been only one of the advanced democracies which have had to face the problem of balancing domestic preferences and accepted procedures with the requirements of *raison d'état* imposed by increasingly destructive technology and ideological opponents.[2]

How 'new' can or should the democracies' 'new diplomacy' be? How much must any nation in war and peace speak with one clear voice, however unrepresentative? How much should war and peacemaking procedure allow for the expression of the increasingly specific and articulated rights and preferences of the mass of citizens, expected both to live with governmental decisions and to march in defence of them?[3] And, especially in the contemporary world, how much will American answers to these questions determine the fate of other republics—unrepresented and increasingly dependent on the functioning of the American deterrent?

Yet the continuing debate does exhibit some peculiarly American characteristics, some recurring ambivalences in the general American approach to foreign policymaking. Two hundred years of experience have left most Americans only more strongly convinced of the uniqueness and fragility of the American experiment, and of the antipathetical (if not actively hostile) nature of the rest of the international system.[4] Accordingly, most Americans believe there is a need, albeit in a vague and usually diffuse way, for a strong popular base for general foreign policy strategies. A perfectible system, surrounded by a hostile environment, can only be strengthened by discussion of basic values, a concern for process and the expression of diverse opinions.

Those most concerned—politicians, statesmen, and scholars— have drawn two quite different conclusions about action strategies. The 'idealists' have seen the primary task as being to expand the number of similar experiments. The method of conducting American foreign policy is seen as an essential part of this ambition: it would serve both as a model and as a stimulus. The 'realists' on the other hand have seen the assured defence of the American experiment itself as the primary goal, whenever necessary and by whatever means, even when those means have run counter to American ideals. Once this security is achieved (note Charles A. Beard's ironic 'perpetual war for perpetual peace') the realists assume that peace and perhaps imitation of the American experiment will follow.

This particular dichotomy of attitudes does not describe group opinions on whether the United States should assume a general interventionist or isolationist military stance. There is, of course, no question about the appropriate response to direct aggression. The American (and Presidential) response must be swift and unified. The punishment eventually meted out must be sufficient to ensure the compliance or deterrence of others who might have similar ambitions. The main concern is not the course of the conflict, which may at first go badly given the aggressor's advan- tage: the main concern is rather with the outcome of the conflict, the victory to be pursued with all possible speed. This will allow the return of normal relations, a condition in which the American experiment might be expected to spread and/or prosper.

What should pertain in periods of tension or even 'normalcy' is a matter of more controversy. Broadly described, the idealists have generally favoured the fullest possible exercise of legislative deliberation and governmental responsiveness to popular will. Under most circumstances, America should be slow to go to war, with priority given to domestic interests and concern over, for example, extensive military preparedness. A strong President with predelegated powers for crisis response might foster more easily the conditions necessary for the development of other democracies, but he might also hasten the moment of direct threat.

Many realists, on the other hand, have seen a strong executive as most conducive to eternal vigilance and swift response. Immediate military responses or even preemption might be necessary before other institutions or the general population become even aware of a threat. Yet attempts to quarantine an aggressor or to keep America in isolation without extended public consideration, might also usefully conserve American defensive capability until the critical moment.

The continuance of this debate, and the emergence of Schlesinger's 'imperial presidency' seem clearly contradictory. Perhaps the only general explanation can be found in the particular coincidence of national and international developments which attended America's emergence as a major global actor after 1890.

Neither warmaking nor peacemaking was a particularly extensive or burdensome American profession during the first century after independence.[5] Wars and war scares were numerous and threatening (by one count 50) but few were without clear possible benefit in territory or prestige for the new state at limited or limitable cost. Most were short or intermittent, truly limited wars, involving actions which were far away or not subject to reportage and which, except for the Civil War, required little major new expenditure or troop deployment. Washington was protected, if also constrained and occasionally punished, as part of Britain's global strategy which favoured American continental expansion. For Washington, all that had to be (and could have been) sought were a series of 'business-like' peace agreements with its betters (England, France, Spain) and acknowledgement of its dominance over domestic foes (Indians and Southerners) and lesser neighbours (preeminently Mexico).

Limitation of military ends and means, however, did not imply a lack of debate about the exercise of war- and peacemaking powers. Much of the period saw strong Congresses, with towering personalities who often overshadowed the compromise party choices for Chief Executive.[6] The threat of ever-impending civil conflict, the stirrings of Manifest Destiny and industrial growth simply enlarged the opportunities for Congressional influence and dramatics in aid of the common defence and Congress' wide-ranging war powers. One need only recall Henry Clay's excoriation of President Monroe and General Jackson on the conduct of the Seminole war, Daniel Webster's criticism of President Lincoln on the Mexican adventure of 1843, and the indomitable Charles Sumner's attack on Lincoln's unconstitutional usurpations in the midst of the Civil War.

After 1890, America's major war experience was shaped by (and shaped) two major political developments—one domestic, the other international. The first was the emergence of national and Presidential, rather than sectional and Congressional, government.[7] Its principal attribute was the seemingly irresistable rise of the President as the leader and spokesman for the nation as well as Chief Executive and Commander-in-Chief. Whatever the area, successive Presidents from the emphatic Teddy Roosevelt to the silent Coolidge expanded their 'constitutional' prerogatives, grabbed control of fast-growing national resources and facilities, and secured for themselves first place in all governmental communication, at home or abroad. The Presidency came to be seen as the only office with a truly 'national' perspective, being the repository of continuous, objective information and expertise. It was seen as the source of salvation in crisis. Its claims to primary authority in all external relations were further buttressed by what appeared to be a long string of successes, sanctioned by judicial interpretation and popular approval.

Yet the new sources of Presidential strength contained some inherent constraints and contradictions. The national system itself was undergoing rapid development and expansion, as broad democratisation of the governmental process accelerated and wave after wave of new participants entered the political system, most with the immigrant's belief in the virtue of the American system. Their principal political identifications were with the local party and the all-powerful national President, but also with what Michael Howard has called 'ideological globalism', the ultimate triumph of American principles and processes. For whatever instrumental reasons, most became partisans of the uniqueness of the American experiment, which permitted no recourse to Europe's adventurism, no dynastic or capricious wars, and no standing armies or military draft save when under direct attack.

Simultaneously, the international system was also expanding rapidly in scope and approaching a new type of 'democratisation'.[8]

The nineteenth-century balance, intermittently managed by Britain, held until World War II. But the new balancers were found among the hitherto peripheral states—Japan, Russia, and the United States—all of whom were increasing markedly in power, ideological ambition, and global commitment. The characteristics of the new international system and its new diplomacy all followed in turn—conference diplomacy, multilateral agreements, complex ideological wars and even more complex ideological collective security or peace-maintaining arrangements.

The United States was clearly one of the primary transformers of the system, particularly in the power it commanded in support of the universality of its constitutional republican procedures and democratic ideals. The issues of war- and peacemaking were basic American, not just Wilsonian, concerns; the most prominent efforts in this sphere were the American campaigns for the Hague conferences, for the regulation of naval armaments, for international constitutional documents such as the Kellogg-Briand Pact or for the creation of the League of Nations itself. Open covenants meant personal diplomacy; and collective security implied personal responsibility for the safety of a global constituency. Statesmen were to be accountable both to their domestic constituencies and to what became called the 'world community.'

But the impact of these changes on norms and expectations was almost as great in the United States as in the system as a whole. Personal diplomacy meant that the President had to give greater attention and show greater responsiveness to the 'attentive' foreign policy public—and at the same time there were ever greater expectations of consistency, speed and strength. Whatever his personal view, Presidents had to recognise the national advantage and the benefits (or sanctions) for the external 'constituency' which the assumption of warmaking and peacemaking as a personal prerogative would ensure. To quote Charles Beard's ironic assessment,[9]

> There is good reason for believing the autarchic tendencies of other governments will force such a concentration of policy and power in the United States, despite all theoretical objections that ingenuity can devise and offer. Again it is a question of a correct interpretation of trends in the world realities of the living present.

And those who would gain the most would be partisan politicians, the dignified Wilson or the exuberant FDR; they would be able at least some of the time to translate international opportunity into domestic advantage, and back again.

The post-war transformations which brought the United States to super-power status merely intensified the process. By the early 1960s, the American President emerged with three quite different powers which made him the focal point of war and peace considerations, national and international.[10] There were the powers he enjoyed firstly as commander of forces, bureaucracies, and resources now deployed world-wide and primarily responsive to his direction; secondly as leader of a far-flung external 'constituency' bound by ties of alliance, nuclear supply, or simple fear; and thirdly as leader and voice of a centralised domestic system enjoying overwhelming popular and intragovernmental support, including bipartisan Congressional support in foreign policy. Involved were few, if any, visibly effective restraints on these powers, whether institutional controls, the existence of potentially countervailing forces, or the existence of prominent public arenas for the expression of legitimate fears, criticisms, or warnings. It was all done in the name of the democratic process and the survival of the Free World, which was shaped in and dependent upon the United States.

Vietnam in many senses was merely the proximate cause of renewed debate, made more dramatic by the horrors, the flavour of defeat, and the determined articulation of a minority opposition. The shrill cries of the revisionist historians, the questioning of the counter-culture movement, the proclaimed end of ideology—all provided secondary stimuli. Furthermore, in an age of purported *détente*, the ever-increasing size of the superstructure necessary to sustain this concentration of powers with the concomitant cost and risk would have been enough eventually to have raised the question of the sharing of war- and peace-making powers. If, to use Kissinger's SALT analogy, the bear could be bound by calculations of advantage and sanction, what need was there for all-encompassing bear traps or indeed an all-powerful bear tamer? And with all these pressures, the familiar search for new organisational formulae and constraints, for new constitutional consideration, began again.

III. The Issues

That the theme of every debate has been the focus of institutional and constitutional responsibility for war and peacemaking is, to restate, reflective of particularly American characteristics. From almost the first days of the Republic, this issue has been defined as establishing the appropriate role for Congress. Should the Congress or its leadership be active participants in debating the onset of war, in directing the efficient use of national resources, and in preparation for eventual peace? Should it not act as the representative both of the immediate popular interest and of the broader values and lessons to be drawn from the American experience? Should its role, and particularly that of the Senate, be rather that of a court of review for purposes both of the legitimation of Executive estimates and arrangements and of an ultimate defence of national interest and sacrifice? How far can or should Congress go in criticising the prosecution of a war or demanding explanation and information while a peace settlement was in process? And do not its powers to declare war logically imply the right to declare peace—or at least 'not war'—in accordance with its own assessment and independent of Executive initiative?

Strict constructionists and constitutional historians have always argued for the greatest possible degree of Congressional participation and responsibilities, basing their arguments on the direct and coordinate powers granted under the Constitution.[11] They have found explicit evidence of the intentions of the Founding Fathers in the records and commentaries surrounding the Constitutional Convention and the various state ratification assemblies. The Senate clearly was expected to function as an executive council, advising and prompting the President in all major aspects of foreign relations. It had so functioned under the Articles of Confederation which left to the more directly popular House of Representatives a share only in the broader rights of making war and peace. There was some discussion of incorporating this war-peace formulation from the Articles in the final constitutional document, as a particularly strong safeguard on the exercise of powers too awesome to be left to any one man. But the exclusive Congressional responsibility for declaring war and raising armies was seen as a strong hedge, and as Mr. Justice Story later commented, the expectation was that peace would usually be made by treaty. Indeed the change late in the Convention enabling Congress to 'declare' war rather than 'make' war was seen as better highlighting the offensive-defensive division of the war powers: the Commander-in-Chief was responsible for initiating short-term defensive actions while the Congress was to authorise and

supervise more significant efforts at defence and the re-establish-
ment of peace.

Most scholars and politicians recognise the evolution of a far
more limited, passive and ultimately self-denying Congressional
role through constitutional practice.[12] All five Congressional
declarations of war have been at Presidential request; almost every
Presidential request for *ex post facto* ratification of war or peacemaking initiatives has been granted. New forms have evolved,
moreover, through Presidential practices which easily escape
constitutional strictures. There are executive agreements, which
may be supported or not by joint Congressional resolutions,
such as the Declaration of the United Nations of 1942; there are
secret understandings such as the Laos settlement of 1962; and
there are simple declarations of the onset of hostilities, such as
Truman's statement on Korea or Eisenhower's speech on the
Lebanon landings of 1958. These are only the most common
forms which have emerged. For at least the last fifty years, once
fighting begins, all war arrangements and peace preparations have
largely been Presidential *faits accomplis*. They have been presented,
rather than submitted, to more or less willing Congresses.

Indeed, debate and discussion in Congress on war and peace
seem to have followed a fairly consistent pattern over the last
hundred years. A known threat of war often stimulates passionate
debate about the interests and responsibilities involved, about the
degree of preparedness needed or at hand, and about the timing
of involvement. Executive initiatives or war preparation are
subject to minute scrutiny and frequent defeat. The onset of
hostilities brings calls for a united front, an end to Congressional
carping and unpatriotic criticism, and full support for what the
President 'needs' or national security 'requires'. As the war wends
on, the level of Congressional criticism increases, often apace
with popular chafing and dissatisfaction. The details of peacemaking and the resulting structure of the international system
have usually been of less interest than the timetable for troop
return or the lifting of domestic restrictions. The 'normalcy'
dynamic usually becomes dominant except for the establishment
of several review committees to assess the lessons of the war, to
correct abuses of power and organisation, or to spotlight domestic
wrongdoing. Thereafter, most Congressmen, like the general
public, are willing to return to the good old days.

At one level this finding is hardly surprising. There may be a peculiarly intense American attachment to patriotic unity in the face of adversity. Primary examples would be the scorn heaped on the Lindberghs after Pearl Harbor or the critiques of Senators Morse and Gruening after the Gulf of Tonkin vote in 1964. But as Truman and Acheson found in 1952, American democratic practices may be particularly inimical to the conduct of long wars. Yet, in the main, Congress has acted as any legislative institution would have: it is the body which is best equipped to enact rules, raise questions for others to answer, and invite pressures to be applied on pending issues.[13] Moreover, parliamentary democracies exhibit the same pattern, made even more extreme by the authority of the party whip or the discipline imposed by all-party government. Given the emotionalism which accompanies any conflict, these legislative functions can perhaps only be fulfilled in the period before a hot war. In modern warfare, nuclear or conventional, this is probably the period of 'war' which has declined most in length.

However, the Vietnam experience lent particular emphasis to two increasingly apparent and disturbing characteristics of the Presidential-Congressional balance in peace- and warmaking. The first is what might be called the ratchet effect, the progressive failure after a war to re-establish the institutional balance at the pre-war level. At issue has been not just Executive dominance in warmaking, but increasingly, Presidential dominance of every governmental function during conflict. In the past, Congress's attempts to regain its powers have sometimes led to deplorable excess; the impeachment of Andrew Johnson essentially in reaction to Lincoln's 'dictatorship' or the Senate's particular delight in Wilson's humiliation over the League. But the experience in the post-war American system seemingly has been far more that of a closed system; accumulated Presidential power has been retained, consolidated, and then used as a basis for greater centralisation in the name of national security during the next conflict or crisis.

The result is what those who sought to curb Mr. Nixon through repeal of the Gulf of Tonkin resolution found. The Presidency has acquired superabundant, redundant powers and controls over such monies and discretionary spending authority as to make short —or even medium-term restraint a futile exercise. Nixon simply shifted his public justifications for his actions in Cambodia and indeed warned Congress of what he would do in the face of further harassment.

The second disturbing phenomenon is that there have been fewer and fewer instances of Congressional criticism of, let alone direct opposition to, Presidential control, even when there is no hot conflict. The last thirty years have seen little opposition to equal that in the House over the Mexican war, or the campaign of Senator Henry Cabot Lodge and the thirteen Republican 'Irreconcilables' against Wilson's peace of Versailles in 1919, or the coordinated opposition to FDR's destroyer deal and Lend Lease in 1940. The bitterness of these experiences and the subsequent public criticism seem to have led the Congress into legislating self-denying ordinances regarding its own powers and responsibilities.[14] An example beyond the resolutions already cited, is the Connally resolution of 1943 which pledged Congressional support for the post-war construction of a new international security organisation two years before peace was achieved and before any details of the Executive's planning or secret agreements were known to more than a favoured, co-opted handful. The stampede effect that Lyndon Johnson engineered for the Gulf of Tonkin resolution in 1964, however, must still lead most lists of Congressional failures and derelictions of duty.

There are, to be sure, many good conventional explanations to be found. Whatever the historic causes, Congress has never had sufficient information resources to challenge the Executive on most of its assessments and pronouncements. As Senator Fulbright painfully learned in the mid-1960s, it has not and cannot command the media attention or coverage available to every modern president. It has little or no assistance in its efforts at oversight and control from the judicial branch which has generally supported the Executive in war and offered only the most narrow, individual relief for Executive excesses once peace has come.

Any systematic analysis reveals a major degree of Congressional irresponsibility, of individual and collective unwillingness to confront hard choices in a time of Presidential 'stroking' and reassurance. The sources seem twofold. Firstly the vigorous assertion of a Congressional role in war- or peacemaking is of dubious electoral value. Outspoken Congressional critics, doves or hawks, have found themselves either swamped by a coalition of the President and a similarly-minded electorate, or undercut by a vigorous minority. American voters in recent years may indeed have become less directly partisan and more oriented toward issues. But even for the minority interested in international actions, foreign policy debates always contain one implicit issue, that of national loyalty. In most contests, Presidential critics will probably find the appeal of 'support our boys' or 'America—love it or leave it' an almost indomitable obstacle.

Secondly, Congress as a whole has been long unwilling to confront what Daniel Webster defined as the major question in the warpowers debate, namely the President's ability to bring war about through his own Executive competences.[15] Polk's attempts in 1843 to provoke a Mexican attack now seem crude. But how different were Roosevelt's programmes in aid of Britain during the 'phony' war—the destroyer transfer, Lend Lease, the patrol (not convoy) of American destroyers alongside the transferred supplies? What of the personal commitments of aid or defence which Presidents have made to other states and leaders, most more acceptable than President Thieu? And what of the probability of major conflict resulting from a Presidential declaration on Berlin or Cuba, let alone relations with South Africa or military assistance to Iran? In the face of Presidential reassurances or declarations of responsibility, Congress has been more than glad to declare 'the buck hasn't stopped here'.

IV Prescriptions and Alternatives

It is therefore hardly surprising that serious attempts by Congressional activists to recapture a major institutional rôle in war- and peacemaking have been few and marked by limited success. The most famous victory, the Senate's rejection of the Versailles peace involved institutional prerogatives only in a secondary sense.[16] The principal factor was rather one of partisanship, involving Senator Lodge's efforts to preserve Republican unity in the face of the opposition of Borah and the Irreconcilables and President Wilson's demands that Democratic Senators vote against the treaty rather than accept any of Lodge's fourteen reservations. While not without precedent, Wilson's call for a solidly Democratic election in 1920 as 'A great and solemn referendum' on Versailles was surely the partisan capstone.

The institutional significance of the Versailles débâcle lies in its impact on the process of peacemaking in World War II. The great 'mistakes' of 1919 were clearly in the minds of all the participants, even those Congressional leaders who had most opposed entry into the war. But it was Roosevelt who drew the most cogent 'lessons' from history and used them not so much to widen significant Congressional participation but rather to ensure against a personal 'Wilsonian' defeat. Congressional leaders were extensively briefed and consulted on the work of groups in the State and War Departments planning the peace and were also told, in less detail, of the negotiating activity of the President. They were encouraged to prepare declaratory joint resolutions and to participate actively in such post-war conferences as that in San Francisco establishing the UN Charter. But whatever they may have believed, few knew much about FDR's secret agreements, or played any active role in the crucial wartime conferences, or could claim—then or now—a major share in the responsibility for key provisions or compromises in the many different documents which essentially stand as the World War II settlement.

The two most serious initiatives to right the institutional balance both took place after World War II: the Bricker amendment debate of 1953–54 and the war powers controversies arising out of the Vietnam ordeal.[17] The first essentially concerned a crude scatter-shot attempt to gain Congressional control of national commitments, primarily through wholesale new restrictions of the Presidency's treaty-making powers and rights to conclude executive agreements. The proximate cause was the executive 'peace' agreements of Yalta and Potsdam which had effectively labelled Senatorial review powers as historical relics. The Eisenhower Administration was drawn into an epic struggle, winning the decisive battles in both the Senate and the nation-wide constitutional debate by very narrow margins.

It was the Vietnam debates of 1967–73, however, which caused Congress to make the most extended, searching review of its powers and led to the development of new, more sophisticated instruments against any future Presidential engagement of military force.[18] The prolonged debate over the McGovern-Hatfield and Cooper-Church amendments did not result, as proposed, in specific binding Congressional limits on the duration and scope of Ameri-

can involvement in South East Asia. But they did lay the ground-
work for the 1973 War Powers Resolution by which Congress
is obliged to authorise or rescind Presidential use of force in
sixty days. The successful over-riding of the Presidential veto
and the extensive research and public attention surrounding the
bill went further toward re-confirming Congressional prerogatives
in the larger issues of war and peace.

The question of operational consequence, however, awaits the
future. Congressional attempts to halt the use of military force
in mid-course may still seem as ineffectual or unpatriotic to the
majority of Congressmen and the electorate as did the attempts
to cut appropriations during Vietnam. Short of a shift in domestic
political incentives, a determined President or Secretary of State
may mobilise massive popular support for his expert 'informed'
policies and easily divert popular attention away from Congressional questions or hearings. A Congressman facing election in
less than twenty-four months will find it hard to ignore the pressures to conform to President or party. Most important of all
is the clear weakness of legislative technique, of attempts by a
representative body at policy prescription or at the imposition of
public accountability. Consider only what even a weak President
can do with a minor drama such as the Mayaguez incident in 1975.

And at some point, the responsibility imposed by a
Congressional demand for troop withdrawal for subsequent
peacemaking activity must be squarely faced. Will a vote to withdraw troops in at most 60 plus an additional 30 days really be
possible without the simultaneous presentation of some plan for
a *post-bellum* settlement? Moreover, as Alton Frye has asked, what
will be the consequence of such an action for the operational credibility of any American alliance commitment (as in NATO, 'an
attack on one is an attack on all') in the eyes of already anxious
allies?[19] Any resolution will almost certainly require far more
extensive Executive-Congressional cooperation than has taken
place in the last century. It seems highly questionable that this
reaffirmation of Congress's right to consult and be consulted will
be sufficient to bring this about in the absence of other incentives
to collaborate.

What alternatives exist? Students of Congress most often place
their hopes in institutional reorganisation and expansion,[20] as
with the information resources now available through the Con-

gressional budget office, or the improved 'early warning system' which the reorganised committee system may make possible. Congressmen as well as private citizens have also found some protection against Presidential secrecy through suits under the Freedom of Information Act or through the anxieties created by the Watergate disclosures. There is also a slight reduction in deference to Presidential judgements and Executive pronouncements.

But Webster's hard question clearly remains the sticking point: How does the republic constrain the Presidency's ability to do mischief under other names, as indeed to carry the nation over the brink to war? Is there any conceivable system under which both authority and representation can be preserved, and by which both efficiency and at least proximate national morality can be attained? Or is the trend toward the centralisation and bureaucratisation of power beyond all but the constraints imposed by individual personality or ethics?

Perhaps one is left only with a list of non-conclusive solutions. The American penchant for organisational answers to questions of power and democratic ideals will not be sufficient in the short or medium term. It is even less likely that the American national character will undergo changes and revision in directions more congruent with the dictates of *Realpolitik*. Least likely of all is a short-run transformation in the nature of the present international system with its multiple actors, diverse arenas of conflict, and accumulations of highly-destructive weaponry.

There remain the archetypal American prescriptions, familiar and unsatisfying, exhaustive and idealistic. There is a need for reasonable, watchful citizens to balance trust and suspicion, to support the resolution of creative leadership and oppose the ploys of overly ambitious politicians, to support new initiatives, but never to forget the lessons of the Vietnam decade. The cycles of involvement and alienation, of passive acceptance and shrill critique must somehow be broken. Individual commitment to public responsibility and accountability must be the benchmark against which present and future leaders, public and private, Presidential and Congressional, must be judged.

In the final analysis every republic must return to the question, 'Who can guard the guardians?'. The traditional answer remains: the community which is subject to their power yet sets the mode of their education, selection and existence. The watch will be long and ever more dangerous.

Notes

1. Perhaps the best brief summary of the War Powers debate in the Congress is found in Alton Frye's *A Responsible Congress* (New York: McGraw-Hill, 1975), chapter VIII, while the *Widening Context*, Vol. III of *The Vietnam War and International Law*, ed. Richard A. Falk (Princeton, N.J.: Princeton University Press, 1972) includes the basic sources on the constitutional debate. For the views of major participants see Thomas F. Eagleton, *War and Presidential Power* (New York: Leveright, 1974) and Jacob K. Javits *Who Makes War* (New York: Morrouj, 1973);

2. By now, the obligatory reference to the impact of governmental structure and level of development on foreign policy behaviour is to James N. Rosenau's 'Pre-theories and Theories of Foreign Policy' in *Approaches to Comparative and International Politics*, ed. R. Barry Farrell (Evanston, III.: Northwestern University Press, 1966), pp. 27–92.

3. Two recent attempts to explore the linkages between the emergence of the mass army and the democratisation of the nation-state are Morris Janowitz's stimulating 'Military Institutions and Citizenship in Western Societies' in *The Military and the Problem of Legitimacy*, (Eds.) Gwyn Harries-Jenkins and Jacques van Doorn (Beverly Hills, Cal., Sage Publications, 1976) and S. E. Finer's encyclopedic 'State and Nation-Building in Europe; the Role of the Military,' in *The Formation of National States in Western Europe*, (Ed.) Charles Tilly (Princeton, N.J., Princeton University Press, 1975).

4. The classic statement of this hostility is, of course, Almond, Gabriel *The American People and Foreign Policy* (New York, Praeger, 1950). See also Frank L. Klingberg's 'The Historical Alternation of Moods in American Foreign Policy'. *World Politics* (1952) pp. 239–273, and Margaret Mead *And Keep Your Powder Dry* (New York: Morrow, 1973).

5. Eagleton (*op. cit.*) dismisses most of this experience as 'in general conformity' with the constitutional prescriptions while Javits (*op. cit.*) finds many disturbing precedents of Presidential supremacy. Perhaps the most authoritative listing of 'wars' of the period is the *Background Information on the Use of United States Armed Forces in Foreign Countries* (revised) prepared by the Foreign Affairs Division, Legislative Reference Service, Library of Congress (Washington: GPO, 1970). In quite different areas, Louis Henkin in *Foreign Affairs and the Constitution* (New York: Norton, 1972), pp. 84–85, and Russell Weigley in the *American Way of War* (New York: Macmillan, 1973) suggest that these experiences led to expectations and benchmarks inappropriate both for the twentieth century and for the behaviour of a major international actor.

6. See, for example, Neil MacNeil's *Forge of Democracy* (New York: McKay, 1963) as well as Javits' rather generous assessments in the foreign policy arena *op. cit.*, chaps. 2–7.

7. For a summary view of this argument by a proponent of Presidential

creativity, see James MacGregor Burns *Presidential Government: the Crucible of Leadership* (Boston: Houghton Mifflin, 1966).

8. Observed (disapprovingly) by Harold Nicolson In *Peacemaking* 1919 (London: Constable & Co., 1933), p. 84.

9. *The Open Door at Home* (New York, Macmillan, 1935). pp. 298–99.

10. See, on this, Schlesinger, *op. cit.* and Emmet John Hughes, *The Living Presidency* (New York: Coward, McCann and Keoghegan, 1973).

11. W. Taylor Reveley III presents a succinct review of these arguments in Presidential War-Making: Constitutional Prerogative or Usurpation,' in Falk, *op. cit.*, Vol. III, pp. 520–83.

12. For a brief summary view, see Merlo J. Pusey *The Way We Go To War* (Boston: Houghton Mifflin, 1969).

13. A similar assessment is made by Michael Foley in 'Congress and United States Foreign Policy: a new myth for the bi-centenary' in *Inter State*, No. 2, 1975/76, pp. 13–17.

14. The most famous post-war examples, of course, are the Congressional resolutions approving Presidential employment of military force regarding Formosa (1953), the Middle East (1958), and the Gulf of Tonkin (1964). However, one of the few Supreme Court decisions in the area, United States *v.* Curtis-Wright Export Corporation, (299 U.S. 304 (1936)) suggests there are few, if any limits, to Congress's authority to delegate its war powers to the President.

15. Javits finds the entire Mexican War controversy a particularly telling portent of later Vietnam struggles. *op. cit.*, chap. VIII.

16. Samuel Flagg Bemis makes a strong argument for this 'partisanship' interpretation. See his *A Short History of American Foreign Policy and Diplomacy* (New York: Henry Holt, 1959), chaps. XX and XXII.

17. See Frye, *op. cit.*, chap. VIII.

18. For a brief introduction to some of the major issues, including the use of Congressional appropriations powers, see Frye, *op. cit.* Garry J. Wooters 'The Appropriations Power as a Tool of Congressional Foreign Policy Making' in Falk, *op. cit.*, Vol. III, pp. 606–22; and Henkin, *op. cit.* chaps. III and IV.

19. Frye, *op. cit.*, pp. 214–215.

20. See on this theme James A. Robinson's *Congress and Foreign Policymaking*, revised edition (Homewood, III: Dorsey Press, 1967), especially chaps. I and VI.

American Attitudes Towards International Organization

Inis. L. Claude, Jr.

Intelligent discussion of this subject requires constant awareness of the dangers of unwarranted generalisation. Americans are never unanimous about anything, and certainly not about international organisation. The conduct of international relations requires that some attitude be designated and treated as the official position of the United States, but this designation always obscures differences of view within the government and, even more, within the vast assortment of human beings who populate the United States. Moreover, the American attitude toward international organisation lacks constancy. Secular trends and ephemeral fluctuations complicate the analysis; prevailing American views had obviously changed between the end of World War I and the end of World War II, and the United Nations inspires different attitudes in the 1970s than it did in the 1950s. Attitudes also vary according to the identity of the organisation under consideration. International organisation is a term embracing international organisations that arouse quite different reactions in the United States. It is true that many Americans think that they have a fixed and general attitude toward international organisation as a generic phenomenon; they have convinced themselves that they approve or disapprove of international organisation in principle. Fortunately, this seldom proves to be the case. For most people, the logic of discrimination is ultimately more compelling than the urge to be consistent. We speak glowingly of motherhood, but we judge child-bearing females according to their individual merits. Similarly, generalisations about international organisationhood tend, in fact, to yield to the instinct for differentiation among things that are different. It matters which international organisation we are talking about.

All this suggests that I should not purport to describe the American attitude toward international organisation, but should discuss some of the attitudes that have prevailed among Americans, at various times, toward some parts of the international organisational complex. This emphasis upon the diversity and mutability of American attitudes suggests the probability that those attitudes have had some currency in other countries; it is unlikely that any perspective on international organisation is peculiarly or distinctively American. At most, we may find that certain points of view have been so prominent and persistent in the United States as to make it seem reasonable to consider them characteristically American.

Let me begin by refuting the notion that America is a Johnny-come-lately, a recent convert, to international organisation. This notion has been nourished by awareness of the American isolationist tradition and by emphasis upon the fact that the United States rejected the League of Nations but joined the United Nations at its inception. In this simplified version of history, America was new at the game in the years after World War II, and this alleged fact is sometimes held to explain qualities attributed to the United States as a participant in the United Nations and other agencies—clumsiness, bumptiousness, excessive idealism, and so forth.

The fact is that American participation in the nineteenth-century beginnings of the international organising process was at least as prominent as might reasonably have been expected, considering the location and the standing of the United States. For obvious reasons, the early organisation movement centred on Europe, but the United States was an active promoter of and participant in agencies that were primarily European, as well as organisations confined to the Western Hemisphere. It was a member of ten international agencies in 1900 and, by 1915, it had joined twenty-seven, as against twenty-eight for Britain and thirty-six for France.[1] Against this record, the decision to abstain from the League of Nations and associated bodies appeared to be a deviation from, rather than a continuation of, established American policy. Moreover, the creation of the League was in large part an American enterprise—a manifestation of the interest in international organisation that the United States had exhibited for a half-century or so. It is open to question whether America's rejection of the League or its initiative in the establishment of that organisation should be treated as the more significant indicator of American attitudes toward international organisation at the end of World War I. This episode clearly illustrates the diversity and volatility of American attitudes. It is interesting to note that some critics have condemned the United States for creating the League, while others have castigated it for abandoning the organisation. The former attribute to Americans a naïve confidence in international institutions, forgetting that the United States rejected the League. The latter deplore the indifference to international organisation shown by Americans of that time, forgetting that the United States took the lead in its formation. These two half-truths combine to give us the whole truth: American attitudes toward the League of Nations included both strongly favourable and strongly unfavourable views.

In any case, America's rejection of League membership was only an interruption, not a reversal, of the policy of participation in the development of international organisations. Although the United States never joined the League, it evolved working relationships with the organisation in many sectors of activity and ultimately assumed a formal role in several League agencies.[2] Developing quasi-membership status, the United States came to play a more active and useful part in the League than many of the officially full-fledged members. In the inter-war period, the United States also continued to join international bodies outside the framework of the League; by 1940, its organisational memberships were more numerous than those of Britain or France.[3] World War II launched the era in which the United States was to serve as the chief promoter, designer, and supporter of the elaborate network of international agencies with which the global system is now equipped. This survey of the record supports the conclusion that America's large-scale involvement in international organisation after 1945 represented not an innovation but the culmination of a line of behaviour that had been followed, except for the aberration in regard to the League, for nearly a century. No state has been more prominent than the United States in the fostering of the international organisation movement.

Americans have frequently been accused of, or credited with, adopting a particularly, if not uniquely, idealistic view of the mission of international organisation. The assertion is probably valid, in the sense that they have tended to think of international organisations as something that the world-at-large, the *rest* of the world, needs, and therefore to conceive American support in altruistic rather than selfish terms. The nature and position of the United States have provided a basis for this view. The organising movement of the nineteenth century was mainly concerned with adapting the European political and administrative system to the requirements posed by the technological fruits of the Industrial Revolution, especially the changes wrought by steam and electricity. The boundaries of Continental states were inappropriate to the new age; regulation and coordination of activities were essential to the solution of the problems and the exploitation of the opportunities presented by the new technologies of communication, transport, and production. These new necessities applied only slightly to the United States, a country far from Europe and blessed with a vast territorial domain. It had its facilities for developing coordination, in its federal system; it had its continental market, within its own boundaries. International organisation might do for European states what Americans had already done for themselves. The twentieth-century knitting together of the world has considerably altered the position of the United States in these respects, but it has not entirely destroyed the basis for the conviction of many Americans that their country needs international organisation less than most other states to serve its own particular economic and technical interests. America's situation is analogous to that of a great rural landowner, in contrast to that of residents in congested urban areas, who constantly confront the difficulties posed by cramped territorial quarters. Moreover, the United States is rich and highly developed, not dependent upon other states for economic and technical assistance. In short, the United States has not been, nor has it become, as reliant upon coordinative mechanisms to facilitate interchange across national boundaries, or upon cooperative schemes to promote economic and social welfare, as most other states. In these circumstances, it is understandable that Americans have tended to regard their participation in international organisations designed for such

purposes more as a contribution to a better world than as an invest-
ment in their own welfare.

This is a morally satisfying view or, if you like, one that en-
genders the unattractive trait of self-righteousness. It does not
provide a solid foundation for sustained performance in international bodies. Idealism, in this sense, is a luxury reserved for
those fortunate enough not to have to worry excessively about
the necessity of realistic pursuit of self-interest. Luxuries are,
by definition, optional and dispensable. If some Americans think
of participation in international agencies mainly as a matter of
'giving', others raise awkward questions about what their country
is, or ought to be, 'getting'. The reply that Americans are, or may
be, getting a better world in which to live may be valid, but its
acceptance as a satisfactory answer requires a degree of sophistication—and perhaps of sheer faith—that is not always to be found
among American critics of international organisations. Organised
international cooperation in economic and social affairs can become
solidly grounded only when global interdependence has become
so intense, and so obvious, that Americans can no longer think
it reasonable to treat their participation in multilateral agencies
as a luxury in which they can freely choose to indulge or not to
indulge. The flourishing of international economic and social
organisations requires that the involvement of the United States
be a necessity for the United States, clearly recognised as such
by the American people. The idealistic view of international
organisation may, in the final analysis, be the source of damaging
opposition to participation in it.

In so far as Americans have conceived participation in international institutions dealing with economic and social problems
as a matter more of giving than of receiving, they have laid the
foundation for insistent limitation of what the United States
receives from, as well as what it contributes to, those agencies.
A prominent and persistent feature of American attitudes toward
international organisation has been the enthusiastic endorsement
of the Biblical proposition that it is more blessed to give than to
receive—with emphasis upon the non-blessedness, or even the
cursedness, of being on the receiving end. This is to say that many
Americans have displayed a marked aversion to having their
society subjected to the impact, or affected by the penetration,
of the influences and pressures generated in multilateral forums.

The concern for national privacy, for maintaining the qualities that have been thought to differentiate American society from the societies of Europe, is deeply rooted in American history. The isolationist tradition combined cautions against America's being drawn into European affairs and against Europe's intruding into American affairs. American acceptance of involvement in international organisation has always been muted by awareness that this entails exposure as well as commitment, and by concern to limit the former. This concern was expressed in an insistence upon the inclusion of safeguards for domestic jurisdiction in the League Covenant and the United Nations Charter. Opponents of American membership in the League worried as much about what might be done to and in the United States by the League as about what their country might have to do on behalf of the world organisation. The belief that the United States has been, or the fear that it might be, improperly penetrated by external influences has figured significantly in domestic criticism of American involvement in the United Nations and in such specialised agencies as UNESCO and the ILO. The drastic shift of the economic and social agencies of the United Nations system from old-style functionalist activities of regulation and coordination to programmes of technical assistance and economic development probably owes something to the fact that the United States is far more comfortable as a contributor to programmes designed to produce results in other countries than as a participant in multilateral activities whose outcome might make an imprint upon American society. This tendency to carry isolationism into American participation in international organisations is clearly related to the relatively low sense of need for the putative benefits of multilateral collaboration.

Dependence upon the help of international organisation carries with it vulnerability to the interference of international organisation; only a state that has little interest in having important things done for it by international agencies can afford to resist having undesired things done to it by those bodies. For most Americans, as for citizens of other developed countries, national engagement in constructive international cooperation has been conceived as a venture in producing effects outside their own boundaries.

The modern development of international organisation has,

of course, not been confined to the economic, technical, and social spheres. The best-publicised enterprises have functioned in the 'higher' realm of international relations, having to do with war and peace, politics and security, law and order. In the nineteenth century, recognition of the increasing complexity of international politics, anxiety about the problems of preventing and limiting war, concern about the orderly balancing of stability and change, and hope for the strengthening of international law combined to inspire the ideal of applying the device of international organisation to the political realm. The League of Nations and the United Nations, along with a number of regional organisations and alliances equipped with organisational apparatus, have been the major products of this movement.

The reaction of nineteenth-century Americans to the notion of what I shall call political organisation was idealistic in the same sense in which I have used the term above. America was not insecure, and it still had considerable confidence in the efficacy of its geographical position and its traditional policies as barriers to its being drawn unwillingly into major international conflicts. In short, the urgency of Europe's need for an improved international political and legal system seemed far greater than that of the United States. For Americans, that need was rather abstract— but it was, nonetheless, quite compelling for many of them. War was an evil that challenged the ingenuity of all civilised men, and societies devoted to its abolition sprang up in some profusion in America after 1815.

The thinking of these peace societies was overwhelmingly legal in emphasis, for reasons that were no doubt rooted in the experience of a people that had built a new state by constitutional contrivance. The international legal system was gravely deficient with respect to the institutions and processes deemed essential to the effectuation of the rule of law; how could a legal system work without the familiar mechanisms for making and revising law, defining its application to particular cases, and enforcing it against violators? The American peace movement concentrated heavily upon the expectation that a general international organisation might complete and perfect the international legal system, closing its institutional gaps. Thus supplied with appropriate and essential apparatus, international law might usher in an era of peace and order. The emphasis upon law bespoke an aversion to politics, which was associated with force and fraud, with selfishness, ruthlessness, and contempt for justice. Law, by contrast, called forth visions of fairness, impartial judgements resting on the merits of the case rather than the potency of the parties, and just settlements reached by rational processes. I shall not attempt a full explanation of the lengthy love affair that many Americans have had with the idea of law. It suffices to point out that those who actively pursued the vision of world order concentrated their gaze upon law as the essential factor.

As indicated above, the legalism that suffused American thought about world order in the nineteenth century—and that has survived, to a considerable degree, in the twentieth century—entailed heavy emphasis upon rationally designed structures, institutions, and processes. In a scoffing mood, we can characterise this as reliance upon gadgetry. Looking at it more sympathetically, we might regard it as an admirably sensible recognition of the fact that disembodied law produces no results; practical-minded people move from praising the idea of law to constructing an apparatus that can give effect to law. Legalism is far more eligible for ridicule when it is not accompanied by institutionalism.

Two versions of the combination of legalism and institutionalism can be discerned in the history of American thought about world order. The first, which might be called 'minimal institutionalism', confined its attention to the potential contribution of a court, brushing aside any serious consideration of the need for the other types of governmental organ with which modern states are equipped. What the world needs, in this view, is simply a court, fully authorised and faithfully utilised, to settle all international disputes by the impartial application of law. The judge looms as the key figure in a system of order, dispensing justice, settling controversy, and keeping the peace.

This version of an improved international system appears to have been dominant among American peace societies in the nineteenth century. Optimism was kindled by the arbitral settlement of the *Alabama Claims* in 1872, and enthusiasm for arbitration as the central element in international reform had an important influence upon American foreign policy for a generation. For the judge-oriented American, however, arbitration was but a half-way house on the road to the real thing: adjudication, the authoritative functioning of a standing court. The quest for the ideal of a

genuine international judicial institution, running from the Hague
Conferences of 1899 and 1907 to the establishment of the Permanent Court of International Justice after World War I, aroused the
strenuous support of many Americans. It is worthy of note that
some of the most prominent opponents of the entry of the United
States into the League favoured joining the World Court, and that
the United States barely failed to do that during a period when
serious consideration of adherence to the League was not politically
feasible. I have observed that, in the aftermath of Vietnam,
American university students tend to be more attracted to the
study of international law than of general international organisation, and that many of them regard the granting of compulsory
jurisdiction to the International Court of Justice as the critical
step toward world order. Faith in the idea of the supreme international judge who can convert international law from a noble
concept into a working system is a thread that has run through
American thinking about world order for more than a century.

The second version of the legalism-institutionalism combination, which I shall label 'maximal institutionalism', insists that
a court standing in institutional isolation would be ineffectual.
If one sets out to make the international legal system a municipal
system 'writ large', what warrant can there be for picking out
judicial institutions from the domestic model and leaving aside
legislative, executive, and administrative institutions? A properly
completed international legal system, in this view, must be equipped with the full range of governmental institutions that give
effect to the rule of law within the well-ordered state.

This idea of world government, almost invariably translated
by Americans as world federation, seems to have been much less
influential among nineteenth-century Americans than the more
modest notion of a judge-run international system, although it
can be found in the literature of the peace societies. (The most
notable of its early proponents were, of course, Europeans.)
It came into its own in the United States after World War II, when
such vocal groups as the United World Federalists gained substantial attention. Many supporters of the idea reacted to the
United Nations in much the same way as supporters of a court
had reacted to arbitration tribunals; they believed that it was
an inadequate but promising first step toward the ultimate goal.
The world federalist surge has subsided without making an impact

upon American policy comparable to that made by the arbitration enthusiasts of the nineteenth century, but it has left a significant residue in the thinking of many Americans who address themselves seriously to the problem of world order. The typical American scholar of international relations today discounts the practicability of the establishment (and, perhaps, of the operation) of a world federation, but regards the creation of such a system as the only effective solution, in the ultimate sense, of the problem of world order, and, consciously or not, judges existing international organisations according to the degree to which they measure up to the standard of world government. Active advocacy of full-fledged world government is a radical stance, whereas the championing of judicial world government is a conservative one by contrast. It should not surprise us to find both in the United States, or to discover that the latter was more prominent in the nineteenth century and has not been entirely displaced by the former in the present century.

It would not be accurate to describe all advocates of world government as legalists. The position is not inherently legalistic; after all, if one contemplates the establishment of international institutions imitative of the whole panoply of institutions that constitute national government, one can choose to concentrate attention upon any one of several factors—legal, political, military, or economic—or to spread it among several. It seems to me, however, that world governmental thought in the United States has been overwhelmingly legalistic—marked by emphasis upon the law-making, law-interpreting, and law-enforcing potentialities of a proper set of global structures. On the whole, it seems appropriate to treat judicialism and governmentalism as the minimal and maximal expressions of the long-standing American conviction that the key to world order is to be found in the institutional perfection of the international legal system.

The tradition of American legalism is as notable for what it rejects as for what it advocates. As I suggested above, fascination with law has tended to imply revulsion against politics, and one is tempted to conclude that many Americans who have favoured the development of institutions to make international law effective have been motivated less by confidence in the potential usefulness of law than by distaste for military, diplomatic, and political factors in international relations. This distaste is evident in the judge-oriented approach to world order, and it appears in the thinking of many world governmentalists, who seem in some cases to harbour the extraordinary notion that the creation of governmental apparatus somehow enables a society to dispense with such unsavoury things as politics and force.

More concretely, both versions of American legalism-institutionalism have displayed a negative attitude toward the undertaking of a substantial political and military role in world affairs by the United States. It is no accident that the heyday of the movement to save the world by arbitration or adjudication came during the period of American isolationism, or that some of the most prominent isolationists of the interwar period were vocal supporters of American adherence to the World Court, or that the revival of student interest in international law and a strengthened World Court has coincided with the post-Vietnam tendency toward diminution of the international involvement of the United States. One meaning of 'let the judges do it' is 'do not ask the United States to do it'. Similarly, the champion of world government loads the responsibility for maintaining peace and order upon an abstract institution, and it may not be fortuitous that this implies the relieving, rather than the burdening, of such a concrete entity as the United States. The vision of the future developed by American legalists in the nineteenth century did not include the involvement of the United States in the international political arena or the assignment to it of heavy political responsibilities— and certainly not the obligation to accept the onerous task of participating in military sanctions against disturbers of the peace. America was not to be contaminated by being dragged into power politics; instead, the world was to be purified by elevation above politics to the realm of law. The world was to be saved by means that did not require American engagement in the difficult, dangerous, and dirty work of an organised political system. This attitude is not altogether missing from the United States of the 1970s.

This analysis provides a background for understanding the political battle over the issue of American adherence to the League of Nations, the first such struggle in the history of the American relationship with the growing movement toward organisation of the international system. The scheme advanced during World War I by the League to Enforce Peace and by similar groups in

Europe, and then embodied in the Covenant of the League under the leadership of President Woodrow Wilson, was not compatible with the brand of legalism that was still dominant in American thinking about world order. The League plan represented an essentially political approach to the objective; it relied ultimately upon the willingness of states to accept and carry out obligations to join in military sanctions against disturbers of the peace. It undertook to institutionalise the diplomacy of persuasion and the politics of pressure. This scheme violated the most basic tenets of the traditional American creed. The American peace movement had hoped for the appointment of a judge; it was confronted by the demand that the United States serve as policeman. Lovers of peace had wished that all states could be invited to rely upon predictable legal processes. Instead, they were informed that all states must assume responsibility for involvement in the uncertainties of political and military activity. True, the new machinery included a World Court, which appealed to American legalists. The movement to join that agency was ultimately frustrated by the fear of involvement in the political League through adherence to its judicial annexe. The American legalistic tradition demanded acceptance of *a* court, but it did not permit acceptance of *that* Court.

If international legalism was the orthodox American creed, then the League of Nations was, for all its Wilsonian inspiration, clearly un-American. But the fact that the shaping of the Covenant was carried out in large measure by representatives of the United States, including, most prominently, President Wilson, ought to lead us to the conclusion that a competing attitude toward international organisation had emerged among Americans. The political approach to world order had taken hold in the United States. It did not win this battle, but it was destined to win the war.

Wilson's scheme was not to take the politics out of the international system, substituting law, but to put the United States into the international political system. He approached this task with reluctance, caution, and shrewdness. He knew that it conflicted with the traditions of isolationism and legalism. He shared the traditional American distaste for the moral shabbiness of international politics, and his instinctive scepticism about the utility of the political system known as the balance of power was sharpened by the evidence that it had failed to avert the catastrophe of general war. He was convinced that it was necessary for the United States to join the international political system as a leading member, but he thought that this was neither possible nor desirable unless and until the system were significantly altered. He proposed, therefore, to change the international political system, to purify and improve it, to make it fit for American participation. This was the meaning of Wilson's talk about abandoning the discredited and derelict balance of power system in favour of a newly designed collective security system. The League was for him the expression and the symbol of the reform of the international political system, its conversion into a system that the United States should and could join. He may have been right in believing that the United States should join the remodelled system. Events disproved his expectation that the American public could be persuaded to enter into it. One of the many reasons for the failure of Wilson's effort at persuasion was the continuing strength of the American legalistic tradition, with its hope for the painless provision of world order by the judicial application of law and its abhorrence of national obligation to engage in the painful business of helping to keep the peace by political and military means.

The triumph of the Wilsonian notion came a generation later, when the United States promoted the establishment of the United Nations and set out to play a leading role in that organisation and in a variety of other agencies. This engagement symbolised the turn in America's relationship to the rest of the world that Wilson had vainly advocated after World War I. It proclaimed the willingness of the United States to accept responsibility for sustained involvement in the difficult business of managing the politics of a turbulent world; it represented a commitment to committedness, an abandonment of the free-floating rôle that the United States had previously played in world affairs. America was no longer beguiled by the illusion that global salvation might be provided, freely and easily, by a court or by a more complete and complex set of international institutions. The job had to be done by states, and circumstances had decreed that the United States was the state that had to carry the heaviest load, if that load were to be carried at all. The act of joining the United Nations registered the American acceptance of political responsibility.

It cannot be maintained that all has gone well—though we might reflect upon the possibility that things might have gone much worse. America has played a prominent role in world affairs, both inside and outside the United Nations and other international agencies. American performance in the world organisation, in its early years, may be cited as an extraordinary example of national support for the purposes and principles of an international organisation, or as a shocking case of national domination and perversion of an international body; we would do well to exercise caution about the total adoption or rejection of either of these interpretations. In any event, neither the world nor the organisation—nor the American national mood—now permits the degree of American predominance in the United Nations that was earlier manifested. My concern is not to evaluate the record of the United States in the United Nations system of organisations, but to analyse the effect of this experience in participation upon American attitudes toward international organisation.

Performance as a great power in international politics and in the United Nations has not proved an exhilarating experience for the American people. There is sharp disagreement and no little confusion among Americans as to whether they have abused the world or been abused by it, and as to whether they ought to abdicate in shame or to resign in disgust. Whether it stems from an oppressive sense of guilt or from weariness in well-doing, there is a pervasive disillusionment about active participation in international organisation among Americans. 'Wouldn't it be nice,' they seem to say, 'if the world were ruled by judges, or by a world government, and we were spared the agony of responsibility and the necessity of dirtying our hands and sullying our souls in international politics?' I am reminded of the unhappiness of the professor who suggested that his dean solve a problem by establishing a committee to deal with it, only to be designated the chairman of the committee!

The American urge to retreat from responsibility has found expression in an increasing tendency to alter the symbolic meaning attached to the United Nations. As I have argued, that organisation was originally conceived in the United States—and not only there—as a device for the registration of America's resolve to remain in the international arena as a leading participant. The United Nations served, as Wilson had intended that the League should serve, to induce that commitment and to facilitate its execution. Of late, however, more and more Americans have come to consider the world organisation a substitute for the United

States as a bearer of international burdens, an agency that can be expected to do more as they decide to do less. This mood was reflected in the presidential campaign of 1968, when Hubert Humphrey, the Democratic candidate and a staunch internationalist, assured an audience that if he were elected President he would reduce America's rôle in the world and work to equip the United Nations for taking up the tasks to be relinquished by the United States. 'The United States cannot play the rôle of global gendarme ... But the alternative to American peacekeeping cannot be no peacekeeping. It must be peacekeeping by the United Nations or by regional agencies.'[4] Humphrey lost to Richard Nixon, whose new Administration was soon described in the press as being disposed to shy [away] from unilateral entanglements and rely more on international organisations to police the peace and good order of the world.[5] These examples indicate the way in which the United Nations is being made to stand for the relief of the United States, rather than for the assignment of responsibility to, and its acceptance by, the United States.

Whether the organisation can and will act as a compensatory agency to cover American retrenchment is open to serious question. This proposition seems to rest upon a false assumption about the nature of the United Nations. It is not an independent actor in possession and control of its own resources, but a receptacle for the combination of resources supplied by member states. Hence, it is probable that the activity of the United Nations will decline, not increase, in proportion to the decline of American activity. Those Americans who talk about shifting burdens to the United Nations seem not to be unduly concerned about this prospect; they appear to be more anxious to be rid of burdens than worried about who will carry them or whether they will be carried. The existence of the United Nations now provides a convenient rationalisation for the diminution of American responsibilities in world affairs.

The trend just noted also finds expression in the reinterpretation of America's obligations as a member of the United Nations. The United States joined the organisation to say what it was willing to do, what it could be relied upon to do. Many Americans conceive continuing membership as a means of saying what their country will not do, what it will refrain from doing. The concept of loyal participation, of 'good citizenship' in the United Nations, is shifting from the positive to the negative, from the acceptance of responsibility to the acceptance of restraint. This change reflects the general devaluation of the morality of responsibility in favour of the morality of innocence. It flows, of course, from the American *mea culpa* that was stimulated by Vietnam. For those who feel a keen sense of guilt, it is less important that America should promise to take part in the solution of the world's problem than that it should promise not to be a part of the problem. For them, virtue lies not in assuming a share of the task of governing the world, but in allowing themselves to be governed; obedience, not service, is the watchword. Many Americans today think of international organisation mainly in terms of rules of restraint that the United States ought to respect. One sees here a reversion to the legalistic tradition, with its emphasis upon the legal subordination of states to international organisation rather than upon their sharing of political responsibility in international organisation.

There is now less consensus and more confusion and uncertainty about international organisation among Americans than at any other time since World War II, and probably since World War I. American dissatisfactions with international organisations and uncertainties about the rôle that the United States can or should play in them are profound, but these are largely reflections of dissatisfactions and uncertainties about the contemporary world and the place of the United States in it. Americans cannot secede from the world, and I suspect that, in the final analysis, most Americans will conclude that they must continue to participate in most of the agencies that constitute the core of international organisation, if for no other reason than because those agencies are *there*—and things happen there from which no important state can afford to divorce itself.

Notes

1. Michael Wallace and J. David Singer, 'Intergovernmental Organisation in the Global System, 1815–64: A Quantitative Description', *International Organisation*, 24, No. 2, 1970, pp. 259, 261.
2. Geneva Research Centre, *The United States and the League, the Labour Organisation, and the World Court in* 1939, *Geneva Studies*, 11, No. 1, February 1940.
3. Wallace and Singer, *loc. cit.*
4. Address by Hubert Humphrey at San Francisco, 26 September 1968, reprinted in *The Washington Post*, 27 September 1968, p. A6.
5. *Newsweek*, 27 January 1969, p. 19.

Notes on Contributors

KEN BOOTH is a lecturer in the Department of International Politics at the University College of Wales, Aberystwyth. Publications include: *The Military Instrument in Soviet Foreign Policy, 1917–1972* (1974); *Contemporary Strategy: Theories and Policies* (co-aurhor, 1975); *Soviet Naval Policy: Objectives and Constraints* (co-editor, 1975); *Navies and Foreign Policy* (1977).

CHARLES CHATFIELD is Professor of History at Wittenberg University. He has served as chairman of the Conference on Peace Research in History, and is Director of the International Education Programme at Wittenberg. Publications include: *For Peace and Justice: Pacifism in America* 1914–1941 (1971); *Peace Movements in America* (Ed., 1973); *The Radical 'No': Evan Thomas' Life and Writings on War* (Ed., 1974); *Devere Allen: Life and Writings* (Ed., 1976); *The Americanization of Gandhi: Images of the Mohatma* (Ed., 1977); co-editor of The Garland Library of War and Peace (1972–77).

INIS L. CLAUDE, Jr., is the Edward R. Stettinius, Jr., Professor of Government and Foreign Affairs, University of Virginia. Previously, he has taught at Harvard, Michigan, and Delaware, and was Professorial Research Fellow in the Department of International Politics, University College of Wales, Aberystwyth, in 1973–74. Publications include: *National Minorities: An International Problem* (1955); *Swords into Plowshares* (1956, 4th edn. 1971); *Power and International Relations* (1962); *The Changing United Nations* (1967).

EDMUND IONS is Reader in Politics at the University of York. He was a Visiting Scholar at Columbia University and Stanford University in 1965–66, and Harkness Commonwealth Fellow at

Harvard University in 1958–60. Publications include: *The Politics of John F. Kennedy* (1967); *James Bryce and American Democracy* 1870–1922 (1968); *Political and Social Thought in America* 1870–1970 (Ed., 1971); *Woodrow Wilson: The Politics of Peace and War* (1972).

CATHERINE M. KELLEHER is Associate Professor of Political Science at the University of Michigan. She has taught at Columbia University and the University of Illinois. She was national conference chairman of the Inter-University Seminar on Armed Forces and Society in 1972–73. Publications include: *American Arms and European Security* (co-author, 1973); *The Comparative Analysis of Military Systems* (Ed. and Contr., 1974); *Germany and the Politics of Nuclear Weapons* (1975).

JAMES P. PISCATORI is Assistant Professor of Government and Foreign Affairs in the Woodrow Wilson Department of Government and Foreign Affairs at the University of Virginia. He spent 1974–75 in Saudi Arabia as IIE-ITT International Fellow, and 1975–76 as Leverhulme Fellow in the Department of International Politics, University College of Wales, Aberystwyth. Publications include articles on the Middle East and international law.

ANATOL RAPOPORT is Professor of Psychology, University of Toronto. He has taught at the University of Chicago and the University of Michigan. His varied academic background includes mathematics and mathematical biology. Publications include: *Science and the Goals of Man* (1950); *Operational Philosophy* (1953); *Fights, Games and Debates* (1960); *Strategy and Conscience* (1964); *Prisoner's Dilemma* (co-author, 1965); *Two-Person Game Theory: The Essential Ideas* (1966); Carl von Clausewitz, *On War* (editor, 1968); *N-Person Game Theory: Concepts and Applications* (1969); *The Big Two: Soviet-American Perceptions of Foreign Policy* (1971); *Conflict in Man-made Environment* (1974); *Game Theory as a Theory of Conflict Resolution* (Ed., 1974); *Semantics* (1975); *The 2 × 2 Game* (1976).

HARVEY STARR is Associate Professor of Political Science and Senior Fellow at the Center for International Policy Studies, Indiana University. He has taught at Yale University and the University of Aberdeen. Publications include: *War Coalitions: The Distribution of Payoffs and Losses* (1972); *Coalitions and Future War: A Dyadic Study of Cooperation and Conflict* (1975).

KENNETH W. THOMPSON is Commonwealth Professor of Government and Foreign Affairs, University of Virginia. He has taught at the University of Chicago and Northwestern University, and has been Visiting Professor at the University of California, Columbia University, New York University, and the New School for Social Research. He is a past Vice-President of the Rockefeller Foundation. Publications include: *Christian Ethics and the Dilemmas of Foreign Policy* (1959); *Political Realism and the Crisis of World Politics* (1960); *American Diplomacy and Emergent Patterns* (1962); *The Moral Issue in Statecraft* (1966); *Foreign Assistance: A View from the Private Sector* (1972); *Understanding World Politics* (1975).

MOORHEAD WRIGHT is Senior Lecturer in International Politics, University College of Wales, Aberystwyth. He read English and American literature at Princeton University, and international relations at The Johns Hopkins University. He has been foreign affairs analyst in the Library of Congress. Publications include: *Theory and Practice of the Balance of Power, 1486–1914: Selected European Writings* (Ed., 1975).

INDEX